The Face of God

The Rediscovery of the True Face of Jesus

Paul Badde

The Face of God

The Rediscovery of the True Face of Jesus

Translated by Henry Taylor

IGNATIUS PRESS   SAN FRANCISCO

Original German edition:
*Das Göttliche Gesicht: Die abenteuerliche Suche
Nach dem wahren Antlitz Jesu*
© 2006 by Pattloch Verlag GmbH & Co. KG, Munich

Cover photograph: The Veil of Manoppello (detail)
by Stefano Spaziani during the private pilgrimage of
Pope Benedict XVI on September 1, 2006

Cover design by Roxanne Mei Lum

© 2010 by Ignatius Press, San Francisco
All rights reserved
ISBN 978-1-58617-515-3
Library of Congress Control Number 2010922764
Printed in the United States of America ∞

For Joseph

"Dentro da sé, del suo colore stesso,
mi parve pinta de la nostra effige;
per che 'l mio viso in lei tutto era messo."

"Deep within, painted in a shade of the same color,
Appeared to me our likeness—
And through this I discovered my own face."

Dante Alighieri The Divine Comedy
(1307–1321), Paradiso,
Canto 33, lines 130–32

CONTENTS

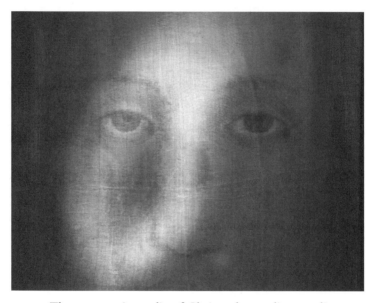

The most ancient relic of Christendom rediscovered?

The Divine Comedy

A rainbow arched over the mountains. Beside it, in the December light, the Rome to Pescara highway turned toward the great tunnel that would let us out onto the eastern flank of the Apennines a quarter of an hour later. Yet even beyond the tunnel, the rainbow would not let up. Sometimes it even grew double, playing in and out of the clouds. Half an hour later, it stood still below us, on our left: straight over the shrine of the Holy Face, which I had left on the right this time, for a last turn up into the mountains.

For first of all, I wanted to show Wolfgang the sea from up here, before we went into the little church down there. "Can you see it?" I asked my friend, and pointed east to the blue mirror of the sea. It had turned into a clear winter morning, and our journey from the Tyrrhenian Sea to the Adriatic had taken us about two hours—the mere blink of an eye for Wolfgang Büscher. Four years earlier he had walked from Berlin to Moscow. A year before that, he had done a complete tour of Germany on foot, by train, and with buses and taxis. In the years since I have known him, he has become a poet among journalists, and yet for me he had remained above all a friend: a modern *homo viator* who had been busy seeking treasures, mysteries, God, and himself and was better than Bruce Chatwin at recounting his discoveries—before now becoming my traveling companion. Years ago, we had both worked for the same newspaper—he in Berlin, and I in Jerusalem and Rome. Both here and there, he had intended to visit me, but it had just never worked out. Yet now he had come on the instructions of his new boss, and what he was about to see was something he had never yet set eyes on in Kiev or Moscow or in the Himalayas. I was going to show him the original icon of Christ. The image of the Messiah was there on a gossamer-thin membrane of mussel silk, which could shine like the spiders' webs of paradise. I had first told him about it two years before.

"Now listen, Wolfgang", I had said to him on the telephone then, "I have uncovered a tremendous story for us here. Perhaps we could get it into the paper for Easter. Now pay attention, this is the basic story. First, there is an authentic picture of God. Secondly, the Vatican had it for a long time. Third, it was swiped from there, about four hundred years ago. And now hold on tight! Because fourthly, I have found it again. The picture has not disappeared. This picture exists—and I have even taken a couple of photos of it. Are you still there?"

He was silent. Then he said, "Paul. Wait a minute, I'll just shut the door." I heard a couple of steps, a door shutting, and then he was on the line again. "Paul," he said then, "do you know what—now I'll have to protect you from yourself." I could understand what he meant; he did not want to have to put this story forward as a suggestion at tomorrow morning's editorial conference of *Die Welt*—and yet of course I could not give it up, either. For here was the key to why only Christians can make pictures of God—and Jews or Moslems cannot. Only the Christians have a picture of God. It is only for them that "the Word was made flesh". In Ethiopia, Christianity was able to develop simply on the basis of icons and pictures, with no Scriptures! With no Bible! My hour would come, I saw that clearly.

This was what it was all about: Deep in the Abruzzis, a mysterious little cloth had been preserved for at least four hundred years by the Capuchins, on a hill behind the little town of Manoppello. It was finer in quality than the finest nylon and could not be made of silk or linen. Yet it was not merely the extraordinarily fine weave that was so marvelous. On the material there was a picture of Christ that was unlike any other—or, rather, almost every picture of Christ on earth resembled that one, as a son resembles his mother, just never quite so perfectly. The eyes here were unforgettable, the nose was thin, the mouth half-opened. The shadows were more delicate than Leonardo da Vinci could achieve with his magical ability in *sfumatura*. In a good many ways, the picture reminded one of a photo, yet the pupil in the eye on the right was slightly lifted above the center of the iris—an effect impossible in any photo. No more could the picture be a hologram, though it was like one, whenever a faint light was shone onto the veil from behind. But a four-hundred-year-old hologram, in the Abruzzis? The idea was even more absurd than nylon.

Four clear folds ran across the little cloth, as if for a long time it had been folded once lengthways and twice vertically. The portrait did not shimmer like a rainbow; the colors of the *Volto Santo*, the "Holy Face", gleamed somewhere between the tones of brown and red and pink, between umber, sienna, silver, slate gray, copper, bronze, and gold. It seemed to be colored with light (Greek, *photos*), since under a microscope absolutely no pigments or dyes at all could be discovered in the weave. When light was shone straight onto it, however, it became transparent like clear glass, and even the folds disappeared.

These were phenomena that could be observed only in the case of mussel silk, the costliest fabric in the ancient world. And that, too, was sensational. For the oldest identifiable fragments of this rarest of all materials were supposed to be from the fourth century. They were in any case much smaller and not nearly so well preserved. And a cloth made of mussel silk with a picture or drawing on it did not exist anywhere at all. You could not paint onto mussel silk. It was not technically possible. Here in Manoppello, however, any layperson could see with the naked eye the most obvious difference from ordinary silk. For the upper right- and left-hand corners were missing from this picture, and at some time these had been repaired with patches of the finest silk. It was like the difference between day and night. Against the light, these patches looked gray, yet the Veil as a whole was transparent, as only mussel silk could be transparent.

So the picture united the qualities of photos, holograms, paintings, and drawings, together with mysterious impossibilities and imprecisions. What the real nature of this Divine Face was, and what we might suitably call it, was completely baffling. It was clear only that it had been greatly revered for centuries and that with all its peculiarities there was only one single object like it in the great picture gallery of the past millennium: that was the "sudarium of Veronica", which was recorded by countless artists up to the beginning of the modern age.

The *Volto Santo* of Manoppello had to be this Veil of Veronica. The many characteristics in which it corresponded to a whole gallery of pictorial documents, in which the artists of the Middle Ages depicted the Veil, were too overwhelming. In Rome, in the crypts beneath Saint Peter's, there are five frescoes in two ancient chapels that show very clearly the old "ciborium" that Pope John VII had had made in 705 for this "most holy sudarium". The altar that then held it, with its pillared ornamentation, was the most important reliquary shrine in Emperor Constantine's old fourth-century basilica of Saint Peter's. Not until 1506 was work begun on the construction of the present Saint Peter's—and they began immediately with a new treasury for the principal relic. The very first of those four towering great pillars that support the dome was provided with a high-security treasury for that delicate veil with the picture of Christ. That was where it was supposed to be installed when the old shrine was demolished in 1608. And that was where it disappeared in the seventeenth century. The "sudarium" was still omnipresent in Rome in a multitude of representations, from a painting in the sacristy of the Pantheon to three frescoes in the basilica of Saint Sylvester. Only the original was no longer to be seen in the city of the Popes. That made the search for the true picture of Christ so very difficult in recent centuries that it was eventually hardly ever attempted any more.

It was much simpler, during this period, to do research in books and ancient texts on where the picture may have been before its arrival in Rome. Researchers did not have to seek for long, though their results were often confusing. A very ancient and mysterious portrait of Christ was talked about in Edessa. There it was said to have withstood all assaults for a long time, built into one of the city gates. Later, the original must have been in Constantinople. Still today, the mosaic of Christ in the dome of Hagia Sophia was quite remarkably similar to the Divine Face of Manoppello. In the early sixth century, in the East, there were a number of reports of an extremely fine picture of Jesus "with four folds", though it was then called "the Abgar portrait" or the "Mandylion"; there were several other names for it. In the course of history, various names had been placed around this one picture, with ever-new overlying layers of legend, like the skin of an onion. Anyone who peeled them off one by one inevitably came up against the Greek word *acheiropoietos* at the heart of these notions. That was probably the oldest name for the original picture in Manoppello—and at the same time it told an illuminating little story.

For even people seventeen hundred years ago must have stood before this picture just as uncomprehendingly as we did today. If it struck us as strange, it must have seemed far more strange to them. So they, too, must have asked themselves, "What is it?" Obviously they ended by setting that question aside, however, and replacing it with the classic murder-mystery question of Scotland Yard: "*Whodunnit?*"—"Who made this?"—"We don't know", they said then. "We don't know whether perhaps God himself or angels painted this portrait. We know just one thing: it cannot have been men, with all their skills. This picture was 'not made by human hands'—in Greek, *acheiropoietos.*" Up until now, no concept had more clearly defined this ancient mystery.

Yet the odyssey of the square of mussel silk back to its origin did not end there. For where did it come from? Did it come down from heaven at some time? But the portrait did not look like a man from Mars. On the contrary, it had a singular mirror effect. This picture was strange and intimate at the same time. The face illuminated like a mysterious point of reference for both sexes, man and woman. Most of all, however, it resembled the face of the man who once lay in the Shroud of Turin. It was just as majestic, and the square of mussel silk was just as mysterious as the linen sheet from Turin— that second, yet far, far larger piece of textile which from the earliest times had been called *acheiropoietos*. And that was perhaps the most remarkable thing of all, because nothing at all could be proved by this.

For among all materials, there were hardly any two that were by their very nature less "exact" than these two woven fabrics: the one linen, the other mussel silk, the two of completely different thickness, density, structure, and weave. Both could be stretched in different ways. Imprecision and extremely problematic measurability were practically woven into these organic materials. Whoever selected these cloths for this experiment seemed to have set down almost with a wink that these cloths not be at all suitable for any mathematical proof.

So it was all the more astonishing how remarkably close the agreement was even so on these two dissimilar cloths. All the measurements and comparisons that anyone had yet been able to make pointed to one and the same original subject. The two cloths portrayed a single identical face, both as original pictures and both quite differently. All other pictures were copies.

That was why Wolfgang Büscher had now traveled from Berlin to Rome. Two months earlier, a book had appeared in which I had collected evidence for an investigation that would now have to be entirely reopened. I had sent the first copy of *The Mussel-Silk Cloth* up to Pope Benedict XVI in his palace. For who should and would have to be more interested? The pontificate of his predecessor had recognized the claims of a "purification of the memory" of the Catholic Church. Must he, too, not be very affected by the question of what the Church's pictures, in the Vatican and in Manoppello, were really all about? The Turin Shroud he knew well. It was a "mystery", he had once told the publicist Peter Seewald, "which has not yet been clearly explained, even though there is much to suggest its authenticity". Yet if it was genuine, then it came from that first Holy Saturday, from the empty tomb in Jerusalem, the first thing left behind when Christ rose from the dead. Joseph Ratzinger himself came into the world on April 16, 1927, on Holy Saturday, and he had been baptized that same night with newly consecrated water. He had always been aware of that. Would it not be bound to startle him if "both cloths" from the empty tomb were now found again, those cloths that John the Evangelist mentioned in his laconic report of the very first Holy Saturday?

In the sixth century, the leaders of the Byzantine army carried this second funeral cloth with them as a banner of victory in their wars against the Persians—just as the ancient Israelites had carried the ark of the covenant with them in their campaigns against the Philistines. The ark of the covenant, too, had been lost and had been rediscovered in exciting fashion, until it had finally gone missing once and for all—Israel's "holy of holies", with the commandments from Mount Sinai. Would the rediscovery of the original picture of Christ not make Christendom rejoice at least as much as a final rediscovery of the ark of the covenant? The face of Christ! The eyes that had gazed down on his Mother from the Cross, the lips that gave us the Sermon on the Mount: "Blessed are the poor in spirit; blessed are those who mourn;

blessed are the meek who use no violence; blessed are those who hunger and thirst for righteousness; blessed are the merciful; blessed are the pure in heart; blessed are the peacemakers; blessed are those who are persecuted for righteousness' sake ... !" God had never shown his face more beautifully.

Years ago, Cardinal Ratzinger proved that the understanding of "person"—as we now have it in our Western world—was first developed in the arguments about the "Face of God". Even the ancient Greeks were not yet familiar with the concept of the person. The "person" was a gift to the world from Christianity—and one that was still far from being accepted everywhere. "Should we not see it as the true fate to which the world is doomed and call all upon God all the louder and more urgently for him to show his countenance?" exclaimed the Cardinal at the time, before concluding his moving appeal with these words, "What was and is new about biblical religion is the fact that ... 'God', of whom there can be no images, nevertheless has a face and a name and is a person. And salvation consists, not in being immersed in namelessness, but rather in the 'satisfaction in seeing his face' that will be granted to us when we awaken."

Yet before we awake, we start to dream again—at least, I do. Wolfgang Büscher wrote up the story of the Divine Face for the Christmas issue of *Die Zeit* in such a grandiose way that it was as if the rainbow that had not been willing to leave us on our journey to Manoppello had accompanied him all the way back to Berlin. The merciful gaze of the Divine Face on the front page moved the hearts of many readers at newsstands, in supermarkets, and in highway rest areas; the issue sold rapidly. *Der Spiegel*'s Alexander Smoltczyk had already reported about "the twin Veronica" in October, in a spectacular piece. The fact that the flagship paper of German left-wing liberalism had reported about relics to that extent—and for the first time without any cynicism or even ironical undertones—in the motherland of the Reformation might almost itself have been recorded under the heading of "signs and wonders". Had a new era begun, perhaps, with the German Pope?

Soon the first busloads of pilgrims from Saint Petersburg were coming from the Baltic Sea to the Adriatic in the middle of winter. Gerhard Wolf, a leading art historian, traveled to Manoppello for the first time and stood impressed before the "living face". The Orthodox Archbishop of Athens started telling people about the mussel-silk cloth. Independent of any research, in Manoppello on December 23, 2005, a holy year was initiated for the sanctuary by Archbishop Forte from neighboring Chieti, which was supposed to commemorate that "Sunday afternoon in 1506", when "an angel" brought the Veil here. Pilgrims had come from afar for the torchlight procession through the icy night to celebrate the start of the Jubilee with the inhabitants of the little town. A written statement by James Francis Stafford, Cardinal Grand Penitentiary of the Curia, had come from the Vatican, promising all those pilgrims who might come with appropriate reverence to visit the Holy Face during this period of the Jubilee Year a "plenary indulgence". The year 2005 ended with a nighttime torchlit procession up the hill to the Divine Face, for a solemn Mass at midnight. We had come over from Rome again for that. Early on the thirty-first of December, Father Emilio had given me a passage to read out in the choir of the church, from Pope Leo the Great in the fifth century. "The birth of the Lord is the birth of peace", I stood and read; "he is our peace, he who has made of two peoples, from Jews and Gentiles, one single people." Suddenly I felt quite wide awake and looked up at the Face of Christ above the balustrade opposite me.

One person made a single people out of two? Such an event is otherwise known to have happened only in Mexico, where in 1531, following an appearance of Mary, the new nation of Mexico suddenly came into being from the Aztecs and Spanish, who had been deadly enemies. This incomprehensible reconciliation was not, however, the work of the appearance, but was the fruit of a mysterious *image* of herself that the Madonna had left behind her! The "image" of the Virgin of Guadalupe on a cheap cloak had changed the course of world history at that time. "God has never done the same for any other people!" Pope Benedict XIV had exclaimed, when he officially recognized the miracle in 1754, so the Mexicans tell us. But the image of Mary could still be seen there today—I had seen it myself, on the outskirts of the metropolis with its multi-million inhabitants; and there, too, no one had yet been able to explain how human hands could ever have created it.

As I asked my wife afterward, in the nearby bar: Could and must not the image of her Son, then—if it came from the empty tomb in Jerusalem—have also played an incomparable role in the mysterious reconciliation of Jews and Gentiles following the Resurrection of Christ, in the emergence of the new people of the Christians about whom the Apostle Paul wrote in such amazement in his Letter to the Ephesians. Must this new image not have played an incredible part, from the very beginning, in the arcanum—in the hidden room of mysteries of the original Christian community of Jews and Gentiles—and in the so incomprehensibly rapid dissemination of the news of Christ's Resurrection? Peter saw "the linen cloths lying and the napkin" in the empty tomb, so John the Evangelist wrote. After that, he himself went in, and "he saw and believed." What did he see for him to believe so quickly? Why did he not believe before that? Only weeks later, the little cluster of people around the scattered apostles had already grown to number several thousand. Did not this image simply have to have played a part here *as well*, more than any book and not merely Peter's preaching? For several generations, after all, the first Christians did not have any new book alongside the Jewish Bible.

"You should have put that into your book", said my wife. "Too late", I said, and ordered another two cappuccinos.

In recent years I had increasingly experienced the exciting story of the rediscovery of the original picture of Christ as a serialized novel about God's humor. This last idea was not necessary in order to complete something in it. Everything was just at the beginning. All that was certain was that there would be a good many surprises yet. A brief survey of the previous places and personages in this ecclesiastical thriller would already indicate that: an enormous vault that had been unable to keep safe a gossamer-thin treasure. A baroque-era pope in a dilemma, with a despicable idea; a Trappistine nun who had taken a vow of silence and then sang like a nightingale. A solitary art historian with strange theories. A fantastical confusion of concepts that swathed the picture on the Veil like a mummy. An age-old forgery that turned out to be the final piece of evidence for the identification of the original. Dr. Martin Luther, whose skeptical remark became an essential witness for the true Veil of Veronica, but only after five hundred years. German professors who rushed off on the wrong track with grandiose investigations. Secretive, conspiring, and smiling cathedral canons. Grotesque mistakes that led to the right results. Damning expert reports concerning an object that none of the experts had ever seen. Saints who were not supposed to exist, yet nonetheless helped—even my Protestant friends. A meal of mussels with the Apostle Thomas that had shattering results. A cardinal playing hooky from a meeting of cardinals to take an outing into the Abruzzis. Finally, a journalist whose closest colleagues were worried about his mental state. I could not complain, not even about the fact that two quite different jubilees, which no film director could have invented, had attached themselves to the story. In this year of 2006, Benedict XVI would celebrate his first birthday in office as pope on Easter Day again. Two days later, the anniversary of the laying of the foundation stone of Saint Peter's in 1506 would be commemorated in the Vatican—a jubilee like that in Manoppello, where they, on the other hand, were celebrating for a whole year the arrival of the Divine Face in 1506.

People who simply believed that an angel had brought the picture here had protected this precious treasure and kept it safe for centuries. Their faith had been quite enough. Yet now, just a few years had been enough for a few restless Germans to see behind this picture the old Roman Veronica—as if here, in a little church in the Abruzzis, the original had survived the storms of recent centuries as safely as it once had, imprisoned in the wall at the city gate of Edessa. For some reason, these Germans could not stop asking: Who was the angel? Where did he come from? What did he bring? Where was it before that?

Why Germans? Was it because the last great dispute about images had begun in Germany? Because it was in Germany—albeit by the hand of the Russian Kandinsky—a good hundred years before in Munich that the first completely abstract picture in the history of art was produced, the complete dissolution of representational art? Because in Germany Catholics, like Protestants and like agnostics and atheists, had all long since passed through the same acid-bath of the Reformation, the Enlightenment, and modern exegesis and were constantly having to question and doubt everything? Probably it was some of all of that.

Yet now the inhabitants of Manoppello could not stop asking, and their question was always the same: "Is the Pope coming? When is he coming?" Even the people in the Abruzzis had noticed that the Bavarian Successor of Peter talked more and more about "the face of God". On January 11, he yet again ended his general audience by saying that "for Christians, God has taken on the loving face of Christ." On January 18, the newspaper *Il Tempo* in the Abruzzis reported on "rumors" that the Pope would be coming to Manoppello "in the spring". On January 23, the Pope's secretary confirmed the news for me: Yes, the Pope had already given notice of his visit to the Archbishop of Chieti and given a firm promise he would be coming soon!

On the same day, in Rome, Benedict XVI was elucidating his first encyclical. He gave us to understand in his explanation that Dante's *Divine Comedy* had inspired him to write it—in which a "cosmic excursion" into the inside of Paradise leads to the most intimate light of love, which is at the same time "the love that moves the sun and the other stars". The most profound and inmost heart of this unattainable light was not, however, an even brighter radiance or an even more glittering light, but the tender face of a human being, which then finally came to meet the seer in his search. This, we were told, was "something completely new". The human face of Jesus Christ, which Dante recognized at the center of the inmost mystery of God, was "even more overwhelming than this revelation of God as a trinitarian circle of knowledge and love", we were told. "God, infinite Light, ... has a human face." I read through this speech three times. Then I took down from my bookshelf the *Divina Commedia* and looked up the passage.

Yet in my Italian-German edition, it was not so simple. In the translation of August Vezin, lines 130 to 132 of canto 33 sounded more dark and equivocal than a Delphic oracle, where "our image made of shimmering gauze, / colored like him, appears in the inner circle, / and (the seer) is lost in renewed gazing". Nonetheless, this was the decisive passage. In the language of Dante, it was simply this: "*Dentro da sé, del suo colore stesso, / mi parve pinta de la nostra effige; / per che 'l mio viso in lei tutto era messo.*" I first of all tried to translate these lines in crude and literal fashion and then, again, somewhat more elegantly: "Deep within, painted in a shade of the same light, / appeared to me our image, / so that I discovered my face." In the following lines, the poet went on to describe this face as an ultimate point of reference, *like a surveyor from the ancient world of the Christians.* I called my wife.

For it was clear that I would not get an exact translation of these lines. Yet it was also clear that Dante was talking about the *Volto Santo* here: about the Holy Face within the divine light! These three lines written in 1320 described it as accurately as a "wanted" poster. The incomparable shades within shades of this "painting", "in its same color", the brush being dipped in a pot of light for the face of Christ, and the remarkable way that it mirrored the face of each beholder. With these three lines, Dante made himself known as an eyewitness of the image on the Veil at Manoppello, someone who had seen it close up—after, just a few pages earlier, in canto 31, he had explicitly referred to "our Veronica". I was speechless. Generations of specialists in Romance literature and in theology had always hitherto seen this vision of Dante as deriving from the vision of God in the Book of Ezekiel, in the first chapter of which we are told about "something" in "the likeness of a throne, in appearance like sapphire", and on this "a likeness as it were of a human form". Upward from the loins, Ezekiel saw "as it were gleaming bronze, like the appearance of fire enclosed round about"; and below this, "as it were the appearance of fire, and there was brightness round about him. Like the appearance of the bow that is in the cloud on the day of rain, so was the appearance of the brightness round about. Such was the appearance of the likeness of the glory of the Lord." Any reference by Dante's verse to this vision was obviously a stretch. The contemplation of what Christians had once had had been lost before the meaning of the lines had been buried beneath incomprehensible translations.

Yet for my book, this discovery had become once more the most important clue of all: finding the true Face of Christ in the heart of Christian literature, at the summit of Italian poetry, was more spectacular than the opening of one final secret treasure chest could have been. Yet more incredible, however, was the fact that the Pope himself had made this discovery. I had sent him some photos. Yet without even having ever once seen for himself the Divine Face of Manoppello, he had already rediscovered it in the heart of the *Divine Comedy*, in the midst of Paradise! "Jesus is clear!" his friend Hans Urs von Balthasar had said to him, years before. Here, Jesus was suddenly clearer than ever before, from within the heart of the light of love, "which moves the sun and the stars". In all truth, no deep stronghold could have opened to show me a greater treasure.

Only a few days later, the war with the Islamic world over pictures and caricatures broke out in Copenhagen, Paris, and Berlin. Writers and artists who had long since forgotten the origins of our freedom in dealing with pictures had ignited it like boy-scouts who wanted to warm themselves at a little fire in the middle of a forest. The Western world was appalled and suddenly became aware that pictures—even pen-and-ink sketches—may be more explosive than bombs, above all in the age of electronic mass communications and with the still half-ancient world of Islam. A new age was again struck, with a rumbling out of the depths of the ancient iconoclastic controversy that has so many times been fought out by Christendom. The era of peace will not come back so quickly. The disturbances, along with the latest news and the new perspectives, however, made it clear that the nice book I had written last autumn would have to be prefaced with this new chapter in the spring. As a narrative, this task was as exciting as a last variation in the construction of Saint Peter's, which played such a strange and prominent role in the story of the loss and rediscovery of the Divine

Face. This basilica, too, had changed its shape several times, since the cornerstone of the new building, laid on April 18, 1506, became the base for the "pillar of Veronica".

This was right in the time of Machiavelli, the great teacher of cunning, whose traces may be found in a good many places in the story that follows. After that, over several generations, geniuses like Bramante, Raphael, and Michelangelo continued to work on this monumental construction, following various plans. The basilica was actually already finished when, a hundred years later, Carlo Maderno put up in front of it a new portal with a baroque façade that has dominated our picture of the entrance to the world-famous basilica ever since. Then again, fifty years later, Gianlorenzo Bernini gave its final shape to the whole complex with Saint Peter's Square—where my story originally began and will in a moment begin again. The book of my life, in our age of unstoppable acceleration, had gone infinitely quicker for me, though less brilliantly. I had to and still have to stop myself from writing and telling it over again. Yet there was still a need for this first chapter—like a newer, more suitable, and somewhat monumental gate to an extremely delicate story that has been being woven for two thousand years already.

The Return of the Images

T he morning sunshine made the marble of Saint Peter's shine a reddish gold; at that moment, a palace of the heavenly Jerusalem could hardly have been more beautiful. Behind the dome, the blue of a new day stretched up into space like a shining tent. It looked as though this might be the first day of summer, this year, in spite of the night-cold stones of Saint Peter's Square. I leaned my head back against a pillar and gazed up at two clouds sailing by. From this point of view, the encircling colonnade opened above like an enormous cosmic volcano, from the center of which the obelisk stretched up to the stars like a direction finder for the world beyond. This was a little trick I normally used to impress visitors to Rome. But this time, nothing was normal. This time, I was lying in the ring of pillars like a boxer on the ropes after being down for the count.

A plane with blinking navigation lights moved across, high up, in the pale gray of morning. The doves were still sleeping on the windowsills. Swallows were chirping as they swooped and dove, high and low. A street sweeper was noisily brushing the black basalt of the square. Some grueling weeks lay behind me. A single great feast of images, about which I had to report almost night and day. Not since the landing on the moon had so many people gazed at one place as had gazed during this time

Saint Peter's, Rome, in the morning

at this square in front of me. The Jewish world was celebrating Passover today: the feast of God's "passing over". Yet three days before, the tableau of a passing over was completed here in a way that people in this age of media had never seen before. From the death of Pope John Paul II to the election of Benedict XVI, this square had been the stage for a unique world theater. Heaven had made it once more the place of the "prophets", as the "Vatican" was called by the ancient Romans, using a word borrowed from Egypt.

The obelisk in the middle was already standing here when Peter the Apostle was crucified in Nero's circus. Now it was a heavenly antenna, broadcasting into the world, for weeks now, ever-new images from a fantastic picture gallery—a return of the images.

I had been here to experience the last wordless blessing from John Paul II, given from his window up there. Later, I had stood in the "love parade" that streamed to Rome, for his dying moments, like a human Mississippi. When the light of life departed from him, I had once more been standing under his window—in the midst of the tumultuous applause that spontaneously greeted the news of his "return to the house of the Father". Here I had joined in singing the Litany of All Saints, which surrounded him on his last journey across Saint Peter's Square to the great porch of the basilica. The stormy gusts, a few days later, that blew the cardinals' vestments about as they stood before his coffin had also run through my hair before leafing through the pages of the Gospel book, there in front on his coffin.

I had been standing there in Saint Peter's when Cardinal Ratzinger, wearing a crimson chasuble like a royal toga, celebrated the final Mass before the election of the new pope. On the evening of the same day, I had stood outside that porch and had seen the first black smoke rising into the sky; and the following evening, I had seen the white smoke—standing in the crowd, in the rain, below the loggia, before that same man had suddenly appeared in white and lifted his arms up above Saint Peter's Square. I could still hear the clanging of the great bells—and still see the fluttering golden vestment of Pope Benedict XVI, in which three days before he had walked out through the porch into a new era. The face of a gothic Christ had been gazing down on him from his Cross, open-mouthed. To report on these sights, I could scarcely at times walk, stand, sit, or lie down. I had written one report after another; the pile of texts was enough to fill a whole book. It was the dawning of a new age.

Two little tractors had driven up to help clear away the last seating from the celebration. The red velvet hanging had been taken away from the loggia. The everyday world was making its return. In a few hours, people from all over the world would be gazing at the square and the basilica and flocking to John Paul II's tomb. There was still not a voice to be heard. The two fountains were splashing. The streetlamps went out. Two policemen strolled through the circling pillars in front, over to the right. I leaned my head back against the pillar again, looked up into the dawn sky once more, and then glanced at the policemen, who were now moving toward the heavy bronze doors. Yesterday, I had walked in through them with my wife—on our way to one last painting, which was going to eclipse all other pictures in Rome.

Over a year earlier, I had made an application to Archbishop Piero Marini, head of the "Office of the Liturgical Celebrations of the Supreme Pontiff", to be allowed to have a close look at the "oldest portrait of the face of Jesus Christ", the so-called "Mandylion of Edessa", which the Vatican had in its keeping in this palace. This "true portrait of Jesus Christ" was the model, so I had read, which had "obviously" become "the archetype of all later pictures of Christ". It was reckoned as one of the pictures "not made by human hands", of heavenly origin, that were supposed to date from Jesus' own lifetime. In a certain sense, it was said, it would have to be seen as "the first icon" of all. Its appearance, we were told, had stamped its impression like a seal on Pope John Paul II's heart, understanding, and thought. For a long time, he had it before his eyes in his private chapel. Edessa had been an important city in the ancient world, in eastern Anatolia, and present-day Urfa was built on its ruins. How this ancient portrait of Christ had found its way from there to Rome was a puzzle, I had discovered; but it could be traced back to the sixth century at least, or even to the third. After that, I had been on fire to see it. In photos, at any rate, the "Mandylion of Edessa" looked almost black.

Archbishop Marini's first reply gave me to understand that the cloth image was in an exhibition in California just now and not in Rome. Later inquiries elicited the reply that it was being restored right then. But suddenly, one day near the end of the celebrations of the great transition, I had received a fax from the "Capella Sistina", which informed me that I could now see the image. I would learn more at the "Portone di Bronzo". Of course I might bring Ellen, my wife, with me, I was told over the phone. So she put on her string of pearls and her red velvet jacket, and even I hauled my best suit out of the wardrobe again. At the bronze doors, the Swiss guards saluted us as if they had been expecting us. We should go straight up the stairs in front of us, the officer said; at the top, another guard would take us on farther. The *Scala Regia* lay before us, the "royal stairs": a cascade of steps climbing up behind the doorway into the Vatican. Bernini's masterpiece was usually barred to ordinary mortals, yet it was not the magnificent drawing power of this ladder to heaven that overcame me or the privilege of actually being allowed to set foot on these steps; rather, it was a feeling as if, without warning, the film of the past few weeks, the scenes of which all the world had been watching on television, were about to be replayed— but this time, backward. Suddenly, I could see the dead John Paul II there in front of me, who three weeks before had been carried down here on a bier for his last journey, to the singing of the Litany of All Saints: "*Sancta Maria, ora pro illo!*", and again and again, "*Sancte Petre, Sancte Paule, Sancte Andrea, Sancte Ioannes, Sancte Thoma, Sancte Bartholomæ, Sancte Thaddæ, Sancta Maria Magdalena: ora pro illo.* Saint Mary, pray for him; Saint Peter, pray for him, pray for him, pray for him, pray for him!"—We were walking up where he had been carried down. At the top of the scala we were taken round two corners. A breathtaking change of perspective: suddenly, through the windows, I could see the façade of Saint Peter's from above, then the Gianicolo Hill, and lastly behind them the domes of Rome in the morning mist. The fax in my hand had become an "Open, sesame". Then we were standing in front of Archbishop Marini's door and looking down into Saint Peter's Square.

Suddenly, a young man with a bunch of keys was standing in front of us, sent by the Archbishop to lead Ellen and me through the labyrinth of the palace to the image of Christ. We went through the "Sala Ducale" and the "Sala Regia". I wanted to linger over an enormous fresco of the naval battle of Lepanto. I twisted my neck to see all the masterpieces on the walls and ceilings; it was like walking through a dream. I even forgot to ask the name of our young guide; and finally I forgot everything else when he opened a door with a large key, and there behind it, hundreds of people were crowded together. We were standing on the threshold of the Sistine Chapel, the threshold crossed by the cardinals, a few days earlier, as they went into the conclave.

Time and again, this door had been shown on television in the last few days, as it opened and closed. "I stand at the entrance of the Sistine", John Paul II had written about this very same threshold in a poem two years earlier. "*Extra omnes!*" the Master of Ceremonies to the conclave had proclaimed several days before, in front of this door, when everyone except the cardinals had to leave this place before the papal election: "Everybody out!"— "Perhaps all this could be said more simply / In the language of the Book of Genesis, the scribal rolls of the 'primal beginning'," John Paul II's poem continues, "but the book awaits its image.—Quite rightly. / It was waiting for its Michelangelo."

I felt almost dizzy. The normal museum activity had started up again, and one group after another swept through this holy place. I looked up at the Judge of the world, in Michelangelo's *Last Judgment*, then looked for our guide in the crowd that was pressing toward us and past us, took Ellen by the hand, and walked forward against the flow, toward the end wall and the altar, and left to where the young man was now beneath the damned, unlocking the door right through the Last Judgment, to the "place of tears". No camera had been allowed to follow events any more when Cardinal Ratzinger went into that room to exchange his crimson cardinal's robe for the white of the pope. This was less a room than a small, asymmetrical corridor with steps, landings, pillars, and simple floor tiles in sienna-brown travertine. "The robes lay here, and the shoes stood here", our guide smiled, pointing to a chaise longue in a corner, and then led us on down a little flight of stairs, beyond which he opened one last door on the left, to the *Sacrestia della Capella Sistina*.

The bare room hardly looked like a sacristy. A young woman sitting in front of a PC nodded to us. There was a bookcase against the wall. Lupines glowed outside the window, blossoming pale pink. Through the stalks I could see walls with old Roman bricks. I was looking in vain all around the room for the heavy baroque frame in which the "Mandylion of Edessa" had been displayed in the Vatican pavilion of the Hannover World Fair, during the Jubilee Year of 2000, when our companion opened a flat cardboard box on a table and folded back a layer of tissue paper: "*Eccola!* The face of Christ."

This was the image. The Pope's image of Christ! The mother of all icons. It was not black, and yet it did require you to look three, four, or five times before the facial features emerged. It was different from what any photos had ever shown. It had been taken out of the baroque frame; gleaming, silvery gold foil covered the outline of the face, as if it were looking at us out of an old window. Ancient nails held the foil down along the inner edge to the picture itself. Down below, a pointed cutaway section in the middle suggested the end of a beard, and two pointed cut-outs to right and left, locks of hair on the shoulders. An image from the world beyond gazed out through this window; so far away, yet so near; so dark, yet so present with us. We bent over it. "Just get the light out of the bag", I asked Ellen. We had gone back once again on purpose to get the flashlight from the flat, just in case. Now Ellen switched it on and asked whether we might shine it onto the image. The young man nodded and even held the light himself, so as to illuminate the face for us. We should be able to concentrate on simply looking—concentrate on the long nose, the mouth, the eyebrows, and the eyes. The image shone slightly wherever the beam of light caught it. Down on the right I was able to discover a tiny corner of plain linen, but otherwise the cloth was evenly covered with one and the same dark coloration.

A good quarter of a century earlier, I had once seen a similar color on the image of the "Black Madonna" at the Jasna Góra monastery of Częstochowa in Poland, which we had gone to see when Karol Wojtyła became pope. "It looks as though gold dust had been mixed in with the paint", said Ellen, "or bronze". Yes, it glittered in a remarkable way, but the image made me feel helpless. "Let us measure it for a start", I said. The young woman at the desk handed us a meter rule. The image as a whole measured 33×22.2 cm ($13'' \times 8.74''$); the inner picture, 28×17 cm ($11'' \times 6.7''$); and the facial area, 24.5 cm ($9.6''$) from the topmost point of the forehead to the point of the suggestion of a beard, and 14.3 cm ($5.6''$) from the left cheek to the right. I noted it all down, because otherwise I did not know what I should be able to fix in my mind. There were no ears to be seen, and even the beard was only a hint. The Pope's icon! The Edessa Mandylion! I took a deep breath, prayed the Our

Father before the icon with Ellen, and then a Hail Mary, kissed the image on the forehead and straightened up. I felt unable to tear myself away from this gaze. The eyes were looking at me, and I looked at them.

I knew those two eyes and that gaze. I had last seen it only three weeks before, in a picture of which this icon was a dim copy; yet I had seen them, not here in Rome in the papal palace, but in a little corner of Italy forgotten by the world. Twenty-two days earlier was the last time I had searched out this face, along with Ellen and Joachim Cardinal Meisner, on a hillside in front of a little mountain town. We had driven out from Rome, early in the morning, 106 miles over onto the other side of the Italian peninsula, merely to see this gaze. It was on April 4, 2005. Two evenings earlier, the Pope had died. "Today I have met with the Easter Lord", said the Cardinal from Cologne, that same afternoon, to the reporter from an American magazine. The memory of it gave him a lion's strength, as other cardinals in the stormy conclave soon noticed.

Yet I am drawn still farther back by this memory—months, years, and centuries back—yet first of all, over the mountains again, like in a film that was starting all over again. Almost all the reporters of the events surrounding this epochal change had already left Rome again. Most of my colleagues in Rome had given themselves a holiday after the strains and tensions of the past few weeks or had fallen ill or both. I was leaning against one of the pillars of the colonnade in Saint Peter's Square, exhausted. My joints were hurting, my limbs burning with pain. Yet now I wanted to—I had to—tell the incredible story of the discovery of the face of the invisible God; tell it once more, on my own, completely afresh, starting at the beginning. First of all, it was the discovery of many discoverers—including various lady discoverers—from several decades and centuries. Above all, however, it was the discovery of a tiny little place in Italian Adria with a curious name: Manoppello.

The Sanctuary of the Holy Face on the Tarigni Hill,
in front of Manoppello

The Holy Face

Dogs had been barking half the night, first one, then, two, then three, and more, and then their hoarse voices joined in chorus in the valleys between the Abruzzi hills and gave us no more peace until dawn. Before the dogs fell silent, the cocks had started up. The twittering lauds of the songbirds began under the window with the first red streak of dawn, as lovely as on the seventh day of creation.

I turned over and dreamed, half-asleep, that in the beginning God had perhaps planted the various trees and bushes out there especially for flocks of the various kinds of birds—the ivy for sparrows, maybe, vines for the titmice, olive trees for nightingales, acacias for black-birds, and almond trees and rosebriar hedges as the seat for clouds of butterflies. When, at seven o'clock, the bell in the campanile next to the little pilgrim hotel called people to early Mass, I must have finally gone back to sleep again. By about nine o'clock, the hill had sunk back again into its everyday peace. A single car was parked in front of the hotel coffee shop, and that was mine. The wind caressing the gentle slopes fanned a hint of the nearby sea into the room. Yet beside the inn a steep wooded gorge plunged down. The winding street that led up here was misleading. It used to be a wilderness here. Whoever brought a treasure here, wherever it came from, really did want to hide it. It was safe here.

The Tarigni Hill was one of the last outlying ridges of the Majella massif, and the sanctuary of the Holy Face lay on it, somewhat aside from the little town, which crowned the summit of the next hill, opposite it. The Majella was a "holy hill", so Petrarch wrote in the Middle Ages; and I have read in a slim volume from the 1960s that Manoppello was a "little Jerusalem". In the classic tourist guides to Italy, however, or even those simply to the Abruzzis, it did not even appear so far, in contrast to many other old places in the district.

There was only this hotel, next to the sanctuary, and then one other inn, farther down, and both closed in the winter—it was already winter—and also three low-end restaurants in and just outside the little town. Fresh fish from the sea was sold from the vans that brought it, and the drivers lured the housewives out of their houses with droning megaphones. Up to thirty years ago, this little town had still been an important market for the surrounding area, but since the highway came, both buyers and sellers could get to Chieti, Pescara, or Sulmona by car quicker than up this hill. If it had not been for the Holy Face, then Manoppello would probably have been completely forgotten. Not far from here, beyond the next pass, the oldest eucharistic miracle in the world was revered at Lanciano, where since the ninth century a Host had been preserved in a monstrance; when the monk whose duty it had been to celebrate the Mass began to doubt whether, after the consecration and transubstantiation, one suddenly was dealing with the transformed Body of Christ, the Host had been transformed into a human myocardal muscle (with AB blood group). Beside that, in a

44

transparent chalice of quartz, a few clots of blood from the same Mass were preserved; when the unbelieving priest spoke the words of consecration, the wine had been transformed into that blood. The world of the Abruzzis was strewn with solitary hidden hermitages and ancient monasteries. Italy had more art treasures and relics than any other country on earth. Above all, however, the Abruzzis were from of old an area of earthquakes. Here, deep down below the Apennine Mountains, the Eurasian and African continental plates ground together on an ocean of seething magma; and now and then one of them got under the other and plunged into the burning mass. There was hardly a house in Manoppello without cracks from the last and the next-to-the-last earthquakes. At the last earthquake, all the inhabitants of this little patrician town had run to the sanctuary in the middle of the night and had spent the rest of the night in and just in front of the church, pleading loudly for help to the Holy Face.

Now the church was completely empty when I entered it through the right-hand doorway. At six in the morning, the Capuchin Father Guardian unlocked it until midday siesta, and then at six in the evening—seven, in summertime—he locked up again. Every one of the handful of women who came from the little town for morning Mass was long gone. I walked along the central aisle toward the altar, my gaze directed to the rectangular monstrance that was set out behind the altar in an armored glass reliquary. With the morning light falling straight onto it, a transparent veil shone milkily in its frame over the tabernacle.

Here, since its first arrival, this Veil had simply been called "Il Volto Santo"—the Holy Face. No one was there. I went left around the altar, up the steps behind it, and at the top I rested my head against the glass, the way I had often done against train windows while on a journey, while the earth was flying past outside, or as I still did sometimes when a plane was taking off or landing. I gazed at the smaller window of the monstrance behind, and now a living face was looking at me from it—with the shape and the tranquility of an ancient icon of the Madonna. A bearded man with sidelocks, who had been struck on his slim nose; his right cheek was swollen, and part of his beard had been torn out.

He had the thin vandyke beard of a young man, so that you could see practically each single hair, and fine eyebrows like those of a young woman. A delicate lock of hair fell from his scalp onto his high forehead. On his lips, his temples, and his forehead there were several areas of skin that, if you looked closely, had the pinkness of fresh-healed wounds—yet somehow "on the inside" of the tissue, like in a hologram. There were patches like that under the eyes, too, within the eye sockets, and on the edema on his right cheek. Nothing could be seen of his neck or of his ears—they were completely hidden in the hair that framed his head. There was an inexplicable peace in his wide-open eyes. Bafflement, amazement, astonishment, too; and a mild pity. No pain, no anger, and no curse on his lips. It looked like the face of a man who was just waking from sleep. The shadows around his eyes and the shades of light on his eyelids were more finely drawn than Leonardo da Vinci could have painted. The color of the skin and the hair changed between brown and bronze and chestnut. The mouth was half-open. The line at the bottom of the upper lip might have been drawn with a kajal pencil. Even the tips of the incisor teeth could be clearly seen; the lower teeth showed only as little points of light. If one had to decide what sound was on his lips, they were making a soft "Ah". A broken splinter of glass was sticking to the picture inside the frame, low down on the right. A living face was looking at me, and he was looking into my eyes as if I were an old acquaintance.

Yet when the Father Guardian opened the main doors to let some air into the church, from up here my gaze—going right through the face—fell on the square outside the doorway and the nearest houses and, beyond them, as far as the Pescara plain in the distance. The picture disappeared completely in the morning light. It had fled like a dream; had become as transparent as a window. This was not the first time I had been here, yet once again I had been alone with him for as long as I liked; him before whom—so I had been told—the emperor of Byzantium was allowed to kneel, under the supervision of the highest-ranking clergy, once a year. Before that, he had had to prepare for the sight by confession and by receiving the most holy Eucharist.

I tried to catch a fly and looked at the face again. It had already been in this church for almost four hundred years, although until 1960 the church had been only half this size. Only since 1923 had it been enthroned above the altar; before that, for centuries, the Veil had been preserved in the shadowy darkness of a side chapel, without any lighting, as a slate-gray relic. It seemed to be breathing. The all but immaterial square of cloth was lit by halogen lamps. A massive silver frame, containing within it a worm-eaten wooden one, surrounded this treasure. Two sheets of old glass, in front and behind, held the cloth image between them. It was 17 × 24 cm (6.7″ × 9.5″) and now looked like an exposed film negative in

47

tones of brown, bronze, and sepia. The gold and silver frame was ornamented with a scourge, dice, nails, a ladder, hammer and pincers, a cock—symbols of the various stations of suffering in Christ's Passion—and with four emeralds and three large and six small, pale-green amethysts.

On the folded-back door of the reliquary was fixed a notice with the "brief history of the Holy Face". "We are told", it said there, "that in the year 1506, one Sunday afternoon, a pilgrim came to Manoppello." In front of the Church of Saint Nicholas, he was said to have asked Doctor Giacomantonio Leonelli to come into God's house with him, and there he handed over a bundle. "Keep this gift lovingly, always hold it dear. God will reward you for that with many gifts and great wealth, either earthly or heavenly." Doctor Leonelli had hardly unwrapped the package before the face of Lord was gazing at him from the gossamer-thin Veil. When he went to thank the donor, there was no longer any trace of the pilgrim. No one in the village knew the stranger, and no one ever saw him again.

For about a century, it continued, the relic had been passed on to his descendants. Finally, in 1608, there was a dispute about the Veil among various descendants. Pancrazio Petruzzi, a soldier married to Marzia Leonelli from the inheriting family, took possession of the relic by force. In Chieti—it is not known why—he was thrown into prison. His wife, in order to buy his freedom, sold the holy cloth to someone else. Thus it came into the hands of Donantonino De Fabritiis.

This text was an abridgment, in a few sentences, of a wordy "*Vera, et breve relazione historica d'una miracolosa figura . . .*"—a "true and brief historical summary of a marvelous figure or true image of Christ, our tortured and tormented Lord, which is now to be found in the priory of the Capuchins at Manoppello, a place this side of the Abruzzis in the province of the kingdom of Naples", in which one Father Donato da Bomba, "Preacher of the Capuchins from the middle province of the Abruzzis", set down for the first time in the year 1645, in a sharp, clear hand on brown, brittle paper, how the Veil had come to Manoppello "through the intervention of heaven" over a century earlier. This was the first document to refer to the singular image in Manoppello.

Even then, Father da Bomba had observed that it was as fine as "gossamer". The original copy of this document was kept in the archives of the Capuchins in the Santa Chiara Priory in Aquila, yet there was another manuscript copy gathering dust in Manoppello, in the tower chamber of the parish Church of Saint Nicholas, and I was able to spend a long time leafing through its yellowed pages. *Preziosa Memoria* was the title written on it by a certain Father Eugenio in 1865: "Precious Memorial". And all the other old books and manuscripts about the Divine Face in the rickety shelves and cupboards of this deserted place, with its wonderful view of the Abruzzi Hills, repeatedly came back to the 1645 document. For centuries, Donato da Bomba's account of the delivery of the Veil "by the hand of an angel" in the year 1506 had been the decisive authority on the origin of the image of Christ at Manoppello.

Because it was not in good condition, the seventeenth-century chronicle continued, De Fabritiis brought it to the Capuchins, "where Father Clemente da Castelvecchio trimmed the frayed edge with scissors and Brother Remigio da Rapino stretched it out between two sheets of crystal glass in a frame of walnut wood". One could see with the naked eye that the cloth had been trimmed: the top corners, right and left, had been patched with a different material. Yet what could have happened to the leftover bits? Were they really "frayed"? It is said to have been "in poor condition" and to have been hidden "in a granary". What remained, though, was in really excellent condition. So, were the edges really only frayed? However that may be, this Signor De Fabritiis was said finally to have made a present of the cloth to the Capuchins in 1638, and they "displayed it to the people for adoration" in 1646.

However historical that may sound, the story thereafter became incredible. In 1703, a Father Bonifacio d'Ascoli tried to take the relic out of the old wooden frame and put it into a silver one. Yet when he laid the veil in the new frame, the image disappeared. It faded from sight like a cloud disappearing from the sky. Several witnesses signed the report of the subsequent investigation. The image remained invisible until the veil was set back in its old wooden frame; only then did it come back into the material. Eleven years later, the same attempt was made again, this time under a certain Father Antonio, with the same result. Only after that was a large silver reliquary made, for a price of sixty-three ducats, in which the relic could be placed together with its old wooden frame. That was the same slightly worm-eaten wooden frame that I was looking at here. Since then, the image had remained visible.—Marzia Leonelli was said to have sold the living image of Christ for four scudi to get her husband out of jail.

I already knew the story almost by heart, with all its questionable events and dubious twists and turns. I had first stood in front of it—through sheer curiosity—in 1999, hand-in-hand with Maria Magdalena, our eldest daughter, who was in a hurry; and then again in February 2000, along with Ellen and Christina, our youngest daughter, on the way to the airport at Rome—and again in a hurry. I wanted to show my wife something that I had not really been able to get out of my mind since my first visit—likely the eyes, which were looking at me like the eyes of my very favorite teacher had done about forty years earlier. That gaze. "He looks like a lamb", said Ellen. "Those eyes are almost foolish with pity." "Yes", I said, and sought for words—humility, meekness, sweetness, resignation, self-restraint, fearlessness—and rejected them, one after another, for this Lamb whom Christendom adores as its shepherd.

The people of Manoppello loved photos in which they were holding a newspaper behind the cloth, and it could be read without difficulty. With no lighting, it was dark gray, and Christ's face was a leaden-hued shadow on woven material that looked almost black, thus "black" and "rueful", as Julian of Norwich, the fourteenth-century English nun and mystic, lamented, when a "true image" of Christ was shown her in Rome. If the delicate cloth was lit indirectly from behind by electric lights, on the other hand, it turned gold- and honey-colored, exactly as Gertrude of Helfta described the face of Christ in the thirteenth century. If the same lamps were lighting it from in front, it turned more of an umber color; and then the weave of the cloth stood out more clearly, a gossamer-thin pattern in relief. Under the polarized rays of a so-called Wood's lamp it showed as little reaction "as if it were not subject to the usual laws of nature". While the penetrating light produced brightness and reflected colors all around the face, its features and appearance remained totally unchanged under this illumination. The cloth was so fine, it seemed as if it could fold into a walnut shell. And how sophisticated the painting was! Yet that was impossible. It could not have been painted or drawn. The material showed not the least particle of any pigment.

Professor Donato Vittore of Bari University and a Professor Gulio Fanti from Padua University discovered, taking microscopic specimens, that the entire cloth offered no trace of pigmentation. Nothing. No brushstrokes, no lead, no opaque white, nothing. Only in the black pupils of both eyes did the fibers seem as if they were singed, as if heat had slightly smudged the threads there. Nothing of that could be seen with the naked eye, however. Even the eyelashes could hardly be perceived, and I first discovered them on blow-ups. And probably, I really became aware of the image for the first time through my own photos—through enlarging and shrinking, in the blow-up at which I looked in a hotel room at San Giovanni Rotondo in the Gargano mountains, after our third encounter—late in the evening on March 8, 2004.

Before that, it had been pouring rain in Rome. A colleague in Berlin had asked me to go to the Gargano Peninsula, where I was to report on the new pilgrims' church that the famous architect Renzo Piano had been building in San Giovanni Rotondo for Saint Padre Pio. Because it was a Sunday, we had planned to take the somewhat longer southern route by way of Bari and have lunch in a simple restaurant I had known for years at the old harbor there. But then it had poured so heavily in the streets of Rome that as soon as we woke up it was clear that we could never drive off in that weather, at least, not immediately. In the end, it seemed for once to be a day to lie in bed with a book and wait for better weather. Yet it was still pouring at ten o'clock. I got up and switched on the computer. "It's no use", I said to Ellen, after I had looked at the weather forecast for Italy on the Internet, "we have to go, and right away. The weather is not going to change for the whole week. So I won't be able to take any time off." The bags were already packed; and half an hour later we were sitting in the car under a torrential Roman storm, with the windshield wipers hardly able to cope. Because of our delay, we were no longer taking the southern route through Bari, but the more twisting, yet shorter eastern road by way of Pescara. Up in the Apennines, the rain finally stopped.

Around midday we passed Sulmona, and shortly after that there was a sign for the Alanno and Scafa exit. "Turn off here," Ellen asked me, "and let's go and eat in Manoppello and then have another look at the Holy Face." In a roadside diner near the highway, we were the only customers. And it was the same at the shrine in Manoppello, to which we drove another six miles up into the hills again after coffee. Once more, there was not another soul, just as on our first and second visits, when a Capuchin opened the side door on the right after the midday siesta. Yet this time—when we were not in a hurry, not hungry, and had nothing to distract us—the image seized my attention the moment we entered the church through the right-hand doorway.

In the upper windows of the central part of the nave, angels carried toward you the instruments of Christ's Passion—just as I had seen them doing on the parapet of the Sant'Angelo bridge only yesterday, in Rome. Yet now, right from the start, I had eyes only for the shining little rectangle above the high altar. First of all, as soon as we had mounted the steps behind to the Face, I took photos of every detail, from in front and behind—the eyes, the beard, the nose, the lips, the frame—and for want of a tripod, I pressed the camera lens against the glass, while Ellen held her coat up behind me to block the reflections produced on the glass by the light of the window in the apse. From behind, it looked exactly as it did from the front—only with the two sides reversed, and the swollen right cheek on the left. I could not get enough of looking at it. For the first time, I found the image overpowering. It seemed to me as if I were seeing it for the first time that day—and letting myself be looked at by it. I took photos until the microchip was full. Then I put my camera away, looked at the face, eye to eye, one more time, and went back down the steps and down the nave to the door. Ellen stayed a bit longer at the lectern. I went back again, to urge her to leave. We did still have about 125 miles to do, and it was already getting late. Finally we walked to the door together, back to our car. We were opening the door in the wooden windbreak in front of the doorway when a nun came through the outer door into the little cubbyhole. "Sister Blandina?" we asked with one voice, in German, deep in the Italian Abruzzis. "Oh, yes!" she replied, and looked at us in astonishment.

An Easter Sister

Neither my wife nor I had ever seen Sister Blandina Paschalis Schlömer, O.C.S.O., or even a photo of her, yet we had read about her several times and had heard that she came from the German convent of Maria Frieden in the Eifel and had moved to Manoppello to live as a hermit. The name Blandina she had been given at her baptism; "Paschalis", on the other hand, "of Easter", was the name she received on entering the order, even if the name was not entirely to her own liking; and O.S.C.O. is the abbreviation for the Latin *Ordo Cisterciensium Strictioris Observantiae*. That meant that she belonged to the order of "Cistercian Nuns of the More Strict Observance", a so-called "reformed" branch of the Cistercians dating from the seventeenth century, who are also known as "Trappistines" after their original monastery of La Trappe in France. This was an ascetic community with a strict rule about silence and rigorous penitential practices, who sang aloud together almost nothing beyond the praise of God in worship. Apart from that, they kept silence. This nun in her black and white habit studied pharmaceutics and had learned to paint icons. Above all, however, for people of today outside Italy, she was probably known as the first person to rediscover the "Holy Face".

For she did not of course need to demonstrate to the artisans, farmers, and fishermen along the Adriatic from

Sister Blandina Paschalis Schlömer, O.C.S.O.

Ancona to Tarento that the image on the cloth was genuine and authentic. They had in any case believed that with unshakeable faith for four hundred years. Sister Blandina was, however, the first to investigate that belief with German thoroughness, with chemist's scales and more and more measurements, through which she has discovered and demonstrated—so she said—that this image entirely and completely corresponded in all proportions and measurements to the portrait on the Shroud of Turin. That, too, had often been asserted in Italy for some time already; but no one had ever shouted it from the rooftops as loudly as Sister Blandina. Without her, I and many other people would probably never have heard of the image on the cloth. Without her, this book would not exist.

"That cannot be true, that we are meeting you here, at this moment", I said in the entrance shelter, while Ellen took hold of her arm; "we are just leaving again." "But it is true", she smiled, and put her head on one side and looked at us assessingly. We went outside together and introduced ourselves. This cannot have happened by chance, she said. Yes, that was what I was thinking—and I promised to call in here again in two days' time, on our journey back from San Giovanni.

Two days later was my fifty-sixth birthday. A new part of my life was beginning. My brother Wolfgang called me on my cell phone in the morning and wished me a happy birthday from the Dutch border. Meanwhile, while I was away in San Giovanni, in looking at the photos in my digital camera, I saw sections and enlargements of the Holy Face that I had never found in any book. And at night, in the hotel room, I devoured that book by Sister Blandina in which, five years earlier, she had expounded her researches into the Holy Face.

Born in Carlsbad, Czechoslovakia, in 1943, Blandina Schlömer came as a refugee to the burning and burned-out waste of the German Reich two years later, holding her mother's hand along with two little sisters; she spent her childhood in the Ruhr. Their father was a pious postal official, who after the war provided an academic education for all five of his daughters, in spite of school fees. Three of his daughters later became nuns, one a dentist, and the other an artist. Blandina became both nun and artist (and time and again felt called to extract ideas from the heads of a good many of her fellowmen). To start with, she wanted only to be a nun, at first a missionary sister "of the Precious Blood", and then ten years later she entered the Trappist order. In the meantime, she had already become a mosaic artist and in 1965 learned all about the Turin Shroud from a book; she was convinced of its authenticity on account of the facts. That became her image of Christ; as a painter of icons, she painted it again and again.

In 1979 her whole convent was down with flu, and she went from cell to cell seeing to sick sisters. While doing that, she discovered on the cross over the bed of one fellow sister the Turin Face. "Oh, you have that as well!" she exclaimed, breaking her vow of silence. The other sister merely nodded and maybe murmured something. Yet as soon as she was better she left a magazine outside Blandina's door, with a report about another image on "gauze" in the Abruzzis and a large black-and-white photo. It was the last, December issue of the magazine *Das Zeichen Mariens* (The sign of Mary), in which a certain Renzo Allegri talked about the "similarities with the Turin Shroud" and about the "mysterious, inexplicable peculiarities" of this other image.

Basically, he was already saying back then all there was to be said about it, but in Sister Blandina he was talking to the wrong person. "I was so angry and annoyed", she recalled, "that I simply took the magazine and stuffed it in the nearest cupboard. Another image of Christ apart from the Turin Shroud? Impossible! There was no such thing." Perhaps she was only jealous ... And then something remarkable happened. In the course of the same day, while she was hurrying along the many long corridors of the convent, seeing to her sick sisters, she could not get the eyes out of her mind. She simply could not get rid of them. She saw them before her everywhere. And that was basically how it had continued to this day, during her long "climb up Mount Tabor", as she called it: the climb up to the mountain where Jesus once appeared "transfigured" to his closest disciples during his lifetime. This was the beginning of a love story with no ending.

That same evening, she took the magazine out of the cupboard again and studied the article quite calmly and critically. Suddenly, she too perceived features that corresponded to the Turin image, yet the image continued to be strange to her—until she discovered that for some reason it must have been printed in the magazine as a mirror image. Then she discovered that it resembled not only the Shroud, but also the icons of Christ that she had been studying for years. It would be another sixteen years before she was able to see the image on the cloth with her own eyes; yet those years were filled with studies of the image—at first, only early in the morning and late at night, but in the end in every spare minute. During that time she was living in the convent of Maria Frieden, in the Eifel, and, for the purpose of further education, in a convent in Provence, where an elixir called

"Blandinin" is still sold in the convent shop today as a remedy for every kind of joint and muscle pain, an elixir she concocted from horse-chestnut essence, lavender oil, and a drop of glycerin while she was there, following an old family recipe from the Egerland. Finally she spent three years in the newly refounded convent of Helfta, in Saxony-Anhalt, where after the fall of the Berlin wall her order was trying to revive the tradition of Saint Gertrude and Saint Mechthild, who both lived there in the thirteenth century and who both had radiant visions of Christ.

Day by day, she lived in the conviction that the image in Manoppello was genuine and not quite of this world, although she had never even seen it. And day by day, she was increasingly living against the resistance that her marvelous love aroused in others—first of all among her fellow sisters and, in the end, in scholars from all over Europe. This was an *amour fou*, as the French say. A good many people regarded her as a "holy fool", of which there used to be so many in Russia; others did not think she was holy. Above all, for many years she was completely alone in her discovery, which she could not get out of her mind. She studied and made photocopies; she played about with film transparencies, laying them one on top of another—she became obsessed with "superimposition", as she calls this technique, of the two images; but then when the experiment was published, the photographic "proof" presented to the public was almost ludicrously shifted out of alignment. Not until 1999 were her findings attractively printed. Professor Andreas Resch, a recognized expert on paranormal phenomena from Innsbruck, had urged her to publish her work after learning about her research. Now, not only were the image of Manoppello and that of Turin printed on two transparencies that could be laid on top of each other so that even details corresponded, but the Veil—when laid over the top of numerous icons and pictures of Christ—seemed to reveal and disclose the true, personal face of Christ ever anew—just as if the Veil were opening a kind of window through the works of art.

She was successful in doing this with the Risen Christ of the Hohenfurt altar in Prague, the Holy Face of Novgorod, the Christ icon of Saint Catherine's monastery on Sinai, and even the mosaic of the omnipotent Lord in the fourth-century Saint Pudentiana basilica in Rome. It seemed incredible: a veil that unveiled and revealed the Face of Christ instead of hiding and concealing it. A piece of cloth that uncovered faces instead of covering them—as if it helped every person and every work of art before which it was held to come closer to its true face. It was incredible. And it was exactly this incredulity she encountered among the academic specialists to whom she first presented her knowledge, especially the one who in his time was perhaps the most important. That was Werner Bulst, a Jesuit Father in Darmstadt who in German-speaking countries had gained a reputation as "pope of the Shroud" because of his comprehensive studies of the Turin Shroud.

In 1983, the nun sent this famous scholar a thick folder with the results of her "research" (into something she had never yet seen). Father Bulst took his time about replying. Finally, he sent a short note informing her that he had handed the matter over to an art historian in Rome who was interested in that kind of thing—to Father Heinrich Pfeiffer, another member of the Society of Jesus, who taught at the Pontifical Gregorian University. A few weeks later, Sister Blandina had a letter from Rome. Father Pfeiffer thanked her for the remarkable Face of Christ; in the light of what she had communicated about it, he could imagine that it might have just as mysterious an origin as the famous image of Our Lady of Guadalupe in Mexico. But it certainly had nothing to do with the Turin Shroud. After that, Sister Blandina went back to her homework: she spent six months in preparing more enlargements, copies, and even more careful super-imposed projections, until the images traced on the material were intertwined to correspond in countless details and the two complementary images "grew into a single new face". Pfeiffer was impressed, but not convinced.

Yet the last mail he had received from Blandina did move him to travel from Rome to Manoppello himself for the first time. When he came into the church through the doorway and caught sight of the Holy Face in the monstrance over the altar, he saw nothing at all. Light was falling through the woven cloth from behind, and to him in the nave it was gleaming snow-white. "It looks like a host", was the first thought that went through the priest's head, "like a rectangular host". From that hour, Father Pfeiffer, too, had fallen for the Face, like a crusader gripped by his longing for Jerusalem. Since then, he had been known in Rome as the "apostle of the Holy Face"—and soon, among other people, as a fool and a dreamer.

And perhaps both were true. Perhaps it really needed the exaggerated imagination of a dreamer in order to conceive of the inconceivable thing that was being reported here. At any rate, the sight of the "rectangular host" marked the beginning of the last great chapter of his life as a researcher—and the beginning of an unholy disagreement. For Father Bulst, in Darmstadt, did not rejoice at the way his learned colleague could fall for the dubious findings of some unknown nun in her convent in the Eifel—or the way that from now on he visited her in her convent in the Eifel all the way from Rome. Together with Heinrich Pfeiffer, Werner Bulst had written a book about *The Turin Shroud and the Image of Christ*, which had quickly become a standard work. Werner Bulst was the actual author, and Heinrich Pfeiffer the critic suggesting emendations. Another book by them was already being prepared, where it was to be the other way around, with Pfeiffer as the main author and Bulst as critic. For Werner Bulst, the image in Manoppello remained so insignificant beside the majestic impression left on the Turin Shroud that he did not even think about going to see it. Various expert opinions that he collected himself were enough for him.

Thus the old cooperative friendship between the two priests and scholars ended in an exchange of letters that was sometimes bitter and sometimes malicious, with stiff reproaches and all the polite disparagements that such a dispute of its very nature produces. Even the General of the Jesuits was brought in, but he was unable to restore peace between the two of them. Professor Bulst distanced himself from their last joint book, which did indeed appear with both authors credited, on the grounds of "absurd unfounded suggestions". Up to his death, neither the former peace nor even mere collegial respect and readiness to listen were again established. He categorically informed Sister Blandina, who would not give any peace to the "stubborn old man" (as she then saw him), that the congruence she had discovered was "an illusion". Yet when Werner Bulst died in Darmstadt in

December 1995, at the age of eighty-three, his desk was strewn with pictures from Manoppello.

But in 1995, even Sister Blandina had not yet seen the image on the cloth itself. The Trappist order was not a community in which any time you felt like it you bought a ticket and whizzed off to Italy. Not until October of that year did she "surprisingly and unexpectedly" set off with Father Pfeiffer and two sisters for Manoppello—because one of her own sisters, who was also a Trappistine, had fallen ill in Italy. The photo taken the morning before her departure from the Trappistine convent of Vitorchiano, near Viterbo, showed her walking on air, she was so happy. "The 'live' meeting with the Veil made a tremendously deep impression on me", she confided to her journal afterward. "In the normal course of events we are not confronted with objects that are beyond anything we have ever experienced. . . . There could hardly be anything more unprepossessing than this little white cloth." And yet, she said, it carried an incredible message. She was already fully convinced that since the fourth century emperors and artists had been using this image, along with the Turin Shroud, as an "unwritten document" of the Christian faith: one of them the image of a dead man, and the other of a living man. There were two sources, she believed, for the authentic pictures of Christ, and not just one. That was why she had always been reminded, during her research, of the principle of mathematics by which two entities that are both equal to a third must also be equal to each other. Hence it was "the Lord", she believed, who was looking at us and meeting with us in the two images. On that account, however, she found the brusque rejection of the Manoppello image easily understandable.

For in contrast to the sublime and mysterious shadow image of Turin, the concrete, "merely human", and thoroughly individual image from the Abruzzis was disturbing. Nobody would want anything as particular as that. And perhaps even the concept of a living God was more disturbing, she thought, than the Face of Christ in the peace of death.

It took a hundred years, she knew, for the scholarly perception to be accepted that every detail on the Turin Shroud corresponded quite precisely to the accounts of Christ's Passion in the Gospels—even invisible details like pollen floating down from the spring flowers on the hills around Jerusalem. Father Bulst himself had made immense contributions to this research. So it should be no surprise to anyone if it took another hundred years for the difficult image from Manoppello to be recognized. That, she said, did not diminish her confidence. Sister Blandina Paschalis Schlömer, O.C.S.O., had a mission—and she had annoyed quite a few people with it. In Germany, she had become the driving force behind an active association, with the Hebrew name of *Penuel*, concerned with the Holy Face of Manoppello; thanks to this, she now had some regular support from outside the convent walls. In the same uninhibited way as she roamed through the preserves belonging to the ivory towers of recognized scribes of the most varied disciplines, however, she also poked her nose into many concerns in the Abruzzis that were "not her business", as they say in England. At one moment she was particularly concerned about the lack of toilets outside the Shrine for future pilgrims. Likewise, the fact that the bells in the tower did not ring properly was a case for her to take up.

In 2003, with this special gift of hers, she obtained from her abbess the rare special permission, while still fully keeping her vows, to move outside her community and into a little house on the slope above the Sanctuary at Manoppello, to live as a hermit there. She went there into the unknown and arrived in front of the sanctuary, with her baggage and boxes, in the middle of summer. She learned Italian at the age of sixty. Now, she spent time every day kneeling and sitting in front of the image, in the Capuchins' little church, which was normally quite empty. Anyone who observed the self-forgetfulness with which she still pursued every new clue she discovered in the ever-new light of the image was bound to fear for her livelihood, which she earned after a fashion by painting and selling icons. "'You are very good at hearing poorly', my father used to say to me", she once answered me when I contradicted her. Wasting time was also something she did well. She came almost regularly late for Mass. That was already so in the convent, when she was cantor—to the delight, of course, of her fellow sisters. When she was already standing in the doorway, ready to descend the little slope to the church, it occurred to her that she ought perhaps to run the iron quickly over her veil or put the jar of honey on the table back in the cupboard or actually look up an important passage in a book before she forgot it. Her joints gave her pain; she used two canes to help her up and down the path to and from the church. And then it was always happening that she stopped on the way down and forgot all else because the majestic view of the snow-covered Gran Sasso in the distance cast its spell upon her.

Sometimes she laughed like a young girl. Sometimes she was irritated by the flies on the wall. Sometimes her face was like an open window beyond which banks of clouds were passing. With nimble fingers she sent entire letters in text messages, with capitals and small letters and perfect punctuation. "Christianity is not just a book of culture or an ideology, nor is it a system of values or principles, however lofty they may be. Christianity is a person, a presence, a face: Jesus Christ! John Paul II on June 5", was the first of her long *short messages* to me, which she sent me on June 8, 2004. "Isn't that an answer? All good wishes, Blandina." Pope John Paul II had panted out that message to the young people of Europe four days earlier, at the exposition site in Bern, as his last message. "Now tell me, Sister Blandina, you are after all a Trappistine", I asked once. "Isn't that one of the orders that keep the strictest silence?" She laughed. "Yes, and I can still keep silent." One would scarcely believe it. When conversation animated her face, she gushed forth like a spring. She laughed aloud. "And you have no idea how much one can talk, even keeping silent: with one's eyes, forehead, nose, teeth, hands, and feet."

When we visited her in June 2004, Manoppello was scented with jasmine. At night, the garden of the Hotel "Pardi" was pervaded as if with gossamer by a web of light from glow worm tracks; one even left its trace right through the bedroom to the window. In the morning we sat together in front of the image. And then in farewell, Blandina sang the *Salve Regina*, the classic Latin hymn to the Queen of Heaven, in a high clear voice, in which one could still hear the leader of the convent choir. "What is that about?" I asked her afterward. "If you are now singing—in front of those eyes—'*et Jesum nobis post hoc exilium ostende*'? When you ask Mary, 'Show us Jesus *after* this exile'! Does that mean for you—in front of those eyes—that your exile is now over?" She laughed again. "Recently, I have often wondered that when I got to that line." There was no question but that she was happy as few people were—with all the trouble she had already caused.

The Veil of Veronica

The so-called Veil of Veronica, however, was preserved and revered, not in Manoppello, but in Saint
Peter's in Rome, in the mightiest church in Christendom, unlike the "Holy Face" of the little Capuchin church
in Manoppello. There were reports about this mysterious image dating from as early as the sixth century: reports
of a portrait of Christ on a delicate veil, said to be "not
painted by human hands". It was "drawn from the water",
said the earliest Syriac source. No one had ever been
able to explain how it came into the world. It was witnessed among the treasures of Rome by the eighth century at the latest. For a long time this image was kept as
a relic in the old Constantinian basilica of Saint Peter, in
its own Veronica Chapel, which had been built in 705
by Pope John VII, one of the last popes of the "Byzantine era" of the papacy. And it was here in Rome, too,
where this ancient *vera eikon*—which means the "true
image" of Christ was wound around from the Middles
Ages onward, by the legend of a woman; people tried to
construct a coherent rhyme to account for the unfathomable nature, appearance, and origin of the cloth—
even though later not everyone was convinced by this
explanation. Concerning the "Veronica, they claim it is
the face of our Lord imprinted on a sudarium and act as
if it were so", wrote Dr. Martin Luther a year before his

Wayside shrine of the sixth station of a Way of the Cross in
Manoppello, by Majolika around 1960

death, in relation to the "diabolical" machinations of the popes in Rome. "And it is nothing but a little square black board. In front of it is hung a piece of clear linen, and they hoist this up whenever they are showing the Veronica. Then poor simpletons from wherever see nothing but a piece of clear linen in front of a black board." "With such gratuitous lies", however, Dr. Luther could explain neither the relic nor the strong attraction it exercised on people; and probably did not want to, by that time.

At any rate, since the Middle Ages Veronica had been represented as a woman who met Jesus on his way to Golgotha and mercifully wiped the maltreated victim's bloodstained face; and he was said to have left the imprint of his face in gratitude. For Good Friday 2005, Cardinal Ratzinger wrote that the longing of the pious of ancient Israel and the longing of all believers to see God's Face, as the twenty-seventh Psalm utters the age-old wish in song, "Your face, Lord, do I seek; hide not your face from me", had been embodied in the idea of that woman. According to another, much older legend, however, Veronica begged Jesus for the image because she was unable to follow him everywhere. After Christ's death at Jerusalem, it was said, Emperor Tiberius, who was ill in Rome, had heard of the marvelous image and had had Veronica brought to the capital so that she could heal him of "a buzzing in his head". Veronica came to Rome, and the Emperor recovered as soon as he caught sight of the image. Before her own death, Veronica bequeathed the precious gem to Pope Clement, the third Successor of Peter. That, it was said, was how the image came to Rome.

Other sources called Veronica "Berenice". By whatever name, the Gospels said nothing about her. And yet the "ways of the Cross" before which Christians since the Middle Ages had mourned the respective sufferings of the Passion and execution of Christ, whether inside or outside their churches, in front of fourteen "stations" every Friday, included her poignant encounter with the mortally wounded Messiah in thousands upon thousands of images and wayside shrines throughout Europe. Throughout the world, there was hardly a Catholic church where the tale of Veronica was not retold either in an old or a modern image: a woman who, in the midst of atrocious violence, in full public view, fearlessly intervened on the side of the victim. Jesus had made a gift to this sympathetic woman from Jerusalem of his true image; there was a firm conviction in the Church of that: "the true icon", or in a Latino-Greek parody of this, *La vera Eikon*. That is how the name Veronica came to be.

About 1350, Niccolò and Matteo Polo, according to the personal journal of their nephew Marco, were supposed to have brought back from a journey to the Far East the first piece of asbestos in Europe, as a gift for the pope from the Mongol ruler Kubla Khan, so the pope could better protect the Veronica from any possible fire. "Tu es Petrus et super hanc petram edificabo ecclesiam meam" were the words of Jesus shaped in gold on the sumptuous covering: "You are Peter, and on this rock I will build my Church." The precious piece of asbestos itself had been lost without trace. The cornerstone of the new Saint Peter's, however, laid in 1506, was also intended to be the base for a massive new safe for this, the most precious relic in Christendom. It took a good hundred years to build. There, in the Veronica pillar, it had lain ever since, locked behind thick walls with five locks.

Four colossal pillars stood around the altar, and the dome of the basilica rested on them. On the inner side of each one there were four marvelously spiraled free-standing bronze columns, which supported the baldachin over the central altar in their midst, beneath which lay the tomb of Saint Peter. Every bronze object in the ancient pantheon had had to be melted down to make these inner columns. The geniuses of Europe of the past had competed with each other to help shape this palace for God. Models for these four entwined columns around the altar again, however—in each case, two of them— were found in the façades of the four crossing pillars that supported the dome. For up on high, these pillars were decorated with four balconies, above which eight much smaller, similarly entwined marble columns could be seen. They used to be called "Solomon pillars"; for these were ancient items, supposed to have come from the Temple in Jerusalem, elegantly turned and spiraled. Vines with plump grapes grew around the oriental columns. Emperor Titus, so the Romans long used to say, had carried them off together with the gold and the seven-branched candlestick from the Temple treasury of the Jews, after he subdued and destroyed the capital of the rebellious Hebrews. These, it was said, were the pillars against which Jesus leaned while he was teaching the crowd in the Temple court. They were the model for the bronze supports designed by Bernini for the baldachin.

Being close to the tomb of Peter, then, they served to frame the greatest treasures—other than the bones of Saint Peter—for which the popes were privileged to be stewards. Behind the altar on the right, on one of the pillars a woman was holding up a cross; a fresh rose was lying at her feet. This was Helen, the mother of Emperor

Constantine the Great, who had rediscovered the Cross in Jerusalem in 324 and brought it to Europe together with other precious relics of the Passion. Helen had also brought from Jerusalem the crown of thorns, the nails, the table from the Last Supper, and even the entire flight of stone steps from the palace of Pontius Pilate, the procurator, down which Jesus of Nazareth had staggered after being condemned to death by him—and, of course, the "true Cross" of Christ. There was still a large piece of that set into the copper cross on top of the obelisk in Saint Peter's Square. Another piece was revered in Poitiers, and yet another in Jerusalem. The largest and most important piece, however, was kept safe here in Saint Peter's.

Opposite Saint Helen, in the second pillar, Bernini had chiseled out of Carrara marble a Roman centurion with a lance and fluttering garments, all so lifelike it might have been molded out of wax. This was Longinus, the Roman officer who had opened Christ's side with his spear so as to establish his early death. Blood and water had spurted out toward him. According to some ancient writings, this officer of the occupying forces then became one of the first Christians, and later he was executed on account of his new belief. His lance, the "holy spear", was tremendously important in the Middle Ages as a treasure and as one of the insignia of the empire. The Apostle Jude Thaddeus was supposed to have brought it from Jerusalem to Armenia, by way of the ancient royal city of Edessa, at an early date, to a little place beyond Yerevan, where the monastery called "Geghardavank" now was. Finally, Pope Innocent VIII received it as a gift from Sultan Bayezid in 1492. The head of the lance was now in Paris; but the actual treasure of the steel that pierced Christ was in Rome.

To the left of the Longinus pillar, the Andrew pillar reminded us of the third of the Vatican's supreme relics. Andrew was an earthly brother of Peter and, like him, was a fisherman on the Sea of Galilee—as were the apostles James and Philip. But Andrew was the very first one Jesus called to follow him. The Apostle's bones came to Amalfi in 1208, and his skull to Rome in 1462. Here it remained until, exactly four hundred years later, Pope Paul VI gave him back to the Greek Church in the harbor town of Patras, where Andrew had been executed in about 60 A.D.

Yet bones may be mistaken for other bones, just as a lance might be—either as a whole or in part—or even pieces of wood that were said to have come from the Cross of Christ. The most splendid of these relics, of their very nature, always lay under the cloud of suspicion of being faked. There was, however, no ground for any of these reservations in the case of the fourth—or, rather, the very first—relic of Saint Peter's and of all Christendom. That was the Veil of Veronica. The "true Face" of Christ could never have been faked. And that is why, as befit the status of this picture, the cornerstone of the new—and highly controversial—Saint Peter's was laid down by Pope Julius II, on April 18, 1506, directly beneath the fourth pillar; the inside of this was constructed by Donato Bramante as the most secure treasury in Rome for this most precious of all relics. The old basilica from the time of Emperor Constantine had not yet been pulled down when this pillar was erected as the first of four. All four relics were supposed to be kept there. There could be no question of any less magnificent church for the true image of Christ in the "capital of all the world", after the Muslims had after all already constructed the

Al-Hussein mosque in Cairo for a single hair from the prophet's beard.

"Sancta Veronica Ierosolymitana" was carved on the base of the massive pillar: the holy Veronica from Jerusalem. From up above, the image of Matthew the Evangelist shone down—he who so movingly described Christ's burial and "sat opposite the tomb", like Mary of Magdala, while Joseph of Arimathea gave the dead body of Jesus back to the earth from which he had come like any other man. Above the inscription, a woman in marble held up a veil on which were the facial features of Christ. Everyone who, on April 18, 2005, was following on television the last Mass before the cardinals went into conclave, celebrated by Joseph Ratzinger, could see it. Francesco Mochi carved that in 1646, but it had never been so well known as now on this occasion. Now, this figure was suddenly standing over the worried Cardinal like a heavenly "Mene, mene, tekel" message in marble. A high wind was blowing about the woman's dress and the cloth in her hands, as if the Holy Spirit were once more breaking into the Church as on that first day of Pentecost. As if he were once more bringing a language that all the world could understand. Above her, a Latin inscription proclaimed, SALVATORIS IMAGINEM VERONICAE SVDARIO EXCEPTAM VT LOCI MAIESTAS DECENTER CVSTODIRET VRBANVS VIII PONT MAX CONDITORIVM EXTRVXIT ET ORNAVIT ANNO IVBILEI MDCXXV. That meant, in English, "That the splendor of the place might keep in seemly fashion the image of the Redeemer taken onto Veronica's sudarium, Pope Urban VIII has built and ornamented this place of its safekeeping in the Jubilee Year of 1625." Urban VIII was the former Cardinal Maffeo Barberini, the creator of baroque Rome and Bernini's open-handed sponsor. The inscription was crowned with a loggia; above this, again in marble, angels were carrying the veil with the face of Christ up to a yet higher level. This work was finished with four cherubs in a golden apse, carrying a banner whose inscription, as it wound and twisted about, could only be made out with difficulty from below, with binoculars: "VULTUM TUUM DEPRECABUNTUR." This is a text from the forty-fifth Psalm, following the Septuagint: "They shall bring petitions before your face!"

Up to the time the new Saint Peter's was built, this image drew millions of pilgrims to Rome. A relic that was also an enormous source of revenue. During the so-called jubilee years, it used to be shown to people, in front of the church, every Friday and on all feast days and, later, even every Sunday and daily during Holy Week. In 1450, the press of pilgrims was so great that it resulted in a catastrophe on the Sant'Angelo bridge, with 172 dead. In those days, people did not come to Rome for the sake of the popes; people made the pilgrimage to Rome in order to see the Face of the invisible God. In those days, people who were coming back from Jerusalem adorned themselves with a palm frond; the sign of the pilgrim to Santiago was to this day a shell. But pilgrims visiting Rome, on their way home from Italy, stitched onto their cloaks little pictures of that very same image of Christ, the "Sancta Veronica Ierosolymitana": the holy Veronica from Jerusalem. Veronica painters constituted a particular trade in Rome, sufficiently large and important to organize their own guild. Since the rebuilding of Saint Peter's, however, it was as though that very pillar had swallowed up inside it the most precious relic in all Christendom.

Inscription on the base of the Veronica pillar of Saint Peter's,
Rome: first half of the seventeenth century

Locked Doors in Mighty Walls

To this day, there was not a single decent photograph of the relic. For comparison, it was as if there were today still not a single photographic print of the Shroud of Turin—and yet since 1898, the best specialists had been able to photograph it repeatedly. Strictly speaking, the modern history of the Shroud even started with photos—it was on them that people could first perceive that in this "image" they were dealing with a photographic negative that was both sensational and inexplicable. No ordinary mortal, on the other hand, ever got to see the Veronica in the light and close up. That was why, at the beginning of 2004, I asked Francesco Cardinal Marchisano, Archpriest of St. Peter's, in a letter whether I might not see the Veronica in the pillar once myself and examine it closely, for a report to appear in my newspaper. The reply came quickly and was most friendly. "I would very much like to give you a positive response", wrote the head of the Saint Peter's Basilica on May 31, 2004; yet unfortunately he had to tell me "that in the course of time the image has faded considerably". He also sent me a revealing newspaper article by Dario Rezza, a canon of Saint Peter's, who in 2000 had retold the story of the Veronica and mentioned in passing how securely the image had long been kept in the upper part of the Veronica pillar. The "visible" part of the image was even described in all the details he thought worth mentioning: "The outline of a human face, about 13 × 25 cm (5" × 10"). Here, on a dark background, a few brown patches can be distinguished, which may be taken as the forehead and may be interpreted as signs of the hair. Similarly, at the bottom there are three pointed patches of the same color, which may be identified with the beard." The nature and origin of this "icon" remained a mystery, and the writer was amazed at this; though it had certainly to be associated with the tradition of images "not made by human hands".

I was not unprepared for this reticence. For the Jubilee Year proclaimed by John Paul II in 2000, the apostolic library in the Vatican had been responsible for an exhibition concerning "the Face of Christ", which brought together everything there was to show. On that occasion, however, the most important image of Christ in the Vatican, that in the niche of the Veronica pillar, had not been shown—as if this were a matter of course. And hardly anyone even asked about it. A long tradition of decent silence had at last been rewarded with indifference and oblivion. For even when, shortly before the outbreak of the Thirty Years' War, Queen Constance of Poland had asked Pope Paul V for a copy of the image, she was put off for over a year before finally, in 1617, receiving a picture, along with a letter of apology for the delay, "because for a long time we doubted whether we could fulfill your pious wishes. For you should know that we could not assign the task to any ordinary artist. For only the canons of the venerable basilica may approach the treasury wherein this precious treasure is kept." Finally, he told her in his accompanying letter, they had found an appropriate clergyman, who was very satisfied with what he was sending her now. This image, he said, was almost identical to the original—it could be admired today in the treasury of the Hofburg in Vienna. The bestselling English writer Ian Wilson discovered it there and identified it, together with the name of the artist: Pietro Strozzi, a Florentine nobleman. Set in a heavy and costly gold frame—and coated again with gold foil, like an icon—it showed the shadows of two eyes, a long nose, and a mouth. You had to look very carefully, though. One thing was clear, however—the eyes were shut! We ought perhaps to recall that the age of genius had begun. In the seventeenth century, Europe was thronging with minds like those of Rembrandt and Rubens, Bernini and Cervantes, Descartes and Shakespeare, Galileo and Newton. A reasonably good copy was the least that could be expected from that era.

Shortly after that, Pope Urban VIII forbade any copies whatever of the Veronica. That did not mean, though, that the original did not go on being revered in the Vatican. Only, no one really got to see it properly any more. In 1849, however, another miracle was supposed to have happened. Then, the image on the veil was said to have taken on color of its own accord for three hours, so that the "Divine Face" of Christ became visible in outline: "It was deathly pale, with the eyes sunken, and animated by a profound stern expression." A hundred and fifty years ago, Pope Pius IX had the hidden relic displayed for five days on the high altar of Saint Peter's, in preparation for his proclamation of the dogma of the Immaculate Conception of Mary, from the third to the seventh of December 1854. No photographs or descriptions of this exhibition had been handed down, but in 1892 the Flemish art historian Andreas de Waal described the Veronica as follows, after being given special permission to examine it personally: "A sheet of gold (31 × 25 cm [12.2" × 10"]) covers the picture, leaving only the face free. Eyes, nose, and mouth, however, can no longer be seen there; only at the top can one see brown coloring that suggests the hair. The beard comes down to three points in the same color, and there is also a brown patch on the cheek."

Nevertheless, about eighty years ago the German author Gertrud von LeFort devoted a whole spiritual novel to the moment of the annual blessing with this image-relic: *The Veil of Veronica*. She depicted the event in two lines, in a single sentence: "I heard a sound from the balcony above us and saw there the white glimmer of priestly vestments; a mysterious object was lifted up—I could make nothing out."—"Stand!" the grandmother exhorted her granddaughter next, severely, "Even reverence does not allow us to kneel when we do not know why."

I do not know how often I have stood in front of the Veronica pillar since reading this somewhat demanding novel. The basilica is not far from us, and I can hear the bells at my desk. Whereas in 1920 Gertrud von LeFort could make out "nothing", it has become quite clear in the meantime that there is obviously a tradition in the Vatican that, rather than displaying that "true face" of Christ, a magnet for pilgrims up to the middle of the last millennium, had since then been hiding it.

"Why is the Veronica of the Vatican never shown to anyone up close?" I asked Professor Brandmüller one evening in his office, which had a marvelous view over the Vatican from its window. The distinguished monsignor and canon of St. Peter's cathedral shrugged his shoulders and stroked the tip of his nose with his forefinger; then he fingered the end of his chin and raised an eyebrow.

He gave the same answer when I asked why there was not a single decent photograph of it. He did not know. The president of the Pope's historical commission was helpful and extremely obliging. He had already said earlier in the year, concerning the Veil in Manoppello, that it could not possibly be the true Veronica. Why? "I have seen it myself," he said then, "and I could see that it is a drawing or painting." When I asked when the Veronica was being displayed, he reached for the telephone— "So that I do not tell you anything that is incorrect"— and called straight to the right number in the labyrinth of palaces on the other side of the road. I could hear from his replies that the relic was still displayed, on the loggia of the Veronica pillar, once a year on the fifth Sunday in Lent, at afternoon vespers, and after that the Passion of Christ was commemorated in the liturgy each day for two weeks, up until Easter. In all the guides to the Vatican that I knew, there was not the least reference to this. Was the Veronica displayed with its own liturgy? Yes, but just at the moment he could not recall the hymns that were sung. He himself had held it up, in the past, I had heard years ago, before I ever knew what it was all about. And in April, Professor Brandmüller had already told me in our first conversation that I would in no case get close to the image—and that it was not worth the trouble, either. There was hardly anything to be made out but shadows. One would have to set an enormous administrative chain in motion in order to come near it. And no, "it is not on wood, it is on linen. And you cannot see any colors there."

"Have you seen it?"

"Of course, often!" he says in his soft, refined voice.

"What does it look like, then?"

"It is simply a dark patch!"

Copy of the "new" Veronica of the Vatican authorized by
Pope Gregory XV between 1621 and 1623 for Duchess Sforza,
on public display again since 2006 and accessible in the Veronica
chapel of the "Il Gesù" church in the historic center of Rome

From Open to Closed Eyes

Yet there could be no question of a "single dark patch" in older descriptions of the Veronica, and certainly not in the early pictures of it—or in the more distinguished pictures of Christ in Rome, which must after all have taken their measure from the original or copies of the original. In the piles of specialist literature that lay beside my desk or in corners, what I had found in my endless leafing back and forth was as follows: perhaps the oldest depiction in which the Veronica was unambiguously shown as a cloth or veil set in a frame came from an illustrated manuscript of the thirteenth century, where Pope Innocent III was displaying it to the faithful together with the Bible. There, we could see—quite clearly and precisely—the friendly face of a bearded man with strands of hair on his forehead and a strikingly long and slender nose whose hair was parted in the middle and whose neck and ears could not be seen: with open eyes. Behind the picture, a black cloth was hanging down (as if the face were easier to see against this background). The Pope was holding up the book and the image at the same level. Later, the portrait was just as unambiguously recognizable on Roman woodcuts—such as those from 1475, 1489, or 1494. It was always the same face, easily identified—with wide-open eyes. It was no different in official copies that were made in Rome in the fifteenth century and by roundabout ways arrived in Spain; since that time, they had been preserved and revered at Alicante in a monastery on the Mediterranean coast as the "Santa Faz" and in the Cathedral of Jaén, north of the Sierra Morena, as the "Santo Rostro": as the "Holy Face" or "Holy Features". These were impressive portraits, with the same inner measurements and proportions—and a gaze that seemed to penetrate whoever beheld them.

In Russia, in the Christian Academy of Saint Petersburg, was preserved an old model according to which icon painters were supposed to learn how they were obliged to paint the true face of Christ: this was a frontal view of a face framed by hair, with a thin beard and mustache, a striking nose, and a piercing gaze—and with a little lock of hair falling down onto the forehead. On the Via Dolorosa in the old city of Jerusalem (on September 11, 2001) I bought a marvelous old Russian icon, which seemed to have been made exactly according to this model. I was looking directly at it as I wrote these lines. Two angels were holding the oriental cloth up to me by two knots, on the top left and right. A ladybird strayed into the room through the window and crawled along the icon.

I found a more Western, yet no less expressive variant on a pouring wet afternoon not far from my old school, the Schiller School, in the Dürerstraße in Frankfurt am Main, in the Städel Museum, and was quick to photograph it; it was by Robert Campin, the "Master from Flémalle", who lived in the fourteenth and fifteenth centuries. The painting was on oak and showed, instead of the angels, a careworn woman of sophisticated appearance in a sumptuous red-and-green dress with blue sleeves, who, with the tips of her fingers, held up the picture on the veil to onlookers by the top corners. With bewitching mastery, each fingernail and every line on the hand was shown in the picture. The fine detailing of the face on the veil followed to a great extent the general rules for a true image of Christ: in the style of the hair and beard, the face depicted without the ears or neck, and the striking nose. The skin and hair were chestnut-colored, like old oriental woven cloth. Four sharp folds divided the gossamer-thin material. Above all, however, the Master of Flémalle had depicted a technical impossibility here—as if he had been trying to link together and combine two modes of existence. For the veil, on which the dark face was shown, was completely transparent. Hence the weave of the veil itself was still more sensational, more delicate, than the minutely painted brocade in the background. It let light through, like a window. Apart from the Face of Christ, it was completely transparent. This was a masterpiece and was not the only one of its kind. For Jan van Eyck, Hans Memling, Roger von Weyden, Mantegna, Dirk Bouts, Israhel von Meckenhem, and the anonymous "Master of the Veronica" had also painted the Veronica. There was hardly any great artist of the late Middle Ages who did not have a try at this theme—and none of them ever painted Christ's face as "a large brown patch". Instead, they always all had open eyes in common.

It is always the eyes that make someone's face alive. The eyes are always what make an impression in any living being's face. "Come," said Sister Blandina on one of my visits, "I must show you my world museum. Here you can study the eyes of Christ as you can maybe nowhere else." She went to her bookshelf and took down a magnificent Italian picture book from the top shelf:

Un Volto da contemplare (A face to contemplate).—"And you can see here that time and again, up to the beginning of the seventeenth century, the greatest painters of Europe took a single model as their yardstick for their portraits of Christ. Yet they have all managed to capture only one expression of that face, or two, but never the whole picture. No master has ever succeeded in painting a real copy." She opened the book like the door of a house with many rooms. "There, look: Cimabue in the thirteenth century, look at the hair on the forehead, the curls, and the beard, the way he is withdrawn into himself! Or look at the universally commanding gaze in Masaccio, a good two hundred years later, the color of the eyes, the emphasis on the white, the hairstyle." She leafed forward and leafed back. "Or here, Bellini, from Venice, forty years later again. It is as if he had really tried to paint a copy of the 'Holy Face', with this innocent, surprised look and with the half-open mouth, the top row of teeth, and the young man's thin beard. It is as if Bellini had tried to paint with his brush the saying from Isaiah, 'After his soul has been afflicted, he shall see light.'—Or this portrait by Antonello da Messina, from London, almost contemporary with it. Is that not a wonderful interpretation of the same image, with the curl on the forehead, the delicate drawing of the hair and the beard, the color of the eyes and that kindly, peaceful gaze, offering peace and blessing? Or look at Titian, here, from 1516, and Raphael, there, his last picture—he died while he was completing it, on Good Friday 1520. Do you see that it is always the same one? Do you see the color of the eyes, in Titian's work, and the feminine eyebrows and light beard—and that calm gaze, testing and reflective? And alongside that, again, the transfigured expression in

Raphael's picture, with all the identical details taken from the Holy Face and its gaze? Or the picture of Veronica by Hieronymous Bosch, from Ghent in Flanders: Just look at that! Here, Jesus is carrying his Cross up the mount of Calvary through the horde of his persecutors, with his eyes shut and his cheek swollen (do you recognize him?), while a woman is moving away from him through the crowd, carrying like a treasure a portrait on a veil of that same Jesus with his eyes open! Or here, a hundred years later again, the asymmetrical face in El Greco's picture from the cathedral in Toledo! This sadness, this *mestizia* of his gaze, in great calmness. The whole eye seems to be pupil. Or that majesty in the gaze of Christ from the hand of Andrei Rublev, in Moscow. These merciful, omniscient eyes! All those pictures were done before 1610."

I took the book from her hands and began to leaf through it myself. "Yes, I shall have to stop there, otherwise I could be showing you more and more pictures until early tomorrow morning. They are disturbing masterpieces, all of them, and yet none of them comes near the full content of the original. Each only catches a part of the expression; they all conjure up just one aspect of the picture, always the same picture, on the canvas—one catches this aspect, and another that one. 'Middle-rate artists imitate details', Father Pfeiffer said to me once; 'the great ones imitate the soul.' In the case of Christ's image, however, even the great artists, again and again, can only filter out details and imitate them. Even so, you can see that these great masters seem to be fascinated most of all by that gaze which cannot be portrayed. In no picture that I know of do the eyes characterize the face of a living person to such an extent."

Deep in the maze of alleys and narrow streets of Traste-vere, in Rome, there was an ancient church where the essence of Sister Blandina's lecture was to be found in a single display, as if under a magnifying glass—that is, if you could succeed in persuading the abbess of Santa Cecilia to allow you into the gallery, which was most often locked. Near the church were houses that had been continuously occupied for sixteen hundred years. In their convent they raised the lambs from whose wool the pope had his pal-lium made, the papal stole that was supposed to remind him of the lost sheep that the good shepherd carried back out of the wilderness. In the gallery of her little church, however, Mother Abbess and her nuns were guarding a quite special treasure. Visitors had come from all over the world simply to admire on an old wall the feathers of the angels' wings that Pietro Cavallini conjured up on the wall here in a shimmering fresco in the thirteenth cen-tury. Still more moving, however, was the royal picture of Christ against a carmine-red background in their midst: with feminine eyebrows, the ears hidden in the surround-ing hair, a thin beard, a long, striking nose, the right cheek swollen, large and expressive eyes—with the white of the eyeball below the pupils—a tiny tuft of hair below the center parting, and a half-open mouth. This was the man in Manoppello: the same man who appeared in countless pictures of Christ, almost identical, from the earliest days of Christianity onward, from the eighth, ninth, or tenth centuries, right up to the seventeenth.

Hence, yet again, on the title page of a book pub-lished in 1618, we find Christ exactly like that: as a small medallion-sized Veronica, the way it had been handed-on and depicted time and again over the centuries. *Opuscu-lum de Sacrosancto Veronicae Sudario*, began the title of this work: "A Little Work on the Most Holy Sudarium of Saint Veronica". It was a pedantically exact inventory, by Jacopo Grimaldi, notary in Rome. By order of the pope, Dottore Grimaldi had to take stock of all the treasures of the basilica before the building of the new basilica was begun and note down their original positions. Hence this *Opusculum* and other writings of Grimaldi's, with their recorded details and their most accurate sketches, had become an irreplaceable source concerning the condition and the buildings of old Saint Peter's. It was no wonder that copies of it were soon made. There was a very fine copy dating from 1620, for instance, in the National Library at Florence, which showed the old face almost even more delicately: the wide-open eyes, the spreading hair, the old open face. In 1635, however, one of the copies of the *Opusculum* witnessed to an unusual and radical change. In the meantime, on November 18, 1626, the new Saint Peter's had been consecrated by Pope Urban VIII. Yet probably the most tremendous revolution in those years was not the building of the new basilica, but a new image of Christ and of God. For Christendom, this must in some ways have been a bigger break than the Reformation—even if it was only in our era that this was becoming clear. For in 1635, the title page of a copy of the 1618 *Opusculum* suddenly showed—in the same old framing of the Veronica—a quite different man as the Son of God!

Otherwise, everything in the copy, which a certain Francesco Speroni made from the original, had remained exactly the same: the text, the symbols (the cock, the pillars, scourge, Cross, nails, sun, and notice fixed to the Cross; the sponge, crown of thorns, dice, and moon; the rock, the lance, the ladder, pincers, and hammer). To the left and right of the image of Christ, in both editions, fluttered tiny seraphim with six wings like hummingbirds. Yet the faces, here and there, could not be more different. Both texts talked about the "holy sudarium of Veronica"; yet obviously, the model that had been copied by Jacopo Grimaldi in 1618 and by Francesco Speroni in 1635 for different editions of the same handbook must have changed. For suddenly, the man had become a corpse. In 1635, Francesco Speroni had sketched in red chalk the coarse and proportionless face of a dead man, with a broad nose, bulging lips, wounds on his forehead, and closed eyes. These were the same long nose, the color of potato-peels, the same closed eyes, the same closed mouth from which in 1617 Pope Paul V had had a copy made for Queen Constance of Poland. Somehow, then, Jacopo Grimaldi must have been drawing the face by memory when he made his inventory in 1618, or his title page had been finished earlier. For in 1617 and 1618, the two, Grimaldi and the Vatican copyist who worked for Queen Constance, must no longer have both been using the same model. Even then, one of them was depicting a living man, the other a dead man.

After this point of divergence, however, almost all the copies were made in that style alone—before they were forbidden altogether: as the face of a dead man, with his eyes closed. We looked at a "mother" for all these further copies in the Jesuit church, *Il Gesù*, in Rome's *Centro Storico*, where a friendly Jesuit fetched it out of the safe in the sacristy one sunny afternoon. *Il Gesù* was a jewel among the churches of Rome, the model for countless baroque churches across Europe. Ignatius Loyola, the Basque founder of the Jesuit order, lay buried here. His tombstone in the left-hand side chapel was more splendid than that of many a pharaoh. In a building nearby, his room in Rome was still shown as he left it, as bare as the cell of a Japanese Zen monk. Over the high altar, the three letters IHS shone out within a radiant halo: the monogram of Jesus that Ignatius—arousing the suspicion of older orders—made the seal of his "Society of Jesus". No wonder that a particularly costly and accurate image of Jesus had ended up in this particular church, even though it was not publicly displayed, but kept in a safe in the sacristy.

I looked on, uncertain how to react, as Father Daniel took the image out of a golden covering and laid it on the Formica surface of the table under the window. He laid a meter-rule beside it for the photos I wanted to take. I saw the rough picture of a man's face without any hair or beard, and with closed eyes, made on silk stretched over a board, 20 × 31 cm (10″ × 12″), with the corners cut away. The copyist had drawn the closed eyelids—without eyelashes—to left and right with a fine pencil, as two lightly swept curves on the cloth, and on the left he had lightly surrounded it with another line of red. It had simply nothing whatever in common with older representations of the Veronica. The mouth was broad and closed. Below the two eyes, two bloodied tears were suggested in red pencil. The artist had given the nose a strong shadow to the left. The entire face was remarkably without contours, with no hair at all, although it was outlined with a thick pencil, in the shape of a down-turned pomegranate, with three bulges where earlier pictures of Christ showed the beard and the hair that fell down to right and left in sidelocks. Yet Michelangelo's dead Son in the arm of his mother, in the *Pietà*—with the mouth half-open, showing the teeth, a thin vandyke beard, the nose, and the cut of his hair—from 1498, had a hundred times more in common with the earlier images of Christ than had this disconcerting puzzle. The forehead was marked by two patches like wounds, which had already struck me in Francesco Speroni's copy of Grimaldi's *Opusculum*.

This image was one of two copies, said a note in old Italian in sharp, clear handwriting on the back, that Pope Gregory XV had had made "from the original of the Holy Face in Saint Peter's church"—one for Duchess Cognata, and the other for Duchess Sforza; this latter was the one that the onlooker had before him. Furthermore, said the note, it was the oldest expressly authorized copy of the Veronica. Gregory XV was pope for only two years, from 1621 to 1623. His successor, Urban VIII, on the other hand, not only had the treasury in the Veronica pillar of Saint Peter's constructed, but also forbade any more copies being made of the venerable image, and under threat of excommunication he had all the existing copies of the Veronica in the Papal States collected in order to be burned. This was important to him. A glance at this copy from *Il Gesù* helped us perhaps to understand him a bit better. For if it came from the quite obviously new "original" in Saint Peter's, then it showed us how at that time, even within the Church, people's trust in relics must suddenly have evaporated dramatically. With copies like that, even the popes themselves must have begun to regard the whole business of relics as a fraud. "No," smiled Father Daniel, "everyone knows, after all, that the Veronica in the Vatican is a forgery." He laughed once more, in a friendly way, as he opened the door for us to leave.

Not everyone knew, by any means; but perhaps Father Daniel only meant everyone in Rome. At any rate, we were speechless when we stood in the open air again, outside the side door of *Il Gesù*, blinded by the afternoon light and stunned—but not, this time, by the exhaust fumes from the Corso Vittore Emmanuele, which ran past the church as one of the main traffic arteries of the city center. We walked back to the house through all the noise as if we could not hear it, too excited to wait for a bus. For obviously, between the years 1610 and 1620, there had been a crucial dividing line in Christian art. Would this dividing line not necessarily have led to a division in theology and the history of spirituality, we asked ourselves on the way. Could the loss of the true Veronica be seen as anything other than the removal of the heart of the world of Christian images? In the middle of the baroque period, without anyone noticing, the "true face" of Christ closed its eyes, just when the art of the Jesuits was beginning to flourish and the last great collective rush of pictures was happening in Europe, from Vilnya to Lisbon. In an amazing silence, the inmost image of God in Christendom had been changed for another in the course of those years. Even on the marble veil held in the hands of the sixteen-foot-high figure of Veronica in Saint Peter's, carved by Francesco Mochi in 1646, the eyes were closed.

The fact that a face in a picture suddenly had its eyes closed, after having had them open for hundreds of years, raised questions. So, there had been a break in historical continuity that was difficult to talk about until now. The old Veronica must have disappeared from Saint Peter's at least four hundred years ago. For four hundred years, likewise, the new Veronica in Saint Peter's could only have been a more or less expensive, or cheap, sham. There had been no shortage of villains in the baroque era. If, however, the "true image" had been changed for another at that time, then the greatest unsolved crime of the era must be hidden behind that change. "And its brilliant cover-up", said Ellen. I was not so sure about that. Perhaps Pope Urban VIII, too, simply could not conceive that the most precious jewel of all Christendom had simply been mislaid, just when the massive treasury built for it had been completed.

The Broken Glass

In the treasury of Saint Peter's, photographing things was forbidden, just as in any better museum of the world. Yet if you switched the flash off, the attendants found it easy to keep one eye closed. I paid five Euros for entry; not for the first time. For I could not get enough of looking at these treasures from Christendom's past. These windowless rooms had nothing to do with the "dungeons of the Vatican", hung round with cobwebs and legends. These were no arched gothic cellars; they had recently integrated sensible museum design into the baroque house. Right behind the cashier's desk, in a black-draped room, the first thing I came on was the last column remaining of the twelve from the Jerusalem Temple that Titus carried off to Rome. This, so the Romans thought they knew, was the one against which Jesus was leaning when they brought before him the woman taken in adultery, before he squatted down and wrote with his finger in the dust *the* one piece of writing about which the Gospels report. In the next room, a Korean nun was crossing herself alongside a noisy class of schoolchildren and gazing, perplexed and bewildered, into a glass display case. There, two golden angels were holding up a golden patriarchal cross with the most costly decoration, into which six large pieces of wood had been set: pieces of the holy Cross from Jerusalem. Two paces farther on

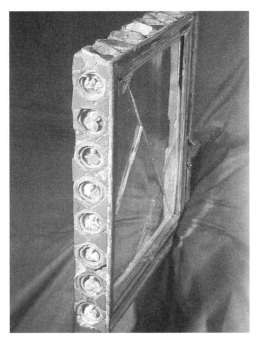

An old frame made in Venice, in the treasury of Saint Peter's.
In this, up to the seventeenth century, the Veil of Veronica
had been kept between two sheets of glass

was an ancient cross belonging to Emperor Justin II, with a medallion of Jesus set in the foot and another of Jesus in the top (both with open eyes, hair centrally parted, and even a tiny lock falling over the forehead).

This treasury was like an open book full of stories that hardly anyone read any more. In the next room but one was kept the silver reliquary formerly used to preserve the top of Andrew's skull, and next to it a glittering piece of quartz, round as an apple, that once held the tip of Longinus' lance. Yet on the left, right behind the doorway, behind an iron instrument of torture with which at one time they used to put the screws on Christians, was the greatest puzzle in these rooms. I waited until all the visitors had left the room before trying for a couple of photos in the dimness, without a tripod, holding my breath. Beneath the overhead lighting I could see in the viewfinder a squarish frame, with a bottom piece, top, left, and right, placed at an angle to the onlooker and held by one corner in a gray, felt-covered block. "Frame of the Veronica", a little notice beside it said laconically, "Late Romanesque. The famous relic was kept in this until the seventeenth century, held between two sheets of glass. Note the skilled modeling of the multicolored figures of the saints along the outer edge of the frame, whose origin may date back to as early as the fourteenth century."

These figures really were worth looking at: on the side turned toward me alone, there were eight little windows from which delicately carved and painted apostles, saints, and angels were looking out, and in their midst a Mother of God in a blue robe, who was almost laughing as she held out her arms. More deserving of attention than the artistic skill, however, was the battered condition of this little treasure. Some of the carmine-red inlaid pieces had fallen out or perhaps been broken off. Had this frame fallen? Had it been dropped? Where? Had it fallen out of the tabernacle in the former Chapel of Veronica, in which it had once been kept, before it had had to be pulled down for the rebuilding? Had this misfortune happened, maybe, during the rebuilding? On the inside framing, at the front, the coloring was peeling off here and there. This was the same frame that was very clearly to be seen in old woodcuts that showed the displaying of the "true image" of Christ to pilgrims. Who could ever have let it fall? Why was it replaced at all? The back of it was in an even worse state. The inner lining of wood had been torn away; there was no trace of the sheet of glass on that side, and the front sheet—still firmly in place in the frame—through which in former times the face of Christ had gazed out upon millions of pilgrims, had a bad crack, running diagonally all the way from the top left corner to the bottom right. Across that bottom right corner there was a second crack, and a third ran diagonally up into the broken pane from the left-hand edge. What was once one had been broken into five pieces. Not even a broken Ming vase could be more touching to anyone who loves beautiful ornaments. I did my very best, both with the magnifying lens and without it, to find traces or threads of cloth in the frame behind the pieces of glass. But there was nothing there.

Soon after that, I found the empty frame with the broken glass as the disconcerting title of a scholarly book, whose author, Gerhard Wolf, was quoted on an Internet page saying that the search by art for a true picture goes to the point of "cutting, crossing out the portrait, to the point of the empty canvas". Probably there was something there I had failed to understand properly. For that same Gerhard Wolf was one of those responsible for an exhibition about "the face of Christ" in Rome, in the Jubilee Year of 2000. That was a true masterpiece of an exhibition, which brought together countless images and paintings of the face of Christ—yet with neither a photo nor a print of that "Holy Face" which is known to have been in Manoppello for at least four hundred venerable years. Would it not, maybe, fit into the broken glass in this frame that I was looking at with such perplexity here? The circumstances in which this precious item came to be in this condition and ended up here lay shrouded in darkness. Would one take the most marvelous relic in Christendom out of its frame so roughly and clumsily if one were going to put it into another one—a frame that was, if possible, even more costly? Would one then simply break the glass and tear out the back pane along with the wooden pieces holding it straight and the relic itself all at the same time? How hasty may we imagine such a ceremony to have been when the relic concerned was avowedly the apple of the papal eye—and a not unimportant source of revenue?

I put my camera away, went down on my knees, and measured the frame—through the glass panes—with a meter rule. The length of each side was 33 cm (13″). The thickness of the wooden frame front to back, with the little saints' windows, was 4.4 cm (1.7″). On all sides, the frame measured about 4 cm (1.6″) from the outer edge inward. Thirty-three minus 8, equals 25 cm (10″). That meant that the area of glass visible within the frame must have been roughly 25 × 25 cm (10″ × 10″). By the time the next visitor came into the room, I was standing up again in front of the instrument of torture. As I went, I cast one last look at the broken glass, which now looked to me like a blind, shattered mirror.

Outside, in front of the main doorway of Saint Peter's, I called up Sister Blandina. From here, the view swept up to the mountains in the east. A seagull was chasing a pigeon across the pillar-encircled oval of Saint Peter's Square, while up on the right, on the Janicula Hill, a row of pines took up the rhythm of Bernini's row of columns. I had to wait a little before Blandina came to the phone. She had been down in front of the holy relic just then and had now come out in front of the door. Could she tell me, I asked, the measurements of the Veil with the image in Manoppello? I happened to have forgotten them. "Of course: it measures 24 cm (9.4″) high, and 17 (6.7″) across, with two small triangles added on the right and left at the top, where a bit had perhaps been cut off with the edges on each side." "Twenty-four cm high?" "Yes."

I tried to recall in imagination what the image on the Veil on the other side of the mountains—right over there, near the Adriatic Sea—looked like; it fit so perfectly into the broken frame. For one thing was crystal clear: for this frame, originally with two glass panes, there was only one corresponding object I knew of. And that was in Manoppello, above the tabernacle. In the frame in Rome then, too, a transparent image *must* once have been set; or at any rate, an image that you could look at from both sides—like a Host in a monstrance. Why else would a frame have a glass pane in the front and the back and not glass at the front and wood behind it, like any other ordinary picture frame? Perhaps, then, that was where the idea of a monstrance came from in the first place—and the idea of eucharistic adoration: that is, the Catholic notion that God could be carried through the streets as a piece of snow-white bread between two panes of glass. That observation unlocked an old mystery like a key. I could not help but think of the curious, thick splinter of glass inside the frame at Manoppello, to the right below the face. A west wind from the Tyrrhenian Sea was driving great mountains of cloud away from Rome.

"Isn't it strange," I said afterward to Ellen, at the dinner table, "that in ancient times the legendary Atlantis is only mentioned once—a couple of lines in Plato; and that ever since then, science has not stopped trying, one time after another, to find the missing city and to probe the depths of the sea where they think it might be? Doesn't Atlantis turn up again in the news every five years at the most, after it has once been found in the Atlantic off Cadiz, then off Crete, off the coast of Libya, and so on? And isn't it even more strange that the Veronica is mentioned not only by writers like Petrarch and Dante—and of course a whole series of popes—and that the élite among the painters and artists of Europe have witnessed to it in a whole selection of masterpieces and that in the East it is represented in countless icons—and yet, today people act as if the whole thing were nothing but a fantasy?! That scholars dismiss this history beforehand, as if this document, which is so well-attested, were nothing but nonsense from the Middle Ages? Or, rather, as if this cloth had simply never existed! The way that no television company and no research department—even within the Church!—even seriously asks where this piece of cloth is and where it can be seen ... It must, after all, be more precious than the lost chamber of amber. Or the Golden

Fleece. Or the sunken city of Atlantis—if that city did ever exist. What item of cultural heritage is supposed to be actually more important than *this* one Face?

"It was taking this as a model that Albrecht Dürer was the first painter in the Christian world, somewhere around 1500, who did a self-portrait in direct frontal view. That was a revolutionary act of modernism: the artist in a fox fur as the image of God! Someone from Nürnberg as a young god! Dürer even took the little lock of hair from the model of the 'true image', which had been reserved up until then for images of Christ alone. The Veronica is the standard measure for the Christian image of man." My wife passed me the breadbasket and put the wine to one side. "It is time you met with Father Pfeiffer."

The Face of Faces

I had actually met Father Pfeiffer years before and had
seen him a number of times, but I was not sure whether
he would remember me. For the first time was the day I
sat at a table with him in Turin after I had just seen the
Shroud for the first time, the "Santa Sindone". A hundred years earlier, on May 28, 1898, the famous piece of
cloth had first been photographed—for archiving pur-
poses. After that, it was going to be shut up, away from
the modern world, as an obsolete relic from the past.
The Turin cathedral chapter did not want to make themselves ridiculous in front of their modern contemporaries, in the twentieth century that was about to begin,
with this old-fashioned cloth with patches of discolor-
ation. The modern era should finally be allowed to begin,
even in Italy! Yet it was these very photographs that had
brought to light the fact that the impression of the figure
on the enormous piece of cloth was like a photographic
negative. Cavalieri Secondo Pia, the photographer, almost
had a heart attack in his darkroom when he took the
plates out of the developing tray. What emerged from
the shadows to meet him were pictures of a dead man
with many and varied injuries, pictures of revolutionary
realism.

In the century that followed, this so-called sindonol-
ogy had grown into a complex scientific discipline, which

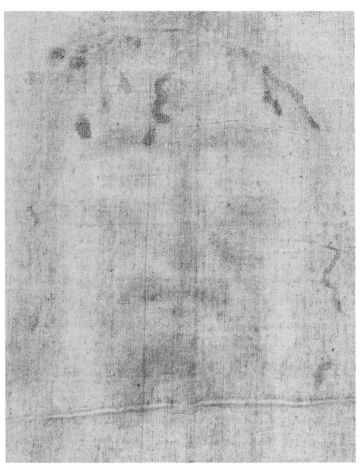

The inexplicable impression of a face on the Turin Shroud

had made the Shroud the most extensively investigated piece of woven material in the world—with all the inside enmities, factions, and petty jealousies that are probably always involved in such a major academic project. The Shroud radiated peace in the way no painting in the great gallery of the past two thousand years did. Yet disputes and disturbance fluttered around it like ravens and vultures around an old-time gallows—and a strange culture of suspicion, misrepresentation, slander, and distortion. The delicate image of blood, drops of water, and faint shadows had been keeping people's minds in turmoil for at least a hundred years. Because of that, Turin had become a center for black and white magic and a place of pilgrimage for satanists, wizards, and witches from San Francisco to Saint Petersburg. Was that not why there were the greatest number of official exorcists here in all the dioceses of Italy, I had asked Giuseppe Ghiberti, the Cardinal of Turin's Vicar General for the Shroud, after a disastrous fire in the cathedral had again set off wild rumors over the cause of it. "There are six exorcists here", said Don Ghiberti, modifying that in a friendly way with twinkling eyes. "Do you think that is a lot?"

In any case, the cause of the fire remained unknown. I had seen Monsignor Ghiberti again, with his short steel-gray hair, on that same evening when I first met Father Pfeiffer. It was at a banquet in an old Savoyard hunting lodge for sindonologists from all over the world, who had come to a congress in Turin on the occasion of the Jubilee. I had been able to smuggle myself in because I had previously written an article about the Shroud and Professor Karlheinz Dietz, who had inherited the academic papers left by Professor Werner Bulst. As I said, however, I had seen the cloth for myself physically before me for the first time that day, in Saint John's cathedral; never previously, either close up or from a distance—but simply on photos.

John Paul II had been there a week earlier, and later Cardinal Ratzinger had subsequently knelt before it; and before and after them, many other bishops and cardinals. Two million people would file past the Shroud as pilgrims in those days. In front of me in line, Ernst Fuchs, the prince of painters from Vienna, was standing patiently with one of his many sons and his little Moroccan-Jewish cap. Many lives were changed by the encounter with the Shroud; probably, mine too. For I had imagined the image to be so delicate and pale, and now it was stretched out so clearly on the wall. The shadow of the Lamb! The impression left by a man badly injured before his death, with many wounds, not bandaged at all. "This is exactly where Christ rose again", Nicolas Mesarites had testified concerning this relic in 1201, in the Pharos chapel in Constantinople, before it was plundered just a few years later by crusaders and the Shroud was shipped to France. "The burial cloths are still exuding myrrh, because they have been wrapped around the ineffable One, dead, naked, and embalmed, after his Passion."

"This is the 'mother of all icons' ", I had jotted down the evening before, in my hotel room; "the Shroud shows us the 'Face of all faces'. And it is older than the oldest manuscripts of the Gospels, in which Matthew describes how Joseph of Arimathea, after Jesus' execution at Jerusalem, asked Pilate to be allowed to take the body, took it, wrapped it in clean linen, and laid it in a new tomb. The Turin Shroud could easily win any circumstantial case that it is identical with that 'clean linen'. No image and no writing in all the world reflects more truthfully, and in more detail, what the four Gospels tell us about the Passion and death of Jesus."

Yet on that day I had suddenly forgotten everything I knew, in the formidable presence of that old cloth, which, with all its patches and burned holes, seemed to light up here so incredibly, entirely undamaged, completely transfigured, at peace and relaxed in its beauty—an incredible photograph, and no one could say how it came to be there. Time stood still in front of it. On the linen sheet—and no one knew how—there was the great double reproduction of a man who had been really badly flogged and then crucified, who was laid on the right-hand part of the $4\frac{1}{3}$ yards of material and then covered with the left-hand part. The back of him was imprinted on the right half of the cloth, and the front of him, with his face, chest, and legs, on the left. His slim hands were crossed over his private parts. Nails had been driven through his wrists and feet. I looked very carefully at the shadows of his slim fingers and traced with my eyes the star-shaped way the blood ran out around the wound on his right side and on the forearm. Forensic investigators had found that he must have thrust himself out from the wood time and again, to get air for his last breath: one patch of blood on the right side of his chest was so large that one could easily have put three fingers into the open wound that the Shroud once covered there. Blood and serous fluid ran out of this wound and down his back while the man was lying here—post-mortem blood.

All the other wounds on his body were made while he was still alive. On his forehead and the back of his head, blood gushed from his hair. The right cheek was swollen right up to his eye, and his eyebrows as well; the nose was broken below the bridge. The beard was partly torn out and matted together. The shoulders had been badly mistreated. His back and all his limbs were covered with scourge marks. Only on the left foot was there so much as a handbreadth undamaged—apart from this, there was nowhere on his body without the marks of blood, most of the drops as big "as the leaves of sweet marjoram", as some nuns in France noted, when they patched the Shroud nearly five hundred years ago. My heart was hammering wildly. This man was covered in blood—yes, but he was also stark naked, front and back, as naked as when his mother bore him. God, naked!

That had been on the morning of the same day. Yet at the solemn banquet in the evening, on June 6, 1998, everyone had been generally boisterous. Five courses were being offered to the illustrious specialists, the best of wines, and strong liquors. There were fancy napkins, fresh salmon with thyme, asparagus risotto, little pieces of sirloin in Riesling—there was everything. I had been warned about Heinrich Pfeiffer; now, suddenly he was next to me at the table. We had been relegated somewhat to the edge of the banquet hall; we toasted each other, introduced ourselves, and fell into conversation. I recounted my impressions, and he listened to me absently, it seemed to me. "The Shroud is one thing", he said finally, in his Swabian intonation, "but the real discovery is another little image in an unknown little town in the Abruzzis. That is the true image! The Turin cloth is only the first thing. The real sensation is waiting in Manoppello." And he had smiled mysteriously at me. "Aha", I thought.

Today I had seen the Face of faces, and now this professor was telling me that there was on earth, supposedly, an even more important picture. A still truer likeness!

With no body, but only the face! A face behind—or above—the Face of faces?! That was simply crazy, and that was indeed the way Father Pfeiffer had been represented, behind his back. I smiled at him and lifted my glass. It was becoming a wonderful evening. After dessert, I got up with a polite bow and had a look around at the other tables and on the veranda. Karlheinz Dietz was there, of course, the man to whom I owed all my knowledge of the Shroud. I had known him in Würzburg, where I had once visited him; since then, we had kept in touch with lively and friendly exchanges of faxes and e-mails. Several Jewish specialists from America and Israel were sitting at another table and were especially concerned to prove to the Christians that Jesus of Nazareth had lain in that sheet. I had been introduced to Ian Wilson, the most famous member of the British Society for the Turin Shroud. He had written the most important book to date on the *Santa Sindone: The Turin Shroud*, a worldwide best-seller. A little bit later, I found him in conversation with another scholar, to whom he was explaining that, really, nobody had any need of Pfeiffer's image on cloth from Manoppello: "We already have enough problems with the Shroud." A fascinating man. We exchanged e-mail addresses.

Back in Munich again, I had immediately bought a second book by him, which he had written in 1990 about *Holy Faces, Secret Places: An Amazing Quest for the Face of Jesus*, and immediately devoured it. Everything to be said on the subject had been brought together here—his collection of material was immense, and he could tell a tale as only Englishmen could. He also mentioned Father Pfeiffer, of course, five times as well as the face in Manoppello that "was painted on cloth with a very transparent paint", before making it unmistakably clear, on page 112, that "the Manoppello copy ... can now safely be dropped from any further consideration", since it exhibited none of the crucial characteristics of true copies of the Veronica—such as the closed eyes. The Strozzi copy (the one with the mouth and eyes closed and the long potato-colored nose), which he had discovered and identified in the Vienna treasury, must rather be regarded, henceforth, as the most reliable point of reference and "guide to what the Veronica looked like at the height of the Middle Ages". As is appropriate for a leader of public opinion, Wilson's books had of course become the accepted orthodoxy; and even I was greatly tempted to quote from them, because they were so persuasive. But then I saw that Michael Hesemann had already done that for me in Germany, in 2000, in his fine book about *The Silent Witnesses to Golgotha*; here he wrote about the "extremely fine brushstrokes" with which the Manoppello image had been painted, "entirely in the style of the fourteenth century". Briefly, and categorically, "We must exclude any identification of the Holy Face with the Veronica. There is not a single picture from the Middle Ages in which this relic, which was regularly displayed in Rome, is shown with an open mouth—a detail that would certainly not have escaped any observant witness." Besides that, he said, the veil was too small. At 24 × 17 cm (9.4" × 6.7"), it did not fit into the old Venetian glass frame in Rome, the display-area of which is 34 (13.3") by 31 cm (12.2"). He rounded off his verdict with a photo beside the paragraph, and beneath it the title, "Not the Veronica: the Holy Face of Manoppello".

There were reasons other than objective ones for this brusque rejection. Before the Turin conference,

Professor Pfeiffer had in fact done something that did not please other professors and colleagues at all. At the end of May 1999, in the *Sala Stampa*, Rome's international press center, he had held a press conference at which he proclaimed, before the assembled representatives of the world press, that he had discovered in Manoppello, in the Abruzzis, a relic with an impression of Christ's face; and that this was "quite certainly" the sudarium of Veronica, which had disappeared from Rome probably in 1608, when the chapel in which this precious relic had previously been kept was torn down, in the course of building the new Saint Peter's. As early as 1991, he said, he had published a book about it, which had not, however, been noticed or acknowledged, either by researchers or by the Church. He was convinced that the image of Christ in Manoppello had originated in fact in Christ's tomb in Jerusalem, where it had probably been laid on top of the large sheet in which the crucified Christ had been laid. That would also explain, he said, why the Turin Shroud bore a negative image, and the veil laid on top of it, in accordance with the rules of photography, a positive one. Everybody had written something about this press conference, and the story had accordingly enjoyed—following the rules of tabloid dailies—"immortality for a day". Thus I had seen for the first time, in the *BILD* newspaper, a photo of the image in Manoppello. More up-market papers like the *Frankfurter Allgemeine Zeitung*, on the other hand, had immediately chosen an Old Master as their illustration, so as to avoid having to present the story in too embarrassing a way.

In the period that followed, I saw Father Pfeiffer twice more, but he was always sitting with people who had no love for the people with whom I was sitting, and vice versa—always in connection with the feuds over the Shroud. On the last occasion, we met in a bar in Turin in September 2002, after we had been able to see the Shroud once more, finally freed from repairs, at close hand. For the first time, then, I had been able to bend over the face really closely, and I had been even more overwhelmed than before. Father Pfeiffer was absolutely opposed to the restoration that had been taken in hand; I was in favor, and still am.

Then, finally, on a rainy day in February 2004, an invitation to a lecture by Father Pfeiffer fell into my hands; it was supposed to begin in half an hour, in the Via della Conciliazione, not far from us. The day before, I had received from Germany the first copy of a book about the image of the Madonna "not made by human hands" in Guadalupe, in Mexico, on which I had been working for five years. In the morning, suddenly in the bath I became weak-kneed, and I didn't know what that meant. I did not want to go to the doctor, so I preferred to go to the lecture instead.

The lecture room was full, and I was sitting in the second row. Don Antonio Tedesco, the southern Italian pilgrim chaplain responsible for German pilgrims in Rome and an enthusiastic supporter of the Holy Face, gave the introduction. He had just recently taken another large group of Swiss guards to Manoppello. He sparkled with passionate enthusiasm. "The sudarium is in the right place!" said Don Antonio. "The Lord has hidden himself in the heart of popular piety, as if in a tabernacle. The people there do not have the difficulties that scholars make for one another. As in the Gospels, the Lord has simply made himself invisible at a certain point in

Church history—and then, the next day, he comes back quite visible!" Then the light went out, the slide-projector snapped the pictures into the slot with an automatic click, and Father Pieffer told, out of the darkness, that unfortunately the depersonalizing of God had begun as early as the work of the great Thomas Aquinas. "Thomas said that God took upon himself the nature of humanity. Yet he did not become humanity; he became a man, one particular individuality, with one particular face. Only the image gives us the individuality, not the word!" Beside me, one of the people invited to the lecture got up and, ducking as he went through the beam of light, went to the restroom. "Well, is that another person leaving the room because of criticism?" asked Father Pfeiffer in irritation, as he disappeared. Meanwhile, I was gazing, fascinated, at the images on the screen, which I had never before seen. The ones that fascinated me were magnified close-ups. For heaven's sake, I thought, don't tell me that is going to be a new book! But I had other work to do, and I was still out of breath from the last book, for which I had had to sacrifice every single day of my last holidays. Now I knew why I had become weak-kneed. After the lecture, I invited Don Antonio and Father Pfeiffer straight back to our place for supper. It was still raining outside. Don Antonio's eyes lit up when he told me about all the great writers who had already described the Holy Face, about Innocent III, who had written a hymn especially for it at the beginning of the thirteenth century, and then Petrarch, and then he was reciting Dante by heart, first in Italian and then in German, from his song of paradise in the *Divine Comedy* of 1320, from canto 31:

Qual è colui che forse di Croazia
Viene a veder la Veronica nostra,
che per l'antica fame non sen sazia,
Ma dice nel pensier, fin che si mostra:
"Signor mio Gesù Cristo, Dio verace,
or fu sí fatta la sembianza Vostra?"

Like someone who, perhaps, from Croatia
Comes to see our Veronica
And whose old longing to gaze is not satisfied,
But thinks to himself—until it appears:
"My Lord Jesus Christ, true God,
How did your human face look?"

Meanwhile, all through the meal, Father Pfeiffer could hardly restrain himself from leafing through my book, because he himself had been in Mexico so many times and was due to fly there again soon for a series of lectures. "When shall I be able to interview you and talk with you?" I asked, finally, as we accompanied the two priests—who could hardly be more different from one another—to the door. It was to be some time. Yet ten days later my wife, on our trip south, made a detour near Pescara to go and lunch in Manoppello, and we came to our first, unplanned meeting with Sister Blandina. I was not to have a detailed conversation with Heinrich Pfeiffer until the summer. By then, Ellen and I had already discovered one thing: while the image of the Passion in Turin well and truly blossomed in any reproduction, the image in Manoppello could not be reproduced in all its multiple aspects. It blossomed only in the original.

The Fair Face of Her Son

"Father Pfeiffer, Sister Blandina may claim to have discovered that the veil in Manoppello corresponds to the face on the Turin Shroud. Your discovery, on the other hand, is not a matter of correspondence, but one of complete identity—this veil is identical with the hidden Veil of Veronica in Rome. How did you arrive at this conclusion?" This was how I opened my interview with him, months later. A remarkable ordered clutter reigned in his room on the top floor of the Gregorian University. This was the den of a collector, with books, pictures, and other treasures on every inch of free surface. His principle for organizing this clutter was: "Like things together", so as to be able to find everything again when he needed it; and, "For anything that comes in, something has to go out." His head seemed to be similarly tidy and full, in a very individual kind of system.

In the meantime he had twice spent two or three months in Mexico, and he was soon going to fly out there again. He was a man much in demand and a sober connoisseur of wine who, for his part, with an opulent meal, would drink simply water. The Jesuits, he believed, were the freest people on earth, ever since Ignatius Loyola, when founding his order, removed all prohibitions with respect to thinking. He himself, however, was not merely one of the best-known experts on Christian art,

The image on the Veil at Manoppello, obverse

but had also long been studying the rules of iconography that had inspired artists in East and West, over the course of the centuries, in their representations of the Face of Christ. Within the city center of Rome, on principle, he went everywhere on foot, even when it was raining— and that had preserved even beyond the age of sixty what you might call a lovely body, which he could look at with a certain vanity. This time, *I* had come to him on foot. Even after decades, his copious Italian vocabulary had a Swabian flavor; and contrary to warnings I had earlier been given, he was by no means a "fanatic looking for a cause", as they say in England. He isn't fanatically looking for a just cause for which to fight. He had found his "thing" long since and, in doing so, had remained a proper German professor, who liked to answer every question with a little lecture—even during my attempt to involve him in a kind of cross-examination, not actually with several people putting questions, but with questions raining down on him from all angles.

I knew that for him, the Holy Face of Manoppello was the model for absolutely all images of Christ, the root of a genealogical tree of all Christian representations of the Son of God. "In view of the complete correspondence that results when you place the Face from the Shroud of Turin on top of that of Manoppello, we have to admit that the image on the sudarium and that on the Shroud originated at the same time", was what he had said years before, somewhat ponderously. As regards their origin, then, only "the three-day period from the time the body was laid in the sepulcher up to the Resurrection of Jesus is possible; and as the place of origin, the inside of the tomb. The sudarium of Manoppello and the Turin Shroud are the only true images of the *Face of Jesus* and are known as *acheiropoieta*—that is, not made by human hands." Since then, the Professor had spent his life—at least, the rest of it, following the serious quarrel with Professor Bulst—in demonstrating the identity of these two objects with this ancient concept.

There were a good many fundamental questions, then, that I no longer had to raise. Yet quite enough questions remained concerning the details of his discoveries—in which, as folk wisdom had it, the devil was always to be found—and perhaps most of all, where something so sacred as the Holy Image was concerned. "I'm sorry", I said, "if I have to pester you with so many questions. I shall simply write it all down, afterward, and then tell it as it was." I did not have to prove anything, I told him. "I always have to prove everything", he returned with a twinkle, before we got down to our talk.

"You were the first one to say, 'Here in Manoppello is where the Veronica is!'—while in Rome there is still a Veronica relic that is lifted up above the parapet on the Veronica pillar, year after year. That is, on the face of it, an outrageous assertion. Had anyone else discovered that before you? Had you read it somewhere else?"

"No, what I had read was all the literature on images of Christ from the very earliest times. I practically knew that by heart. The discovery was then a process to which a number of different experiences contributed. The most important event, however, was my first encounter with the Veil in the autumn of 1986. I had just published my book about images of Christ. Then I saw the image for the first time, and I knew straightaway, 'That has to be the Veronica!'"

"Why?"

"Because I already knew the picture so well from the literature. And because it is so transparent. There could not be two things like that—I realized that, right away. With the best will in the world, no one could paint that; it is simply not possible. People can in fact paint both on one side of a cloth and on the other; the Byzantines were already doing that on silk. But you cannot paint a picture that—in practical terms—*disappears*. There is no technique by which you can achieve that; it is not possible. And I knew that there was only one object that people have always been enthusiastic about in this respect: in the West, the Veronica, and, in the East, the so-called Camuliana cloth. That is how I arrived at the idea of seeing it all in one object."

"But then you came back to Rome, where the Veronica is still honored in its treasury. How did you ever come to think that this image in Manoppello and the original Roman Veronica did in fact amount to the same thing? That once upon a time, then, the Manoppello image used to be revered in Rome?"

"Strangely enough, it only gradually dawned on me—first of all, though, with the recollection of Luther's 1545 pamphlet against the papacy, where he writes about the Veronica with which the pope deceived the poor pilgrims; in which 'poor simpletons from wherever' could see nothing more, he said, than 'a piece of clear linen': that is, a little transparent cloth. 'That must have been the same cloth' suddenly went through my mind."

"Yet does this text not argue rather for a deception? Is he not saying, rather, that a sham was being shown to the pilgrims as early as 1545?"

"No, no. I, too, saw only *white* at first. And only when I was looking from different angles, and going up to it, did I see the image itself, properly. That is what must have happened to the person who told Luther about it—with this difference, that when he saw the *white*, he did not look any more closely, but immediately moved on. That is how the pope was deceiving the poor people of Christendom! Instead of making sure, he stuck with his first impression. I can quite well imagine that. Luther was disappointed about so many things that he was only collecting evidence to confirm Rome's mismanagement. And I had always been annoyed at the way art historians simply assume that the pope could have misled people with just any old picture. You can mislead the masses, but you cannot show something like that to any king or emperor. The original Veronica in Rome must have had a miraculous character."

"Can you describe the moment when the penny dropped for you? It must have been quite electrifying."

"The whole story is electrifying, but the realization came little by little. The first thing was my great love for the Shroud of Turin, which I first got to know about from a lecture, when I was eleven years old. When I studied the history of art, later, I always used to wonder why the Shroud of Turin was always stubbornly ignored by art historians. That did not seem scholarly to me; it was well known in the Middle Ages, after all. It must have had an important influence on iconography, anyway, I thought. Then I really set to work and tried to derive all images of Christ from the Shroud. Yet there was always one little problem with that. The rounded, oval face of Christ cannot be derived from the Shroud. The little lock of hair on his forehead cannot be derived from the Shroud, either. That always created difficulties for me. Besides that, I had read again and again that there were several objects, among which there were *two* that were most important. According to the ancient sources, there were also *two* translations of images to Byzantium, those of an image from Edessa and a Camuliana image."

"Well, how did you discover the statements about the Veronica that are consistent with the image of Manoppello?"

"I already knew them all. As early as 1983, in a catalogue for an exhibition in the Palazzo Venezia, I had written an essay on the Veronica. I had made a thorough study of the sources for that and had tried to derive all the data about the Veronica from the Shroud. At that time, along with many other people, my view was that the Veronica image might be some kind of a copy of the Shroud. But I have had to revise that opinion. I have often had to correct myself."

"And how did you come to believe that the old *Relatione Historica* of Pater da Bomba, from Manoppello—dating from 1645—must be a fiction and that the true story must have been quite different?"

"For various reasons. The first thing that struck me was the way the dates were parallel. For anyone can see that. Every false story carries within it traces of the truth that underlies it—most particularly, the harder the author tries to deceive people and the more sophisticated the means he uses. And then in that story of Pater da Bomba's, now, we have the year when it was allegedly brought there, in 1506; and then 1608 as a second date, when we have the account of the way the Veil was forcibly purloined from the house of the brother of the wife belonging to the family who inherited the image. These dates fit too perfectly with those of two events in Rome to avoid the suspicion necessarily arising today that they must have been used to construct an alibi. For the author of the *Relatione Historica* does not mention any date at all between them—for an entire century! After that, on the other hand, the story continues with several dates one after the other: 1618, 1620, and so on."

"Yet why did Donato da Bomba choose 1506?"

"That is simple. That was when the cornerstone of the new Saint Peter's basilica was laid in Rome. That was a date at which, as everyone knew at that time, the Veronica was still being kept safe in the Veronica chapel of the old basilica. Also, the fact that the whole thing, in the *Relatione*, is set within a framework of data such as that Julius II was pope at that time; Maximilian was Emperor of the Holy Roman Empire; Ferdinand of Aragon was King of Spain; and all those things—that only actually makes it all the more noticeable that someone is trying very hard to construct something that fits into a historical context. That someone is going all out to give something an earlier date than it did have."

"When was the Veronica publicly displayed for the last time in Rome, then?"

"In 1601. There is no way anyone can quibble about that—yet the author of the *Relatione* does not seem to know that."

"And why did he choose 1608 for the date of the theft by that Pancrazio Petruzzi?"

"In 1608, the Veronica chapel in Rome was pulled down, thus making it necessary to transfer the famous relic into its new treasury. Perhaps it was not deliberate when Pater da Bomba chose that particular date. Yet nonetheless, for the historians of today he makes himself suspicious by doing it. At the time, he was trying to say, 'At that time, the *Volto Santo* had already been here with us for a hundred years. So it cannot possibly be the Veronica from Rome'—the loss of which was being felt most painfully by the popes of the time, who were searching for it!"

"Yet going back to you, Father Pfeiffer. You believe that the Holy Face in Manoppello comes from the empty tomb of Christ in Jerusalem; you think it is a 'small' or 'second shroud'. Why do the Gospels not tell us about this important piece of cloth, then, or the Acts of the Apostles, or the Letters of Paul?"

"In the world of Judaism, objects from a grave were seen as being extremely impure. It is hardly possible to imagine anything more unclean for Jews! That was the ultimate scandal. Yet Christianity originated entirely within the world of Judaism. It would have been quite impossible to start telling people about that, right away—first, on account of preaching the message and then, on the other hand, on account of the cloths themselves, if people were trying to keep them safe in a responsible way. If anyone had talked about them openly, they would have been in enormous danger!"

"But when and where is there first clear evidence concerning the Holy Face in the sources?"

"The earliest reference to this image on a cloth? The earliest source, you mean, that is unambiguously talking about that?" He did not pause long before answering. "That is the so-called Camuliana legend from the sixth century, which was presented in the fullest possible detail by the great Prussian scholar von Dobschütz, as early as the end of the nineteenth century, in Berlin. This is an old Syriac fragment about an image of Christ that in 574 was translated from Camuliana, an insignificant little spot in Cappadocia, in the east of the Byzantine Empire, not far from the city of Edessa, to Constantinople. This image was from the beginning held to be *acheiropoieta*, that is, 'not made by human hands'. And besides that, it was supposed to have been neither painted nor woven by human hand. We are dealing with several mutilated fragments of text; yet all of them recount how one day, in a spring in her garden, a pagan woman by the name of Hypatia finds a cloth in the water, on which she at once recognizes the image of Christ. She pulls it out of the water, and in an instant it is dry. The story was said at that time to have happened in the past, at the time of the persecution of Christians under Diocletian—and yet no one seems to be able to say exactly when it was supposed to have happened. Copies of it are said to have been made very quickly, and yet this 'Camuliana' was regarded as the original."

"And that is all?"

"No, there is another text, which has only come to light very recently and comes from Tiflis, in Georgia. Wait a moment, I must have it here with me." He stood up and went to one corner of his bookcase, pulled a book out, and took a piece of notepaper out of it. "Here it is; it comes from the library on the floor below, and I published it some years ago in one of my essays. A Flemish Jesuit discovered it three decades ago and translated it into Latin for the first time, when the Soviet Union was starting to crumble and become more open. This text, which talks several times about an 'image of the Redeemer', also comes from the sixth century, and the most important passage in it goes like this: 'After the Ascension of Christ, the Immaculate Virgin kept by her an image, which had originated on or over the Shroud. She had received it from the hands of God himself and kept it with her at all times, so that she might always be able to contemplate the wondrously fair face of her Son. Each time that she wanted to adore her Son, she stretched the image out to the east and prayed before it with her gaze on her Son and with open, uplifted hands. Before the burden of her life was finally taken from her, the apostles carried Mary on a stretcher into a cave. In this cave, they laid Mary down to die before the Face of her Son." I gazed at Father Pfeiffer; in Jerusalem, not long before, evening by evening for nearly two years, I had visited the basilica of the Dormition, which had been built, according to a tradition in that place, above the old cave in which Mary died.

Father Pfeiffer took off his glasses and looked me straight in the eye: "That must have been the image on the Veil at Manoppello. Everything the text says and the way it is structured point to that: 'the fair Face of her Son'; and also the format, and the way it is used as an image to focus meditation. A good many solid researchers are indeed of the opinion that it is the Shroud that is being talked about; but the mere idea of stretching out a piece of cloth four meters long in front of oneself is just as nonsensical as identifying the 'fair Face' with the double impression of the crucified Christ. And finally, if you ask me, who—apart from Mary, his Mother—could have taken away this fine little cloth after the crucifixion and Resurrection and kept it for herself? Who else, from among the first early community, could have been permitted this privilege? I regard it as quite self-evident that it was in Mary's keeping! Who else could have had it?"

"And what is the next report?"

"That is a sermon from the seventh or eighth century, which assumes that the Camuliana image is well known and in which—just as in the familiar scenes of the Annunciation made by the Angel Gabriel to Mary—a decorated chamber is mentioned, in which a white cloth covers a table on which stands a pristine glass bowl that Jesus uses to wash his face; after that he dries it, and in miraculous fashion the cloth preserves the impression of his face. At that time, this image is supposed to have been brought to Caesarea in Cappadocia."

"When did this image leave Camuliana or Caesarea?"

"That is not clear. It is simply certain that in 574, together with some pieces of the true Cross, it arrived in Constantinople, where great celebrations were held for it; here, at this period, a whole series of legends talk about miraculous reproductions of the original. In the Eastern empire, the image was regarded as having been lost without trace after 705. Right after that, in 721, the iconoclast controversy had begun, and countless icons had gone up in flames. In the capital of the Eastern Roman empire, the miraculous image that was held to have been created by Christ's own miraculous powers had, before that, become the standard and the flag of the Byzantine armies in their struggle against the Persians invading from the east. Perhaps it was already there, as the 'Palladion', when they were victorious in the battle at Constantina in 581. General Philippicus displayed it to his soldiers before the battle on the river Arzamon to give them courage by this marvelous sight, in the face of the enemy's superior strength. In 622, the poet George Pisides enthusiastically hymned the image on the standard as an 'image of the Logos, of the Word that shaped the universe' and as an 'original image made by God'—exactly as if it were a being that had been bred without human seed. In 586, Theophylactus Simocattes explicitly confirmed, yet again, that the image was of supernatural origin. 'Divine art' created it, he says, because, as he says, 'no weaver's hand' produced it, and 'the pigment of no painter colored it.' There can be no doubt whatever that all these statements are consistent with the image on the Veil that is at Manoppello today and with no other object currently in existence. Even the sermon to which I referred, which is said—probably wrongly, though perhaps not—to come from Gregory of Nyssa, a few years after 394, calls Camuliana on that account a 'new Bethlehem' and says the origin of the image is comparable to the birth of Jesus itself, because it came into the world 'through the Holy Spirit from the Virgin Mary'. The image effects a direct continuation of the work Jesus himself achieved on earth. He remains present here, it says, together with his power."

"Yet how do we come to have a legend? Why is it not enough that this concrete image is simply there?"

"No, that is not enough. That is why the legend is so important. The legend always has to justify the image's belonging in a particular place. If the image shows up in a godforsaken hole like Camuliana, then it seems clear and right to everyone that it belongs in Constantinople and should be transferred there, to the capital of the empire. If it had been in the important border fortress of Edessa, then the transfer would not have been right—unless, that is, the city of Edessa had in the meantime fallen into the hands of unbelievers. Legends have always served the purpose of clarifying and legitimizing questions of possession."

Father Pfeiffer had become somewhat heated while talking and paused for a while. I poured some more water into his glass. "And is it not remarkable", he continued then, "that the very same image is being kept in a place by the name of Manoppello? 'Bethlehem' means 'house of bread' in Hebrew. 'A handful of wheat' is what the old Latin word *manipulus* means. Is that not remarkable? Has the insignificant Manoppello in the Italian Abruzzis not really become something like a new Bethlehem, like the place in the Judaean hills where, two thousand years ago, the Bread of the World came into the world? However that may be, at some time in the eighth century, the miraculous image from Camuliana disappeared from all Byzantine sources. At the fifth session of the Seventh Ecumenical Council in Nicaea, in 787, the chamberlain Cosmas reported again with a declaration that iconoclasts had unashamedly cut out of the martyrologium in the patriarch's chapel the story of the miraculous image of Camuliana. In Constantinople, the image had simply disappeared from before the eyes of contemporaries. In the East, at that time, the Arabs had appeared as new enemies, in place of the Persians; they were self-proclaimed iconoclasts, and they were more radical than the Jews had ever been in that sphere. It is said, from that time, that when the iconoclast controversy broke out under Leo the Isaurian, Patriarch Germanus I entrusted the miraculous image to the waves of the sea. As if of its own accord, it swam from there to Rome, it is said, where Pope Gregory II himself gathered it from the waters—after it had first protected the ships of the Byzantine Admiral Heraclius in just as miraculous a way as it had saved the great city of Constantinople when it was besieged by the Scythians. It was an uncommonly powerful image, and it is all the more astonishing how quietly it then disappeared out of Constantinople. Germanus I was Patriarch in Byzantium from 715 to 730, and Gregory II in Rome from 715 to 731. Earlier, in Egypt—as early as the sixth century!—an anonymous pilgrim from Piacenza recounted that he had heard there about an image, the radiance of which was as blinding as that of Jesus' face at the Transfiguration on Mount Tabor. It was said to have been an image whose appearance was constantly changing."

"Just a minute", I interrupted the little lecture. "Whereabouts exactly was that in Egypt?"

"In Memphis."

"Do you have the text there?"

"No, but I know where it is in the library. If you like, I can get it right away."

I asked him to do so. Professor Pfeiffer stood up and took his bunch of keys; in the meanwhile, I gazed at the many pictures in every available corner of his room, stuffed full of books as it was, and hardly five minutes later he was back with an old 1898 folio from Vienna tucked under his arm, because unfortunately, he said, almost all the photocopiers in the university were out of order. He soon found the place he wanted, on page 189, and right away he started to read it out—first in Latin before he then added a translation: "*In Memphi fuit templum* ... In Memphis there used to be a temple that is now a church. There we saw a linen cloth, on which there is the image of the Savior; and they say that he wiped his face with it, and the exact image of him remained on it afterward and has in all ages been revered. We, too, prayed to him, but on account of the shining radiance we were unable to look upon it carefully enough, because it changed before one's eyes, while one was looking at it."

"But that is like an early description, point by point, of the Veil at Manoppello", I interrupt him.

"No," says Professor Pfeiffer indignantly, "that can only be something like the Shroud. On the Shroud, too, you see hardly anything at first, when you are standing in front of it."

"Yet how is that, then? This is explicitly said to be the description of an image of the head. And that way of changing as the light falls is precisely the phenomenon that can be observed today in Manoppello. But tell me, is this Memphis not identical with that place in Egypt near Antinoë and the El Faiyûm oasis, where almost eight hundred pictures of mummies from the first to third centuries were discovered, at the end of the nineteenth century? Pictures that, so people say, became the earliest precursors of icons?"

"Yes, that is exactly where it was. And that is quite right—nowadays, those Faiyûm pictures are to be found at the beginning of almost all books about icons and photo collections of icons."

"Might it not be, then," I asked in astonishment, as if I had made a groundbreaking discovery, "that there is perhaps a connection between this image that the anonymous pilgrim from Piacenza was describing there—and these mysterious pictures of mummies? They are, after all, without exception pictures of dead people painted on wood, and no one who has seen one can ever forget their eyes and their expression. Years ago, Hilde Zaloscer, an art historian from Vienna, once told me that she regarded these boards as the very first Christian pictures simply because they all seemed to be depicting people risen from the dead, for the first time in the history of the world! Yet is it not far more probable that they had above all one single model, especially with regard to the expression of their eyes?" Professor Pfeiffer hesitated. "Perhaps", he said, and stroked his hand over his hair. "One would have to go into that more thoroughly, sometime—even though I do still regard this text as making an early reference to the Turin Shroud. Not only I, but many other scholars see it as such. Yet one really would have to investigate that more carefully sometime." I asked him to continue his account. It was a pleasure to him to continue; I listened eagerly.

"An image of Christ 'not made by human hands' comes to light in Rome in 753, in the papal chronicle; Pope Stephen II carried it barefoot through the city in solemn procession in order to prevent the Lombards under Aistulf from attacking the city. In the so-called *Liber Pontificalis*, this image is called 'Acheropsita'. A good many people today regard this as having been the so-called 'Uronika', an old full-length icon, which is still preserved today next to the Lateran basilica. Yet *that* icon would in fact have been too large to be carried about. It is at any rate a long time after that that a Veronica is first mentioned in Rome, as having been supposed to have wiped the Lord's face on the way to his crucifixion. Or so-called 'Abgar images'—that is, a mysterious self-portrait that Jesus himself is supposed to have sent to King Abgar in Edessa."

"How can one tell the Shroud of Turin and the Veil of Manoppello apart, in the tradition, then? Is it not possible that in many cases either the one image or the other might be meant without it being possible to identify a distinction today?"

"No. Nonetheless, it may be that both of them together remained in Edessa until into the fifth century. Ultimately, we may say that both cloths were probably soaked with a solution of aloes and myrrh, which made them photosensitive. The Shroud is quite clearly a photographic negative, and the face on the Veil that probably lay over it is clearly a positive. On the basis of what we know of photography, it must have been lying on the outside."

"Are you trying to tell us that God is a photographer?"

"The Greek word *photos* means 'light' in English; *graphein* means 'to write'. And there is no better way of describing the technique of these two *images* with a single word: they have been 'written with light'. Who could have done that?"

"What was the first copy, in Rome, of the image on the Veil?"

"That must have been the mosaic of the bearded Christ, which was put into the apse of the Lateran basilica in the reign of Constantine himself, around the year 320. There must already have been at that time, in Rome, the first reports and accounts of that true image of Christ from Camuliana. Irenaeus was already talking about genuine images of Christ being made and about this being done following a model that was said to have been made in Jerusalem as early as the time of Pilate."

"When did the image itself come to Rome? And why is it that for quite a while after that we hear nothing more about it?"

"It probably arrived in Rome in 705, under Pope John VII. It was probably purloined from Constantinople later than 695, after the Byzantine Emperor Justinian II had been hounded into exile from there. So that he should never dare to return, his nose had first been cut off. When in 705 he nonetheless recaptured the city, he was unable to discover, even by means of torture, where the image had gone. It remained missing from Constantinople. And later, for a long time it could not be displayed in Rome for the simple reason that Byzantium could still assert, and enforce, its right of possession. At that time, it said in a chronicle that the pope had a Lady chapel made in the old basilica of Saint Peter's, which was called later the 'Veronica' and which he owed to the 'true image'. Finally, in November 1011, Pope Sergius dedicated its own altar to this sudarium, as it was known at the time, in that same chapel. Down the centuries thereafter, time and again there are clear references to this cloth, on which the Face of Christ was 'clearly to be seen'. As early as the twelfth century, there were in Rome priests who served in a Veronica chapel. In 1143 the tradition says for the first time that 'the sudarium' was also 'called the Veronica'. For Saint Birgitta of Sweden, who took part in celebrating the holy year in Rome in 1350, it was clear that the Veronica was miraculous and reproduced the Face of Christ in a quite unique way. One could find many more voices from the Middle Ages to agree with this."

"When was the image on the Veil first publicly displayed in Saint Peter's, then?"

"Certainly not until after 1204, when the Byzantines could no longer have any say in the matter from Constantinople. We have to say that there was a decisive breakthrough in 1208. That was when Pope Innocent III—under whose authority, on April 13, 1204, Constantinople was captured and sacked by the crusaders—first decreed that thereafter, on the second Sunday after the Feast of the Epiphany each year, the image, in a frame, should be carried in solemn procession from the old Saint Peter's to the church of the old Hospital of *Santo Spirito in Sassia* and back again. Do you know that church? Behind the Hotel Columbus and next to the Jesuit Generalate? It is interesting that that is the very place where nowadays the picture of 'Merciful Jesus' in accordance with the vision of Saint Faustina of Poland is quite especially revered, the image of Christ that seems to be the most beloved of all for John Paul II. It is a large painting in the Nazarene style, and yet the Christ is nonetheless somehow quite amazingly like the *Volto Santo* of Manoppello. Perhaps more like it than any other picture. Be that as it may, from the Pietà chapel, just on the right in Saint Peter's, where the old Veronica chapel was at that time, to the Santo Spirito church—I paced it out myself once, exactly—you still today have just about a quarter of an hour's walk, whether you go straight along the Borgo Santo Spirito after Saint Peter's Square or over the Via della Conciliazione and then turn off into Via dei Cavalieri del Santo Sepolcro.

"To this day, however, that Sunday is known in the liturgy of the Catholic Church as 'Omnis terra', after the first two words of the psalm that is sung for the introit. 'Omnis terra': that means, "All the world'. 'All the world worships thee, O God', it goes on. And in a way that is suitable, because from then on, all the world could be told about the image. A plenary indulgence from all punishment for sin was promised to everyone who came to Rome for that occasion. It was a feast day. The Pope distributed gifts to the poor and, at the end, gave his blessing, with the Holy Face, to the entire festal assembly of people who had streamed into Rome for that. It was above all through this feast that Saint Peter's attained the standing it has today. Naturally, as in all such cases, that did not come about without some tensions. For the pope's real church, then as now, as you must know, is in fact the basilica of Saint John Lateran. That was the first basilica that Emperor Constantine had built in Rome, about nine hundred years earlier, as the 'mother of all the churches in the world'. Now, however, the procession between Saint Peter's and the Santo Spirito became an anticipation of the *visio beatifica*, the 'blessed vision', as Sister Blandina once recounted to me. The great Saint Gertrude of Helfta had several visions on that day, which she narrated in her work *The Herald of Divine Love*. Before her, in Helfta in Thuringia, Saint Mechthild of Hackeborn had already had the vision, on that Sunday in January, of a high flowery mountain with fruit-trees and a throne of jasper and precious stones, 'on which sat the Lord. The Face of the Lord was radiant as the sun; it filled all vessels like food and drink and clothed all those present like raiment.' Sister Blandina seems to know all these visions by heart. I have also learned from her that Gertrude of Helfta set her nuns the task, for that day, of praying 150 Our Fathers on behalf of other people—to commemorate the 150 miles a pilgrim traveled from Helfta to Rome." He smiled: "But Saint Gertrude must already have been thinking in terms of heavenly miles, there."

"When was there, then, the first picture in Europe of a woman who is holding this Veil—that is, a symbolic Veronica figure, like the one we can see today in Saint Peter's?"

"The first sculpture of that kind was in France in the fourteenth century, in the cathedral of Écouis, where a woman is displaying a veil with the face of Jesus on it. This is a statue from the period around 1310. And then, this gesture certainly appears in the Passion plays, in the late thirteenth or early fourteenth centuries. The way of the Cross had developed in Jerusalem. Birgitta of Sweden had followed the way of the Cross there, more or less as it is today—though as yet still without the Veronica station! Henceforward, the Franciscans helped to spread it farther. The Veronica legend must therefore have arisen after that—and in fact, in a bloody version and a non-bloody one. The oldest form is non-bloody; that is why the famous fifteenth-century "Veronica Master" from the Cologne area painted both versions—a veil with a crown of thorns and one without any such thing. And the Master of Flémalle shows Christ, on his image on the Veil, without any sign of the Passion. In Rome itself, however, before the time of Dürer, there was no representation whatever of Saint Veronica. Dürer was the first to bring her to Rome, in 1510, when he combined two traditions and showed Peter and Paul on a woodcut, with Saint Veronica and the Veil standing between them."

"In February, in the Via della Conciliazione, you spoke of three factors veiling the true nature of the Holy Face in Manoppello. What did you mean by that?"

"The first veil cast over the true image of Christ is the Western legend of Veronica: that is, that a woman by the name of Veronica, who took pity on Christ, is supposed to have captured his image with a sudarium, so that the true image of Christ is supposed to have been the result of a woman's being merciful to Christ on the way of the Cross. That is the first veil. Countless 'station shrines' in Europe and the New World recount that. That has sunk deep into our memory. The second veil, however, was woven in Manoppello itself, by that legend that as early as 1506 an unknown pilgrim handed over this image in a little packet to a respectable citizen of the place. Yet that is simply impossible."

"Why was it told like that, then, and asserted to be true?"

"To preserve this precious object from the pope's efforts to search for it."

"And why could it not in fact have been brought to Manoppello as early as 1506?"

"Because, as was said earlier, about a hundred years later the image was displayed again in front of many pilgrims and witnesses in Rome. This legend is thus trying, in a fairly sophisticated way, to conceal the fact that this was indeed the original Roman Veronica in Manoppello. That is the whole reason for it. This story is a little deception by the *Manoppellesi*, by means of which at the time they told Pope Urban VIII and his prelates, who were investigating the matter, 'We have had this cloth for a hundred years longer than yours has been missing. This cannot be what you are looking for.' That is why the *Relatione Historica* of Donato da Bomba was written, in which he narrates in 1645 how the cloth was handed over to a Dottore Leonelli by a messenger from heaven, in front of the door of San Nicola, as long ago as 1506. For in an edict of May 29, 1628, Pope Urban VIII had directed, under threat of excommunication, that is, exclusion from the communion of the Church—which was almost the heaviest penalty of all—that all 'copies' of the Roman Veronica had to be returned to Saint Peter's in Rome! That is why we have ended up with this story, and any fool can see that it is a fabricated legend. It simply served to legitimize the existing state of affairs, to establish the right of possession of the relic in Manoppello. That is why, with the public reading of this *Relazione* before the most prominent citizens, we have the very first documentary reference to this image in Manoppello. There was a notary's statement of April 6, 1646, in which thirteen elderly and respectable notables of the little town declare, solemnly affirming together, that 'their image' has been in the place much longer than the 'copies' the Pope is demanding to have returned to him. That means, 'Nobody can come and get it or claim it on that account!' That was an incredible step to take—and in retrospect, that is why it is incredibly easy to see through it."

"But just a moment, Father Pfeiffer. In the meantime, I have been making an intensive search through the Vatican's secret archive for this alleged edict of Urban VIII's. Yet there is no mention of it to be found there. Nor does the *Indice 767* of the *Segretaria dei Brevi*, which is relevant here, make the slightest reference to such an edict. In the Chapter Archive of Saint Peter's, likewise, there is no evidence to be found concerning it, nor is there any in the libraries of the papal universities. Not a word about it! It does not appear here anywhere. Is this alleged edict not a fabricated legend, then? Or a conspiracy projected into the past?"

"No, no!" The face of the white-haired scholar flushed in a malicious smile. "It is after all hardly surprising that such compromising documents are not preserved after they have been found to be of no use." His voice took on a triumphant tone, as he stood up and took a large envelope from the bookcase. "But just look here at what I received only yesterday from Don Filippo Lupo, the parish priest of San Nicola di Bari in Chiusa Sclafani, in Sicily, where there is still an old copy of the Veronica. That is the second of those mentioned on the back of the copy in *Il Gesù*, here in Rome. It is one of the so-called original copies that Pope Paul V had made in 1617." He took from the envelope a whole bundle of copies of old manuscripts. "Here, on the outside, some old writings have been preserved that have the news about the edict. Here, read it for yourself." He handed me a large magnifying glass and then nonetheless himself read out from a manuscript of 1628 belonging to the parish archive a passage where it said that Pope Urban VIII "has become aware of various copies that, contrary to all rulings and apostolic prohibitions", supposedly "represent the true and sacred image of the Holy Face" and concerning which His Holiness had urgently to be informed, in order that these images might be withdrawn from circulation. Any contravention of these strict instructions would have to be punished by irrevocable exclusion from the communion of the Church.

Then he smiled again. "It will be a pleasure to copy this for you. You see: Urban VIII had a real problem. Without the Veronica, he would not have been able to keep his Holy Year in 1625. The pilgrims did not want to see him; they wanted to see the image of Christ. They wanted to see the image of God. He urgently wanted to get that image back. If he had had it at the time, then he could not have cared less about any copies—even those contrary to the rules of art. So it must have been otherwise: the Veronica was simply no longer there! For Urban VIII was not stupid; on the contrary, he was a crafty diplomat and a friend of the Society of Jesus. But that was perhaps the only positive thing about him. Otherwise, his behavior sometimes bordered on the despicable. He put the Church's treasure at Richelieu's disposal; and Richelieu had nothing better to do with it than to hand it to the Swedes. That was how the Swedes were able to carry on the Thirty Years' War against the emperor. I can still remember that from grammar school, from the mouth of our Protestant history teacher, who always took particular pleasure in explaining that to us."

"Are there no other historical sources that show that the image was nevertheless already in Manoppello in the sixteenth century, as the *Relatione Historica* maintains?"

"No; but that very silence is significant. In 1574, for example, a Dottore Rozzi traveled all around that area, that is to say, in Manoppello and in all the neighboring villages and little towns, where he meticulously recorded every image of any saint and every relic down to the smallest little bone in every single chapel he went into. In Manoppello, on the other hand, he had nothing to report—apart from the name and the fact that he had been there. That would have been quite impossible if the image had been there already. Unless, that is, it was buried in the churchyard at the time. And yet even that is an impossibility for anyone who has ever once seen the image. It needs to be seen. It demands to be seen."

"'The holy lance was carried through Borgo by way of the Vatican, amid loud cries', it says in a contemporary text about the *Sacco di Roma*, however, when in 1527 German and Spanish troopers plundered Rome; 'and the Veronica was passed from hand to hand through the lowest dens in Rome!' What do you say about that?" This argument was the last trump I had to play against Father Pfeiffer, but he looked at me unmoved.

"That was a hysterical rumor that was appropriate to the mood of catastrophe in those years—and which was at the time strongly denied. The Veronica was in fact displayed in Rome again in 1533, and then in 1536, 1550, 1575, 1580, and 1600."

"And what is the third veil you were talking about?"

"That is the cover-up and concealment of the fact that the Vatican lost the most important relic in Christendom four hundred years ago. The Veronica was stolen at that time—but to this day, no pope has openly said so. In 1608, the old and venerable Veronica chapel was to be pulled down, and each of the relics was to go to a new place in the new Saint Peter's. There was an enormous amount of resistance to that, however. Think a moment: the old chapel—which was intact and beautiful—had been standing there about nine hundred years. To many people in Rome, the demolition of the chapel by the pope must have seemed a matter of sheer arbitrariness. Assuming the best-case scenario, the popes of the last four hundred years probably did not themselves have any slight suspicion that something must have gone wrong with the splendidly planned translation of the relics from their old places to their new ones. In the curia, however, all down through the centuries, there must always have been quite a number of people to whom it was quite clear that the cloth that has been preserved in the Veronica pillar for four hundred years is nothing but a fake. It is not without good reason that there is not a single photograph of it. Not without good reason that you will not get to see it, in however friendly a fashion you may ask."

"That is by no means a trivial allegation, Father Pfeiffer. And this is not the first time you have made it. You were making that assertion as long ago as your 1991 book, and then you did so again at your press conference in 1999. It is, after all, the Vatican you are directly accusing and incriminating—how have they reacted to it?"

"Not at all! Yet a year after my press conference, in the year 2000, the hitherto carefully sheltered 'Edessa Image', which is supposed to have come to Rome from Edessa during the Middle Ages by way of Constantinople, was brought out of the pope's apostolic palace to the world exhibition in Hanover. That was an all but revolutionary thing to do. That image on cloth, according to the German Monsignor Kemper's semi-official statement about it on behalf of the Vatican, was 'the oldest likeness of the face of Jesus Christ'. Besides that, he said, this image had 'not only significantly influenced our idea of what an icon essentially is, but in a certain sense it is the first icon of all'. That was the Vatican's response—if there was any—to my discovery of the image of God in Manoppello. The most recent investigations and research into this Mandylion of Edessa, on which this account was based, had been commissioned by Professor Arnold Nesselrath, the German Director of the Vatican Museums.

From the Lord of the Images
to the Image of the Lord

In contrast to Father Pfeiffer, Arnold Nesselrath was less talkative. *Voci di corridoio*, using a somewhat more polite expression, was what they called gossip in Rome; and reliable "voices in the corridor" had told me that he regarded Professor Pfeiffer, together with his convictions concerning the Holy Face in Manoppello, as being no more deserving of respect than me and my own researches—to put it most politely. I had to look into that. The queue in front of Nesselrath's kingdom wound along the wall of the Vatican for nearly three-quarters of a mile. At the end of it, whistling security doors like those at airports made gaining access to the Vatican Museums even more irritating than it already would have been in all that crowd. The five-hundred-year-old rooms full of world-famous treasures, in the quarters formerly occupied by many popes, house what is perhaps the most valuable art collection in the world, including that of the Louvre. Michelangelo and Raphael were among the artists who worked on paintings directly intended for these rooms. The paintings did not have to be bought later. And nowadays, in any case, the guardian of all these pictures was the German art historian Arnold Nesselrath, director of the department for Byzantine, medieval, and modern art of the Vatican Museums since 1996 and

Father Heinrich Pfeiffer, S.J.

professor at the Humboldt University in Berlin. "Ah, you want to see Dottore Nesselrath", said the security official in the entrance hall appreciatively, "to see the capo in person!"

Dottore Nesselrath had already been in Rome when the Sistine Chapel was cleaned, though his predecessor had still been in charge then. It was under his supervision that Raphael's world-famous *Stanzas* were restored at that time. He seemed to know his way around every single stone of the pope's various palaces and when it was put in place there. It was hardly any different with the pictures among his immeasurable treasures. It was under his aegis that the Edessa Mandylion in the sacristy of the Sistine Chapel had been investigated, on the occasion of the fiftieth anniversary of John Paul II's ordination to the priesthood, in 1997; and he was soon telling me, too, that following that investigation he could well imagine that this image of Christ "goes back to the third century", and not—as some other people maintained—to the fifteenth. He had also had the *Uronica*, the full-length Christ icon from the Sancta Sanctorum Chapel of the Lateran, investigated, and also the ancient icon of Mary from the basilica Santa Maria Maggiore, which the Romans call *Salus Populi Romani*, "the salvation of the people of Rome". "All these images 'not made by human hands' are surrounded with layers of legend, which lead back to a point quite close to a very early origin—if you strip them away very carefully", the experienced art restorer said, cautiously, in his cozy little office above the rooftops of Rome.

The walls were covered with bookshelves. Through his open window, the view swept over the Prati quarter of the city to the Monte Mario hills and the Villa Miani.

His desk was piled with things. Beside the museums, he also took care of the art treasures of Rome's churches; he could not complain of having nothing to do or that he did not have the greatest consideration paid to each one of his specialist judgments. Nonetheless, he made an impression of youth, of being alert—not fossilized or wrapped in dreams, like other scholars who have sat too long in libraries and have not had enough fresh air. Only his short black beard was slightly unkempt, as if he had often rumpled it while he was thinking. In his eyes, the pupils darted here and there with great rapidity. The names of other specialists, all of whom one ought presumably to know in order to carry on any meaningful further conversation at this level, came tumbling out of his mouth quite casually as he talked.

What did he have to say—this was what I wanted to know from him on that glistening bright early morning—about the Holy Face of Manoppello? After the debates about this that had already taken place in Rome following Father Pfeiffer's initiatives, I could and had to take it for granted that he knew about it and that he rejected any identification of this Face with the Roman Veronica. And he did not deny this at all; he was quite unable to conceal how well informed he was about everything, even about his early-morning visitor and his daughter. "What am I supposed to say about a picture I have never seen?" he responded, cautiously, to the question for which he had certainly been waiting. He, too, had heard of the image, of course. He had also "heard" of an article that I had written about it—and even, incidentally, that I was now writing this book. "But does this image not interest you?" I asked, dumbfounded. He shrugged his shoulders. "Well, you know, the evidence concerning the provenance of this object is not particularly good." Yet its mere existence, I said, to add more fuel, is extremely well attested for at least four hundred years. And had he not heard about the sources relating to it that his colleague Professor Pfeiffer, for example, had discovered? And ultimately, in this connection, did not the Gospel of John have to be taken seriously as a source, as so many people had believed when confronted with this image? "You know, there we are getting into territory where various different specialist areas are relevant, and it is very difficult to decide where to draw the line as to where one of them ends and another begins." Yet was he not at least curious, as a specialist and as the master of so many images, at least for once to see this object in the nearby Abruzzis, which a good many people—and more and more people all the time—regarded as simply the "matrix and mother of all images of Christ"? "It takes only a scant two hours from Rome", I added carelessly. "Not really, because you see, if this is a relic, as other people say, then it is no longer my responsibility. It is does not then fall within my area of jurisdiction." He left me speechless. This was, after all, a picture—to say the least!—even if it was a relic a hundred times over. Would that not have had to make it that much more fascinating, the fact that this might really be an object not made by human hands—without any legends—and that all other images going by that designation were merely early copies of it? It was impossible to get any answer to that. Nor did he let a single word slip as to what he thought about me and my reflections and investigations. I was not supposed to have brought any tape recorder along for this interview; but not by one single question did the clever art historian allow himself to be drawn. When I left him, after an hour, I was still completely in the dark as to why this object did not have him bursting with curiosity and why he did not take the freeway to Pescara the very next Saturday. How was it—this was going through my head while we were once more talking about quite different subjects: about cheap flights to Rome, about the threatened sale of all its art to private individuals by the Italian state ("A state that sells off its cultural heritage is destroying itself!" "We start wars with the click of a mouse, and we are surprised that we cannot end them the same way."), and so on—how could it be that a man with this degree of expertise and this position in Rome could go to such lengths to avoid this image? Yet I did not get an answer even to that.

I should have liked some comments "from the horse's mouth", and I asked him for them, but all in vain. Even a compliment, to the effect that he was as sly as a fox and stubborn as a mule poised at the edge of black ice on to which he obviously did not want to let me draw him, tempted him only to a brief laugh, but not to a single extra word on the subject. We talked on, about this and that, before I picked up my hat and stood up to take my leave. "Will you not, just for once, drive over to Manoppello?" I asked this highly cultured scholar and specialist, making one last attempt as I stood in the doorway. He merely shrugged both his shoulders and lifted his arms up like some great bird, before laughing as he gave me his right hand.

One more mystery. I took it with me as I made my way along the corridors outside, through groups of Japanese, back to the entrance to claim my passport, which I had had to leave there as a security pledge. The winter morning still stretched gleaming over the Vatican when I stood once more outside the walls. I was so overcome with hunger for the ready information given by Father Pfeiffer, it was as if I had missed breakfast that morning. I had taken the day off—and the *Apostolo del Volto Santo*, as Rome's endearing wits had recently christened the art historian from the Gregorian University, also had the day free. I would be most welcome to come round, he said over the telephone. An hour later I was again in his scholar's den, where our conversation flowed on as if it had never been interrupted. "So the Vatican's image of God was replaced with another?" I asked. "Yes." "But why was that?"

Father Pfeiffer laughed happily. "I don't know. As a Jesuit, however, a member of the Society of Jesus, I am very touched and amused by the typically Jesuit character of the whole business! Is it not almost as if, here again, he himself had passed through walls and locked doors? Does it not show something of his sense of humor and that of his Father that at the very moment when the greatest and mightiest treasury in all the world had just been built for it, with more locks than the high-security wing in a prison, the image found its way out onto the street again right then, completely unprotected, like one man among others? That at that time, the authentic image of God took a walk out of the palaces of Rome to visit the Capuchins, the poorest mendicant order of Catholic Christendom!"

"Back to the alleged theft. Who do you suppose committed it, then, and why, exactly?"

"That is unclear and will perhaps always remain unclear. The one certain point is that Paul V had people who were strongly opposed to what he intended, building a new Saint Peter's. It was not only the Christians in

Germany, those around Luther. The people opposed to him in Rome were scarcely less passionate—even members of his own family. For he belonged to the Borghese, whose bitter enemies, at that time, were nobles who had long lived in Rome, such as the Colonnas. They were a powerful clan of nobility, and the Palazzo Colonna is still there in Rome today to tell of their greatness. They had property and lands throughout Italy; even the little market town of Manoppello belonged to the Colonnas in those days. Monsignor Pietro Corsignani, Bishop of Venosa, near Benevento, reported as late as 1738 that a particularly large number of the high nobility 'of the House of Colonna' took it upon themselves to follow the long and difficult road to Manoppello to venerate the relic there. So it seems certain to me that the old Veronica disappeared from Rome at the very same time as the Pope had the Veronica chapel of old Saint Peter's demolished. After that, the irreplaceable relic was simply replaced."

"You have been asserting that for a long time now. Yet is it not very remarkable that in 1618 Jacopo Grimaldi quite consciously made a fairly accurate drawing of the original Veronica with open eyes once again, for the title page of his inventory—yet that at the same time, he mentions that the old frame had been broken 'through the carelessness of one of the canons', as he says; although you assume that it was broken in the course of the theft? Does Grimaldi not have to be disregarded as a witness on account of that contradiction? He is no longer much good as the primary witness of the loss because of that."

"One could look at it like that—if one were to misunderstand the Vatican as being a unified and monolithic construction. Yet the opposite is just as true today as it was then. How many opponents do you think the present Pope has in the Curia?! Or do you really believe that he faces no opposition at all in the Vatican? The opposite is always more probably the case, and that was how it was, quite particularly—as I said—under Paul V. Grimaldi's work should probably also be seen in that context, when he documented the treasures of old Saint Peter's with such precision. That was the very first inventory of all the treasures of the magnificent basilica of old Saint Peter's, which did, after all, go back to the early Church, in the days of Constantine. This was no ruin they were pulling down. And even now, in many documents you can feel how the hearts of a great many people who loved the old basilica must really have bled. That, I think, will also have been the case, quite especially, for Canon Grimaldi, who knew the church so well. I have no way of actually proving it, but given what we find in the sources, I could even imagine that on that account Grimaldi himself also played a particular role in the 'loss' of the relic, if we may call it that. A particular indication of that, it seems to me, is that in 1618 Grimaldi talks about the 'very great similarity' of the copy made for Queen Constance—the one, as you say, with a nose like a potato and the eyes closed!— that at that time, then, he explicitly confirms this copy's similarity to the original, which in fact he knows, and after all he did himself execute a quite marvelous drawing of it on the title page of his inventory, with the eyes open and the slim nose—more like the image on the Veil at Manoppello than anything else."

"Yet how is it possible, then, that after the 'theft in Rome' the cloth remained so unknown here that nowadays hardly anyone in his senses will or can believe the story?—How is that possible?"

"There are several reasons for that—some of them quite banal ones. First, up until a few years ago the Abruzzis were still the most distant part of Italy. Far into the twentieth century, until the freeway was built, this part of Italy was the end of the world. Palermo was nearer—by ship. In contrast to that, Manoppello might have been on the far side of the moon. Drive there from Rome by way of the ordinary roads, and not the freeway, then you still get some idea of that. In that area there are *trulli*, Stone-Age huts built of untrimmed stone, in which people still live. In short, you could hardly take the image anywhere that was farther away than Manoppello, and there was scarcely anywhere better for hiding it. In 1811, the Capuchins were chased out of their priory in the Napoleonic wars and, until they were able to return in 1816, entrusted the relic to the Poor Clare nuns.

"In 1866, the Fathers were expelled once more, this time by aggressively laicist laws; under pressure from those, they had to leave the relic alone in the church for three years, up to 1869. The people in Manoppello believe that the Archangel Michael kept guard over the image during that time. Yet sometimes it almost seems as if they had forgotten it themselves."

"Yet the Romans cannot possibly have forgotten it. And it would be still more impossible for them to keep it secret that it had been stolen out of Saint Peter's!"

"Yes, they could—and that is a remarkable phenomenon of human nature, which has been very well understood in Rome for a long time. You have only to read in what a frustrated way Ian Wilson runs on, in his book about *Holy Faces*, about how, for all his efforts, the Veronica here remained so completely inaccessible to him. The stubborn wall of all the guardians who would not let him get to it increasingly convinced this clever guy of the immense value of the fake. He did not even get any answer at all to his last question as to whether he could not at least take a photo; only silence amid the forest of pillars of Saint Peter's. It makes me laugh, the trouble he took with archbishops and monsignors, 'simply to be able to investigate the Veronica directly, himself, for once'. And all that time, Manoppello was completely open to him and could easily be reached by a little journey in a rental car. The drawbridge that was pulled up in front of the sham Veronica had so drawn his attention to itself, however, that he simply did not see the wide-open door to Manoppello. He did not think about it. The idea simply did not enter his head. Just as for many other scholars with a fixed, scathing judgment about the true image on the Veil when they have never seen it, it probably seemed to him simply too easy. It seemed to him so simple that he could not even imagine finding the true relic there, perhaps next to a little mother who is weeping loudly about her daughter before the image and another who is praying her Rosary, or—what would have been equally probable—that he could have stood or sat or knelt in front of it, all on his own. Impossible! Too much in his book, so Wilson writes regretfully, is unfortunately dependent on second- or third-hand information—because of the inaccessibility of the essential relic. Only the object so firmly protected that he was not even permitted to see it could be for him the 'holy' original; not something as utterly unprotected as the Veil of Manoppello. That seemed simply too cheap, too easily available, too ordinary. This incredibility was in some sense also the best protection for it—for the swindle in Rome, just as much as for the true relic hidden in Manoppello."

Father Pfeiffer, of the Society of Jesus, smiled again with malicious mischief.

"Yet that cannot have been enough to ensure that the story of the Veronica also fell into oblivion the way it did at the time?"

"Perhaps it was, though. And most recently, there has also been a defensive front that is just as remarkably absurd on the part of the so-called sindonologists and Shroud researchers in Turin against recognizing the authenticity of the cloth in Manoppello. This conflict goes along with a conceptual confusion that encloses and conceals the true image of Christ with many and various names. Sometimes people talk about an image on a cloth, sometimes an image on a veil, an *acheiropoietos* that was 'not painted by human hand', and then again about a sudarion, sudarium, or kerchief; in Russia about a Mandylion, or again about an image from Edessa; about the Veronica, the true image of Christ, the *Volto Santo*, the *Santo Volto*, the Holy Face, the true icon, the *Santa Faz*, the *Santo Rostro*, the second shroud—there is no end to the concepts and names surrounding this image. We hardly know what to call it ourselves. The lovely word 'countenance', for instance, somehow gives the impression now of being like old currency that is no longer in circulation. Who could be surprised that all this confusion has completely bewildered many and that hardly anyone asks about the hard core of truth behind all of it?—A second great difficulty is that we have an infinite number of copies that are set beside this relic of the image—and must be set beside it. Copies of the most varied kinds, whether they are miniatures or icons or pictures that have been given the same title as the relics. The Mandylion concept alone is itself most complicated."

"But what is the Mandylion, then?"

"That is the Turin Shroud! There is no question about that! In the Arabian period, the Shroud had been given the Arabian designation of *mindil*—for 'cloth'. The Greeks made *Mandylion* out of that."

"Yet why, in Russia, are many old icons called 'Mandylion' that show only the face of Jesus and look as if they were painted—directly or indirectly—as copies of the Veil of Manoppello?"

"The reason for that throws a quite significant light on the mysterious events in Rome in the first two decades of the seventeenth century. That very same Pope Paul V who kept the Queen of Poland waiting so long when he was asked to have a copy of the Veronica made for her—that very pope, in 1617, forbade any artist in Rome to make a copy of the Veronica without being authorized to do so by the Vatican. Henceforward, such copies could be made only by selected members of the clergy of Saint Peter's! A more than remarkable occurrence. Even more remarkable, however, is that starting at that very time, the early seventeenth century, countless icons of that very image of Christ turned up in Moscow looking as if they had been copied from the old Roman Veronica. So at the same time as that kind of art virtually stops in the West. There can be almost only one explanation of that: those artists who now found themselves without work must have moved from Rome to Moscow at that time. Since then, the Russians have consistently called all Veronica icons 'Mandylion'."

Portrait of Christ (detail), ascribed to Simone Martini from Siena (1284–1344), in the convent of Saint Francesca Romana, Rome

The light-image of Christ over the high altar of the Capuchin church at Manoppello, where the first evidence for it is from a text dated in 1645: The fragile old document says that "the hands of an angel" supposedly brought it into the Abruzzis in 1506.

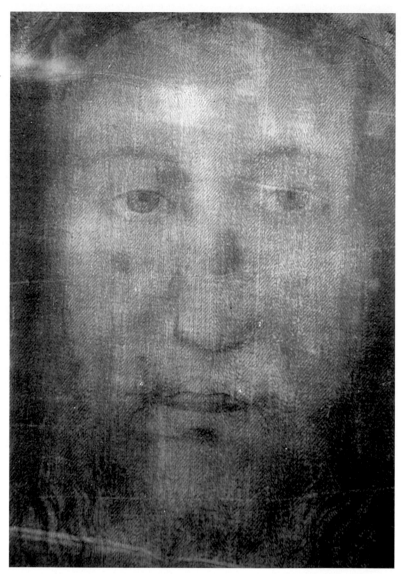

A semi-transparent slide-picture with the face from the Shroud of Turin in front of the image on the veil at Manoppello: so-called "superimposition" by the Trappist nun Blandina Paschalis Schlömer, made on July 16, 2005. This technique, in the original scale, clearly shows in the two images laid one on top of the other, right through the structure of the linen-weave, the identity of one single person, in all its proportions, and even in the wounds—a degree of correspondence scarcely ever attained by any "wanted" photo.

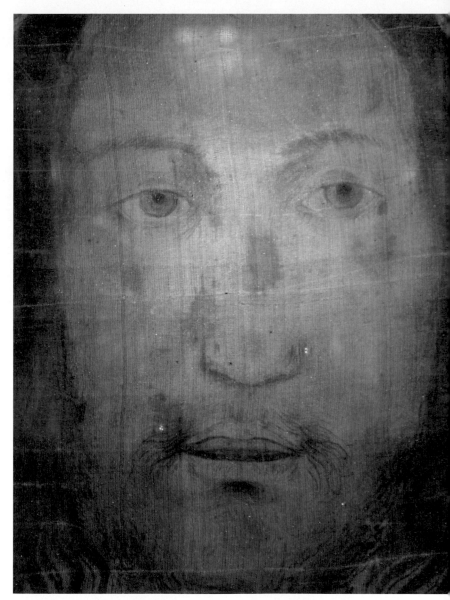

In a similar fashion, however, the "Holy Face" corresponds to old sources and texts that, for around two thousand years, have mentioned a true Image of Christ—and one "not created by human hands"—and about the "veil of Veronica". On this photo, we can clearly see the "folds", by which an inexplicable image of Christ was said to be able to be identified as early as in the ancient "Acts of Thaddeus".

In 1545, Dr. Martin Luther described the Veronica relic in Rome as "a transparent linen cloth" on which scarcely anything could be made out. Even today, the cloth relic in Manoppello has the appearance of completely transparent material when light is shone directly onto it.

Sister Blandina Schlömer uses her hand—on which her wrist-watch can still clearly be made out, right through the veil—to demonstrate the phenomenon of the partial transparency of the Image of Christ, on the morning of April 4, 2005, in a room adjoining the pilgrim church.

Only since the middle of the last century has the image on the veil been displayed in the light of electric lamps. Before that, it was for centuries kept hidden in a treasury, and after that preserved in the shadows of a side-chapel, where the facial features could hardly be made out at all.

The so-called "Mandylion of Edessa", in the sacristy of the Sistine Chapel in the Vatican, is regarded by many experts as the "oldest picture of Christ". The most recent investigations suggest a date for this image, executed in tempera on linen, probably as early as in the fourth century.

A related, if perhaps more recent "Edessa image" has been preserved in the Church of Saint Bartholomew of the Armenians, in Genoa, for at least the last six hundred years. There it is revered as being likewise the "true and oldest image of Jesus".

Pietro Cavallini's masterpiece in the Church of Saint Cecilia in Rome. This fresco, from the thirteenth century, shows Christ with his eyes open, his mouth slightly open, and his teeth visible, his right cheek swollen and a delicate lock falling down from the central part in his hair.

The Flemish "Master of Flémalle", regarded as having been Robert Campin, probably lived between 1375 and 1444. No other artist has painted the "Veronica" as he did: as a portrait of Christ with no neck shown, on an extremely delicate, gossamer-thin transparent veil.

Around 1460, Giovanni Bellini from Venice painted the Risen Christ giving a blessing, with his wounds, thin beard, slightly open mouth, flax-colored locks of hair, and a crown of thorns that is already turning into a radiant halo, while still in his hair.

Albrecht Dürer introduced into Rome the standard pattern of picture of the image on the veil of Veronica, in 1510. Ten years earlier, in Nürnberg, he had painted himself in a full frontal portrait, which up till then had been reserved for Christ in all paintings everywhere—and painted himself with a lock of hair falling onto his forehead.

In the caves under Saint Peter's basilica, beneath the high altar in the so-called Chapel of "the Virgin of women giving birth", this fresco has survived; it still shows the old treasury in which, up to the reconstruction of the Basilica that was begun in 1506, the principal relic of the Church was preserved behind an iron grill in the earlier building—roughly in the place where nowadays we may admire Michelangelo's Pietà. "Ciborium of the most sacred veil of Veronica, erected by John VII", it says in Latin to one side. Pope John VII reigned from 705 to 707.

Public display of Urban VIII's Veronica-reliquary, on the balcony of the Veronica pillar in Rome, on Passion Sunday 2005, between the two pillars allegedly from the temple in Jerusalem. Above is a bas-relief of the school of Bernini, with the veil of Veronica.

Foundation-stone and treasury: the Veronica pillar in Saint Peter's. "That the splendor of the place might preserve in seemly fashion the image of the Redeemer taken onto Veronica's kerchief, Pope Urban VIII has built and ornamented this place of its safekeeping in the jubilee year of 1625."

The pilgrim church of "The Holy Face" was built about 1620. After 1960, the old building was renovated and extended. At the same time, the new façade was constructed, which reproduces the patterning of the romanesque Basilica of Saint Maria di Collemaggio in Aquila.

The little town of Manoppello on one of the outlying arms of the Majella Massif, with the Gran Sasso in the background; this still gives us some idea what a barrier the Apennines constituted to traffic between the east and west coasts of Italy, up to a few decades ago.

Twice every year in Manoppello
the luminous image of Christ
is carried in solemn procession
in the natural light of the sun:
first in broad daylight on a long
route from the sanctuary to the
nearby village and back; then,
in the evening twilight, only
a short way to the bottom of
the hill and back. Both times
there are fireworks, showers of
flowers, and decorated homes
along the way.

The longer procession has been
held, since 1712, on the third
Sunday in May. The shorter
procession is more ancient.
Since 1690 it has taken place
each year on the image's own
feast of the "Holy Face", August
6th, when the Catholic Church
celebrates the Feast of Christ's
Transfiguration on Mount Tabor
in Galilee.

Father Cucinelli shows Cardinal Meisner the "paschal Christ" on April 4, 2005, in the cloister of his friary—before, a few hours later, the Archbishop of Cologne accompanied the dead Pope from the Sala Clementina, down the Scala Regia into Saint Peter's.

The face of John Paul II is being covered with a veil of the finest silk—immediately before his funeral, on Friday, April 8, 2005. The Pope himself had introduced this ritual in his order of service "Ordo Exsequarium Romani Pontificis". (photo: AP)

▷▷Exactly two years later, Benedict XVI visited Manoppello, and spent quite a long while in silent prayer before the "Holy Face". With his visit that day, the Pope made the forgotten image world-famous. Two weeks later he raised the little church to the status of a papal basilica.

Chiara Vigo, from the Sardinian island of Sant' Antioco, is the last master-craftsman in the Mediterranean in the harvesting, spinning, and weaving of mussel-silk. On September 1, 2004, she recognized the "Holy Face" in Manoppello as being a cloth woven of mussel-silk.

"Many people talk about God; in the name of God even hatred is preached, and force is used. That is why what we have to do is to discover the true face of God. In Jesus Christ, who allowed his heart to be pierced for our sake, the true face of God has appeared to us."

—Pope Benedict XVI, on August 20, 2005, in Cologne.

The Master of the Living Child

O n the left, in front of the main door of the Gregorian University, where Father Pfeiffer dwelled on the fifth floor in his narrow room, which was stuffed full of books and pictures, a little gateway in the Via Pilotta concealed one of the loveliest central courtyards in Rome. The courtyard, with its palm trees, orange trees, and fountain, belonged to the Biblical Institute, where, nearly twenty years ago, one of my finest reports had had its beginning, about the "Heavenly Jerusalem"—the plans for which an old Jesuit from Hungary had reconstructed here, beside the laundry room, with fantastic models that he had put together following discoveries in the ruins of the ancient church of Santo Stefano Rotondo and had hung from the ceiling. One of those models, made by Brother Sándor Ritz, was still standing in my bookcase; it touched me and consoled me whenever I remembered him, even though he himself had long since moved on to the Heavenly Jerusalem himself. His inner courtyard, however, where in summertime he used to water the hedges and trees, had remained unchanged in twenty years. Time seemed to have stood still here: the blue heavens high above the quad, the peeling rust-red plaster on the walls, the green of the cypresses, and the white marble of the fountain. It was a little vestibule to paradise. Beside the arcades, I could find my way back, almost without looking, to the refectory, where Brother Ritz had invited me for a meal that last time we saw each other. "Here, take some", he had said mischievously, pouring me some more wine and putting an artichoke on my plate. "Take some, take some! You still need to grow!"

Everything had stayed the same within the high vault of the refectory, yet I had never before noticed the great mural at the head of this room where the professors took their meals, even though it had been there for decades. For at that time I had eyes for nothing and no one but Brother Ritz, who could not turn his inner gaze away from the many-towered architecture of the golden city that God was going to lower down to earth from heaven at the end of the days. Up to that time, I had never encountered a more fantastic story. He was always merry when I met him, but above all else he was possessed by the idea of the kingdom of heaven. Hence, I now became aware for the first time of the great mural beneath which Brother Ritz had then been telling me about that kingdom for the last time: it was a living fresco in the colors Michelangelo used for the Sistine Chapel, yet in the athletic and realistic style of the first half of the twentieth century. Dawn was just breaking. Six life-sized men were standing on the shore of a lake, surprised, astounded, puzzled, each in another incarnation of perplexity, almost all of them half-naked. In front of them, an older man was kneeling in the waves and handing a fish to an eighth—and younger—man, who in return was handing him a loaf of bread. These two were also only scantily clad, in cloths that were slipping from their shoulders. A small fire of coals was glowing between them on the shore, and a fish had been laid in the embers. Behind the feet of the kneeling man, the water was teeming with fish, glittering silver with fish in a net that the men had just pulled up to the beach. The youngster who was sitting on a stone beside the fire had an open cut on his right foot.

The composition here was a little masterpiece and recounted one of the loveliest stories in the Bible. This scene opened the closing chapter of the powerful Gospel of Saint John. After Jesus had come into a room on Mount Zion—through walls and barred doors—to meet the apostles in Jerusalem, following his Resurrection (and Thomas had asked to be allowed to put his hand into his wounds), he showed himself to his disciples on the Lake of Tiberias, it said at the beginning of this chapter, and it happened this way:

> Simon Peter, Thomas called the Twin, Nathanael of Cana in Galilee, the sons of Zebedee, and two others of his disciples were together. Simon Peter said to them, "I am going fishing." They said to him, "We will go with you." They went out and got into the boat; but that night they caught nothing.
>
> Just as day was breaking, Jesus stood on the beach; yet the disciples did not know that it was Jesus. Jesus said to them, "Children, have you any fish?" They answered him, "No." He said to them, "Cast the net on the right side of the boat, and you will find some." So they cast it, and now they were not able to haul it in, for the quantity of fish. That disciple whom Jesus loved said to Peter, "It is the Lord!" When Simon Peter heard that it was the Lord, he put on his clothes, for he was stripped for work, and sprang into the sea. But the other disciples came in the boat, dragging the net full of fish, for they were not far from the land, but about a hundred yards off.
>
> When they got out on land, they saw a charcoal fire there, with fish lying on it, and bread. Jesus said to them,

"Bring some of the fish that you have just caught." So Simon Peter went aboard and hauled the net ashore, full of large fish, a hundred and fifty-three of them; and although there were so many, the net was not torn. Jesus said to them, "Come and have breakfast." Now none of the disciples dared ask him, "Who are you?" They knew it was the Lord. Jesus came and took the bread and gave it to them, and so with the fish. This was now the third time that Jesus was revealed to the disciples after he was raised from the dead.

There was a time, not long ago, when almost every baptized person in Europe could have recounted that scene from memory. This heavenly breakfast in the gray of morning was in some sense part of the essential core of the gallery of the Christian subconscious—and a modern artist would find it hard to paint it much more beautifully than here. Every stone on the shore of the Sea of Galilee here was familiar to me. Each of the men seemed to embody a different remark, a different thought, a different amazement. "Piczek I. 1950" was written in the waves of the lake, in plain block letters, to the left of Peter's knees. It was on account of that artist, Isabel Piczek, however, and not on account of Brother Sándor Ritz, that I had come back to the Biblical Institute that day. I had found out from Ian Wilson that the picture to be seen here was the earliest of all her murals, over two hundred of them. It looked tremendously mature.

Yet when she finished this picture, Isabel Piczek had been just fourteen. It seemed almost incredible. Today, the artist lived in Los Angeles, where she specialized in mosaics and painting on walls and glass. In 1999 she was appointed Dame of the Order of Saint Gregory by Pope John Paul II, and in 2000 she was honored with the famous "Cardinal's Award" by Roger Cardinal Mahoney for outstanding services in the archdiocese. Above all, however, Isabel Piczek was an experienced and committed expert in the worldwide circle of sindonologists, in which context she had demonstrated, using many lines of argument, that in the "picture" on the Turin Shroud, according to all the rules of art, we could not possibly be dealing with a painting. Her name cropped up time and again in the relevant literature as a primary witness for the inexplicable and unique nature of this "work of art" on the linen sheet in Saint John's Cathedral in Turin. Yet it was not only in connection with the Turin Shroud that she was regarded as a reliable expert. "Isabel Piczek's story was a particularly fascinating one", wrote Ian Wilson in his book about the quest for the true image of Christ.

During the 1950s, when only thirteen, she fled from the communist suppression in Hungary, arriving in Rome, where her artistic abilities quickly won several awards, including a competition to create a fresco at the Pontifical Biblical Institute, across the road from the Gregorian University in Rome. It was this work which brought her into contact with several very senior individuals within the Vatican hierarchy, ones who could literally open any door. Isabel was not yet fourteen when one of these took her into St Peter's, entered the sacristy, and kept her waiting nearly an hour. Such was the secrecy insisted upon that to this day Isabel declines to make public the name of the individual concerned (though she has disclosed this to me). But to her astonishment the sacristy door suddenly opened, and the illustrious cleric and his companion were revealed a few feet inside holding a framed cloth that she was told was the Veronica. According to her description: "On it was a head-size patch of colour, about the same as the [Turin] shroud, slightly more brownish. By patch, I do not mean that it was patched, just a blob of brownish rust colour. It looked almost even, except for some little swirly discolorations ... Even with the best imagination, you could not make any face or features out of them, not even the slightest hint of it." As she further recollects: "The light was not that good at all, and there was glass on the object [i.e., the Veronica]. He did not bring it out in apparent fear that people would gather."

Right out of the blue, her name came up on my computer screen when, in 2004, I was trying to report convincingly on my discovery in Manoppello to Professor Karlheinz Dietz in Würzburg. Since Dietz had, some years earlier, acted as my *cicerone*, both humorous and informative, in Turin, we had become friends over more than one glass of wine and a good many plates of pasta in the trattorias of the Piedmontese capital. "I'll eat my hat", I wrote to him now in an e-mail from Rome to Würzburg, with photos attached, "if this is not the genuine Veronica—if there is such a thing as the genuine Veronica." Still on the same day, he had asked me in his reply "to spare the hat a little longer"—not least, because a certain Isabel Piczek had said that she knew of other such images on cloth, and in those cases, as in that at Manoppello, "Sienese paintings from the sixteenth century" were involved.

This was also the offer of an honorable means of saving the honor of, at the very least, the still mysterious image. For paintings of the Sienese school counted among the most lovely and delicate of the many treasures that Italy had to offer—by no means simply in Siena, in Tuscany, but in the finest museums of the whole world. So even if the Veil from the Abruzzis could not be reckoned as supernatural as the linen sheet in Turin, everyone—whether "for" or "against" it as a "relic"— could without loss of face regard it as immensely precious:

indeed, from the artistic point of view, as far more valuable than many other relics. It was clear that Karlheinz Dietz, in however friendly a way, was determined not to be convinced of anything further. Even new photos and e-mails, however often I tried, could not move him to go and see the image for himself. "I do not feel annoyed by the fact that other people regard as genuine what I regard as false", he gave me to understand, after I had written to him once more about the image in Manoppello and the Easter Liturgy in Saint Peter's Square, in which "seeing", as I had then for the first time become aware, played an almost central part. I wrote to him again, "When the women came to *see* the tomb, alleluia. Come and *see* the place where they have laid the Lord, alleluia. Fear not! You will *see* me in Galilee, alleluia. And so on. And the sudarium was almost as prominent in the texts today as Peter himself."

It did no good; my critical friend from Würzburg simply could not relate the cloth from Manoppello to the Risen One in Jerusalem at all. Nothing would really prompt him, he told me several times, because of everything he already knew about the cloth so far (and, especially, what he knew about the association of friends linked to it that had grown up in Germany), to come to the Abruzzis and look at the cloth with his own eyes for once. This refusal did not even require citing the many duties he had at the university, which prevented such a visit almost as much.

I could thus continue to visit the image, particularly alone with Ellen, on many Saturdays—with never-diminishing amazement. Months later, I asked Mrs. Isabel H. Piczek personally, in a fax, to please send me her expert opinion, to which Professor Dietz had referred in making his judgment. Eight days later, the fax-machine sounded during the night; in the morning, an extremely friendly letter from the lady in faraway Los Angeles lay on my desk. She had taken several days over her careful response. First, there was something she must explain, she wrote at the beginning: "I have not investigated the actual object in Manoppello. I am principally an artist by calling. For me, it was enough to have enlarged reproductions, transparencies, and close-ups of this work of art in order to know exactly what it is. The Manoppello image is in every respect a painting. It is a product of the so-called Sienese school, from the mid-fourteenth to the mid-fifteenth century."

In a most systematic fashion, in the next paragraph she then passed into a little essay on locating the picture in its historical context: "Paintings that showed the same picture from two sides on a very thin screen first appeared in Spain in the Middle Ages. The single coloration, with the dark outlining of the eyes, teeth, and so on, show Islamic influence, as does the material on which it is executed. This technique quickly spread to France, where it became very popular. Italian artists from the area around Siena brought the technique home with them from visits to France; the most important of them was Simone Martini. In Siena, too, this technique became very popular in the second half of the fourteenth and the first half of the fifteenth century." That was why, she said, faces in the same style as Manoppello were to be found in gothic paintings in Spain, such as those of Ferrer Bassa (1290–1348), but most especially in the paintings of the Sienese school, like the *Maestá* by Simone Martini (1284–1344), and his *Madonna with Saints*; likewise in the Camposanto of Pisa, in the art of Taddeo Gaddi (1300–1366); but most vividly and most accurately in Gherardo Starnina's *Madonna with Child and Musical Angels* from 1410. "Starnina lived from 1354 to 1413 and, significantly, was active in Spain between 1379 and 1403."

The technique of painting two pictures on both sides of a very thin screen, she said, had unfortunately not survived to our own time, "and in fact this was precisely on account of the very fine material used." This veil probably had to be stretched out on a very strong frame, and then the artist must have used a most sophisticated technique, which must in some ways have corresponded to that used nowadays for painting on silk. "Hence it comes about that this image is exactly the same, both from the front and from behind, and there is in general a lack of brushstrokes and very little coloring. This kind of work done on silk should make the image appear faint in its details—as in the case of the eyelids, the outline of the eyes, the lips, and so forth. In these areas, in Islamic art, finer and stronger brushstrokes were applied: obvious brushwork."

After that, the final paragraph of the two-paged expert assessment was then a categorical summary responding to the question of whether the cloth might perhaps be a relic. "There is nothing miraculous about the picture in Manoppello", the artist wrote. "In contrast to the Turin Shroud, it is a work of art. Nor can it be the sudarium of Veronica, in which—according to tradition—Christ, on his way to Golgotha, wiped his bloodied face. Even if we were not to take into account obvious technical details, why should anyone at all wipe his face on a cloth with his eyes wide open, so that even the pupils leave an imprint on the cloth and the eyes look out directly from the cloth into the eyes of the beholder? To sum up, therefore: the

Manoppello cloth is not the Veil of Veronica. Nor has it anything to do with the Turin Shroud. It does, on the other hand, have a great deal to do with the old Sienese school of painting. At any rate, it shares characteristics with a quite particular technique, once so popular in Siena, and these suggest that we might suspect it to be the last remaining painting of this type. Isabel H. Piczek, DSG."

This fax was an enormous help. If I had correctly understood it all, the findings amounted to this: If everything in the analysis was right, the picture in Manoppello would have to be a quite extraordinary treasure—the last remaining work of art of a very rare type, showing Islamic influences in the heart of Christianity, centuries old and preserved in the very best condition. That the Muslims, among whom the representation of any human face was forbidden, had contributed their most delicate techniques to this image of the Messiah's face in particular was at the very least amazing—in fact, it was sensational! It was revolutionary. For that reason alone, the Holy Face of Manoppello would have to be more valuable than Leonardo's *Mona Lisa* and Michelangelo's *Pietà* put together.

"But that's incredible", said Ellen. "And merely because it shows the Face of the Most High, the art historians are behaving as if it simply were not there? As if it were nothing! That cannot be true." What was there that could not be true? I asked in return, and took down from the bookcase my illustrated volume on Sienese painting. I spent the whole evening studying this luxury volume and looking up on the Internet every single name that Isabel Piczek had, in such friendly fashion, mentioned and offered by way of comparison—Ferrer Bassa, Simone Martini, Taddeo Gaddi, other masters from Siena, and finally

Gherado Starnina—and each one of their works that I could find. It was enormously enjoyable and a real feast for the eyes, especially Starnina's *Madonna with Child and Musical Angels* from the J. Paul Getty Museum in Los Angeles, the expression of which supposedly came "closest" to the Manoppello Face and "in the most vivid manner". The alabaster hue of the Madonna was breathtaking, and the jewels in her crown still glittered in print. Gherardo Starnina had painted this picture in Florence, around 1410, in tempera on wood. He was also known as the "master of the living child", because he was able to create such incredibly lifelike pictures of the Christ Child—and here, looking at the Child on the Madonna's lap, one could understand the title. It was a feast for one's eyes: the golden brocade, the angels' plumage and their joyfulness, and the heavenly balance of the composition. I could not tire of looking at it. The delicate colors, shapes, and composition would overwhelm anyone who loved painting, and especially the Sienese gaze of the Madonna, which had become world-famous, looking out of her narrow eyes.—Only, that picture on wood had not even the least thing in common with the gaze and the expression and the lifelike character of the face above the tabernacle of the Capuchins' church in Manoppello. The Holy Face in the Abruzzis corresponded, not so much to any Sienese picture on wood, but far more to all that the oldest sources tell us about an ancient and legendary so-called picture of Abgar.

Jude Thaddeus before King Abgar. Detail of the altarpiece
picture in the Piccolo Casa San Giuda Taddeo, Rome,
by Prof. Ballerini, 1940

Jude Thaddeus

No one who was nowadays still seriously seeking the true and authentic image of Christ could in fact bypass King Abgar of Edessa. One evening, in the Saint Anna Church, the little parish church of the Vatican, just behind the Saint Anna Gate where the Swiss guards monitored all visitors of the mini-state, Ellen showed me on the literature stand a little brochure, on the title page of which a man in a red cloak was holding out to another man, sitting on a bed in front of him, a Veil with the face of Christ on it. The title leapt out at me. The picture shone like a revelation. It was a semi-transparent picture of shining light on a thin white cloth, which was astonishingly similar to the first of Jacopo Grimaldi's drawings of the Roman Veronica from old Saint Peter's: the open—green!—eyes, the hairstyle, the slightly asymmetrical face. Even the hands of the man who was holding the image were lit from within by the cloth, as if that were a source of light. *S. GIUDA TADDEO APOSTOLO prega per noi* was written beneath the picture, however: "Saint Jude Thaddeus the Apostle, pray for us!"

I put the brochure in my pocket and, out on the street, took it out again at once and unfolded it. "That cannot be true!" I said, "Here is the actual Apostle Jude Thaddeus represented together with the subject of an image that has otherwise been reserved for the figure of Veronica; that is, this time there is a real man of flesh and blood in the place of an allegorical figure." Saint Jude Thaddeus, I gathered from the booklet, was especially revered in a small church on the western side of Rome, where the picture could also be seen. The next evening we were there, in the "little house of the holy Apostle" on the corner of the Via Gradisca and the Via Roverto, not far from the Piazza Istria and the Corso Trieste. The large original of that little picture was hanging over the high altar in the dusk. It was an academic historical painting, which had been painted in 1940 by a Professor Ballerini. We were able to take a close look at it after the nuns had finished their evening Rosary. The Mother Superior switched the electric lights on for us and told us that the picture showed how the Apostle Jude Thaddeus was said to have brought an image of Christ "not painted by human hands" to King Abgar on his sickbed in Edessa and that the King had immediately been healed at the sight of it. We could now also perceive a small tongue of fire that was hovering over the slim Apostle's head. He stood barefoot on the cold pavement, holding a large pilgrim's staff in the crook of his arm so as to have both slim hands free and to be able to stretch out the light image in front of the King. He had a small forked beard, and his hair was bound back in a ponytail behind his head; he was dressed in a red cloak and a white tunic. At his belt was hanging a kind of case for holding manuscript scrolls. Heavy curtains screened off this oriental room behind them. A lion skin was lying in front of the King's bed; a servant was looking on skeptically at the scene in the room from the entrance; behind him there was a sand-colored wall and, behind that, a date palm.

"Aha, someone has put the legend of Thaddeus into the form of a modern painting", laughed Professor Pfeiffer, when I told him about it on the telephone. "Of course, there is absolutely nothing in it. That Apostle certainly had nothing whatever to do with the *Volto Santo*—and besides that, we know next to nothing about him." What I knew about Jude Thaddeus, on the other hand, was that his grave, here in Saint Peter's, lay almost as close to the Veronica pillar as did that of the Apostle Peter. Together with the Apostle Simon, he was regarded as a son of Clopas, who was supposed to have been a brother of Joseph, the foster father of Jesus. Consequently, he would have been a cousin of Jesus. The brief Epistle of Jude in the New Testament was ascribed to him. The Jesuits had been very committed to fostering a particular cult of him in the seventeenth century. Personally, however, the first I was aware of having heard of him was over sixteen years earlier. My mother was still alive then, and I was confronted with an extremely difficult decision and did not know which way to turn. The whole world was oppressing me. In the walls of the houses across the street I could see only the mullions and transoms of the windows—apart from that, no tree, no shrub, and no other living thing in the street. At that point, I called my mother. "What is it?" she asked. I told her. "I cannot help you or advise you about that", she said; and then, after a pause, "There is only one thing that can help: you have to pray to Saint Jude Thaddeus! He is the patron of hopeless cases, lost causes—and he always helps!"

"But there is as good as nothing about him in the Bible", I said. "How is he supposed to be able to help me, then?" "I don't know what there is about him in the Bible," my mother replied, "but I know how often he has already helped me when I was at a loss about something. He can also help people learn to pray again." Whether I took any notice of her advice then I can really no longer remember—but since then, I have never forgotten the name of the Apostle. I later saw for myself that in Mexico, in almost every church, he was almost as much revered as the Madonna of Guadalupe—usually, as a figure with a cudgel on his arm, in remembrance of the blows with which he was beaten to death in the city of Edessa (and often with a picture of Christ on a medallion hanging round his neck). Some weeks earlier, we had read his legend again, in a kind of pictorial narrative, set in a costly picture frame, in a remarkable church in the Ligurian port of Genoa.

We had been in Germany and Switzerland and were on our way back; we had stopped for the night in Pavia and intended to go and see the splendors of Lucca the following afternoon, where a miracle-working *Volto Santo* was revered in Saint Martin's Cathedral. According to the photos of it we had seen, this was the figure of a crucified man with his eyes wide open, his hair centrally parted and a forked vandyke beard; Father Pfeiffer thought it was the only item of old-Syrian plastic art to have survived both the Byzantine and the Muslim iconoclasts. Next, however, out of the blue, there was a heated quarrel between us over our evening meal. What about? Neither Ellen nor I could remember later. The next morning, in any case, we woke up much too late, with nothing to say to each other; each drank a cappuccino, separately, at the hotel bar and got into the car in silence. The foggy plain of the Po came flying toward us on the freeway, silvery rice-fields flickered past us, and it was dreadful. We had been far too late getting on the road to visit

Lucca. Shortly before Genoa, Ellen broke the silence for the first time: "Haven't you always wanted to see the Edessa image in Genoa?" "I don't know where it is", I murmured. "Shouldn't we simply look for it?" "The city is far too big for that." So we drove to Genoa—after we had first missed the right exit for it on the freeway.

Nor could I later recall how we found the church, whose name we did not even know, nor could Ellen, my most beloved wife. Suddenly, we had parked the car in the Via Assarotti, which seemed to run down to the sea in the distance, not far from the synagogue, and then suddenly we had to climb up just one more flight of steps, and then yet another, and then we were standing in front of the Church of *San Bartolomeo degli Armeni*. The church was open, Sunday afternoon! From the outside, it looked like a large old dwelling, with many windows, which might equally well have been standing in Prague or Kraków, and tenants like Franz Kafka or Gustav Meyrink might still have been living there. There seemed to be rooms behind the windows of the upper floors into which no doors would ever lead you. And it was probably much the same with the depths of history, deep into the cellars of which this remarkable building reached down. "AVE SACRA CHRISTI FACIES", an inscription over the white marble doorway read: "Greetings, O Holy Face of Christ!"

In the sacristy was kept, in a glass container made of quartz, a complete foot of the Apostle Bartholomew, with a golden sandal. Bartholomew's right name was Nathanael Bar-Tolmai; he was one of the seven whom Jesus met in the gray light of dawn on the shore of the lake, after his Resurrection, with a fire of coals nearby; and he was the one concerning whom Jesus had prophesied at their first meeting that he would "see greater things than these", after Philip had enticed him to meet his new Lord with the words, "Come and see." What he was to see in the end, in any case, was that before his own crucifixion in Armenia, the skin would be cut away from his living body; that was called "flaying", in the technical terminology of torturers. Because of the stripping of his skin, Bartholomew was, funnily enough, the patron of shoemakers. In this church, however, what was more moving than the Apostle's foot was a dark old image of Christ, inside to the left, in the *Cappella del Santa Sudario*, by the side of which an inscription said, in lapidary fashion, "This *Santo Volto*, which has been kept for six hundred years in the Church of Saint Bartholomew of the Armenians, in Genoa, is according to tradition the oldest image of Jesus; and it is probable that it is a genuine portrait of the Redeemer."

It was a tremendously suggestive portrait: the great eyes were almost Indian in their almond shape, with the whites showing beneath the pupils, and the nose was long and slim. The face gazed out at the beholder as if from a window, from a frame that gleamed gold and silver, in the finest early Byzantine decorative technique. Sophisticated filigree patterning in gold and silver wire was twisted into ever-new flowers around the frame. Apart from ten pictures of scenes worked in relief, the entire frame was covered with this patterning, very strange and beautiful. From the midst of this, two incredibly familiar eyes gazed out at us. A strong floodlight illuminated the dark-brown coloring; but if I merely held my hand in front of the light, the face immediately disappeared in a darkness as deep as night. If the light was entirely covered, the face sank into shadows like those of the ocean deeps. In Jerusalem, years ago, I had discovered a similar pitch-black icon of Christ in the Veronica chapel on the Via Dolorosa, behind the altar, which would only disclose the face it hid on photos taken with a flash.

"In one passage of the Gospel of John," it said in this accompanying text, "we read that one day 'some Greeks' appeared before the Apostle Philip with the request to see Jesus. These 'Greeks' are supposed to have been the emissaries of King Abgar V of Edessa. A very ancient tradition, going back to the first centuries of the Christian era, bears witness to an embassy Abgar sent to Jesus." In Edessa, at the time of Jesus, Aramaic was spoken, just as in Jerusalem. The two cities lay only some 370 miles apart; and the Roman road system at that time was already excellent. It was thus not improbable that Jesus' reputation had spread that far in his own day.

For the first time, we were standing alone and completely undisturbed in front of one of the famous Edessa or Abgar images. As on our later visit to the sacristy of the Sistine Chapel, in April 2005, it was entirely clear at first glance—or at least, at the second—that we must be dealing with a very old, very venerable, and very powerful copy of the image on the Veil at Manoppello, or with a copy of a copy, albeit without the overpowering mildness of the original. There was nothing surprising about the great veneration in which this masterpiece was held; it was a "living image", and it was terrifyingly beautiful. As was the case with the Edessa Mandylion in the Vatican, this portrait, too, was painted on linen, which had been stretched over a board of cedar wood. And perhaps, at the time when this was made, the transparent model now in Manoppello was for a while stretched over wood, so that at the time the image on the Veil was perhaps similarly dark and opaque in appearance, like those paints, darkened to match those egg-dying colors that were used, as long ago as in ancient Egypt, for finishing portraits.

A priest of Saint Bartholomew's Church, whom I had found in the sacristy, told us that earlier the image on the cloth had been revered as a relic, because the legend about it said that it had come into contact with the body of Christ himself. I had searched him out so that he could tell us about the portrait itself and the sequence of ten pictures around the frame, in which an artist from Constantinople, a thousand years ago, had recounted the story of the Abgar image in relief images in beaten gold, as if in a modern comic-strip. "The legend begins here, at the top left", our guide told us helpfully. "Do you see that man in bed there? That is King Abgar, who is just sending the man standing in front of him to Jesus, in Jerusalem, to ask him to come to Edessa, the city on the Euphrates, in order to heal him there. The messenger was called Ananias. And look here," he continued, moving his finger around clockwise, to the right, to the next picture, "you see here how Ananias is in Jerusalem, trying to paint the portrait of Jesus. Yet his efforts are in vain. After that, we see how Jesus washes his face and hands and dries them—and how, in the next picture, one picture farther down, he gives Ananias that very towel he used, to be taken back to King Abgar as a letter. In the picture below that, Ananias comes back to Edessa, to King Abgar's sickbed, and the King is instantly made healthy the moment he sets eyes on the image of Jesus' Face that he had left on the towel."

Here, the man paused briefly, went round to the left-hand side of the frame again, and pointed to the golden vignette just beneath the opening scene, high on the left. "It continues here," he smiled, "and just see there what happens—and I wish it still happened like that for us today: as soon as King Abgar sets the image of Christ up high on a pillar, the old pagan idols all around fall down like figurines from their pedestals. Yet in the next picture, following the death of King Abgar, a bishop is already climbing a ladder to a treasure vault with the image of Christ, to hide it there from enemies of some kind who are looking for this image and want to destroy it. That was probably after the capture of Edessa by Emperor Caracalla, when the Christians had to go underground again and a bishop hid the image away in the city wall. After that, knowledge of the relic was lost for awhile—though probably not completely. Those are at any rate the essentials of the story we know from the so-called Acts of Thaddeus, from the sixth century. What can be traced back historically out of all that is as follows: there was indeed a King Abgar V, who lived at the same time as Jesus and ruled in Edessa until A.D. 50. And at the latest under one of his successors, Abgar VIII, Christianity was already tolerated and was an officially approved cult and promoted as such."

"And what about the three pictures at the bottom?" I asked. "None of those three has anything to do with the legend; they recount actual historical events that are also well-attested in other sources. Look here, on the left: the picture with a bishop and a ladder, which looks almost the same as the previous one, where the image was being hidden? Here the picture enters the realm of history that can be verified if desired. For this picture, together with the next one, recounts how in 544 the Holy Face was first rediscovered by a bishop in a walled-up hiding-place in the city wall; and then after that, the inhabitants, with the help of the image, miraculously broke through the circle of Persian enemies—far more numerous than they were—who were besieging them. The historian Evagrius Scholasticus writes about that, and he also calls the image 'made by God, and not by human hand'. Another chronicler, Procopius of Caesarea, writes that it was found again in 525, in a hollow space in the city wall of Edessa, following a flood. According to the monk Niaphoris, however, the cloth is supposed to have been hidden and to have disappeared as early as 325."

"And the last picture, on the bottom at the right? What story does that tell?"

"That is four hundred years later again, when the image was being solemnly conveyed by ship from Edessa to the port of Constantinople. That was in 944. This event is as well-attested, historically, as it could be. Only a little while ago, the manuscript of a speech by the Archdeacon Gregorios was found in the Apostolic Library at the Vatican—a speech he made that same year, on the occasion of the translation of the Edessa image to the old capital of the East Roman Empire. The Emperor himself, he tells us, went on foot in front, when the image made its solemn entry into the city; after him came the patriarch and the clergy, all barefoot and carrying lighted torches before the people, who welcomed the relic to Constantinople in procession with cymbals and elaborate hymns. Archdeacon Gregorios—whom we should call an archbishop—calls the image an 'image of the impression of Christ', and he imagines that it was imprinted on the cloth, not in ordinary colors, but by drops of blood and sweat. He describes the head pretty accurately, with the large eyes, the locks of hair and the thin beard on the chin. This priest was already saying, even then, that nobody could copy this image, as it was an image 'which could not be called an image'."

I looked the portrait straight in its darkened eyes once more, looking right into this gaze, which was deep as a well. It got under the skin; yet it was certainly an image that could be called an image, a picture. In the light of the lamp, the gleaming, three-dimensional surface of oil and tempera colors applied here shone so much it was hardly possible to photograph it. To the left of the temple, TO HAGION had been hammered into the gold plating with delicate skill, and MANDYLION to the right— The Holy Mandylion. "What does that mean?" I asked. "The Holy Sudarium," the man said. "And besides that, according to Gregorios' sermon, it is not supposed to have been Ananias who brought it to King Abgar, but Jude Thaddeus, one of Jesus' apostles. 'I will not be able to come until I have accomplished everything here', is the message Jesus is supposed to have sent King Abgar by Ananias. 'After that, however, I will send one of my apostles to you with my image, so that he may heal you with it.' That is why, after Jesus' Ascension, Jude Thaddeus is said to have come to Abgar, together with this image. The Apostle Thomas gave it to him to take with him. He had been given the cloth by the Lord in person, after he had dried his sweat on it, after he had been sorrowful even to death. Thomas said he had received it 'after Jesus had come down from the mount on which he had been praying'. That would certainly have been the Mount of Olives, with the Garden of Gethsemane."

"But the image has painted colors on it, so it is painted after all", I said. "So that cannot have been a sudarium."

"Perhaps it was, even so", the priest replied, taking the keys out from under his cassock. It would now be time to close the church for midday. Even we were getting hungry. "Perhaps, underneath the paints, there was sweat on the cloth, and perhaps an artist merely went over the outlines with his brush, later, to reinforce them."

"But where does the Abgar legend come from, then—the one that is retold in the little pictures round the frame?" I wanted to know, before asking the parish priest about a low-priced restaurant in that part of the city. "That is much older. Correspondence between Jesus of Nazareth and King Abgar is first referred to by Eusebius of Caesarea in 325. Eusebius is regarded as one of the first Church historians. In 544, during the Persian siege of Edessa, the chronicler Evagrius wrote about 'a divinely wrought image of Christ' that had come into existence 'without involving any human'. The oldest version of the story of King Abgar handed down in any of the documents known to us is probably that in the so-called Acts of Thaddeus from the sixth century, first in Syriac and then in Greek."

The restaurant that his reverence had recommended to us in Genoa was, unfortunately, closed; we drove on, still hungry; yet we could not get the eyes of the Edessa portrait out of our minds, all the way along the Tyrrhenian coast to Rome. The Genoan captain Leonardo Montaldo had brought the image back from Constantinople, so we had read, in 1362—presumably "as a gift or reward for military services"—and had presented it to this church in 1384.

When we got back, we found in our mailbox a large packet containing, in a ring binder, a thick stack of photocopies that a certain Matthias Henrich had sent to my friend Martin in the Allgäu. Among these was the speech of Archdeacon Gregorios, from the Apostolic Library of the Vatican, in a rough typewritten translation. Behind that was a transcription in Greek letters and, finally, the sixteen-page copy of the original manuscript. To me, all three texts were almost equally incomprehensible, and perhaps most incomprehensible of all, indeed, was the overblown and pompous German version of this truly Byzantine speech. What I could understand of it largely corresponded to the explanations we had been given in Genoa. What I understood less was a description of the image, which sounded like this: "In these instances, is not painting, with its wealth of content, a door made to correspond with the meaning? The root-word of the image, schematically, in one form—the prototype. In such cases, even the outer radiance of light is carved into it. On the one hand, painting puts together the bodily form in its intactness for the manifold areas of skin appearing there. Burnt with red, strongly for the cheeks, colored red around the edges of the lips. A lock of hair springs out, holds firm, gleaming somewhat black for the eyebrows. With beautifully adorned areas of skin, at the same time the eyes in their entirety. As it is built up, the nose takes shape likewise through the mixture of the elements. The curvature of the character gives shade below to the cheek near the chin, and the locks of hair strung together are laid around it."

It was bewildering. Did these statements correspond, even in the vaguest way, to the image we had been looking at in Genoa? Or to the Turin Shroud, when the almost unanimous opinion among scholars was that in 944 this very Shroud had been brought from Edessa to Constantinople? What I did understand was above all the description of a face with the open eyes. "Everyone is able to see for himself that the face of our Redeemer has been imprinted on the cloth by a miracle." The rest of the body remained vague and approximate. More concrete were the statements from a few pages of another text, from the nineteenth century, that Matthias Henrich had added after that from the tenth century—a text with the long title, "The Poor Life and Bitter Sufferings of Our Lord Jesus Christ and His Most Holy Mother Mary, together with the Mysteries of the Old Testament, according to the Visions of the Blessed Anna Katharina Emmerick", edited "from the diaries of Clemens Brentano". These were visions she had had in dreams, which the visionary from Dülmen in Westphalia had recounted to the poet-count Clemens von Brentano. This was most astonishing, yet I had long since ceased to be astonished by anything, not even by the varied and contradictory visions of the nun, who bore stigmata on her hands, feet, and heart.

On July 15, 1820, so Brentano wrote, she saw "Jude Thaddeus, a blood relative of our Savior, for I am able to make this out in my visions", as he "came to a king in Edessa. He had a written document in his hand, and as he came in I saw a manifestation appear beside him. It was the radiant form of Jesus, as he had walked on earth, only smaller. The king was looking neither at the Apostle nor at the letter, but was bowing deeply to the manifestation." After that, Thaddeus laid hands upon him and healed him from a serious illness.

In May 1822, Katharina "saw" the king again, "in the distance. A king in a city not far from Damascus. He was ill. He had a rash, but not yet quite externally. It had got into his feet, and he was limping." The sick king had a great love for Jesus, about whom he had heard a great deal, and not least about his power to heal sick people and to raise the dead.

A little later she "saw" the king sending a "young man who could paint" to Jerusalem with gifts; and how this young emissary then set out "on a camel, with six companions on mules, for Judaea", with "materials and fine sheets of gold wrapped around each other and several pairs of very fine wool-bearing lambs, which they were leading by ropes". At the Jordan, the emissary watched Jesus "with great amazement, observing him carefully", and then started to draw "on a little white board of something like boxwood. Then first he sketched with something like a pencil the outline of Jesus' head and beard, without his neck. He worked on this for a long time and could never get it quite right; and whenever he looked at Jesus, it was as if he were surprised by his face and would have to start work over again." The emissary found that nothing was any use; he simply made no progress with the picture until finally Jesus took pity on him, called him to come to him through the crowd, accepted the gifts, and straightaway had them distributed. He also received the letter from King Abgar, read it, and then wrote on the back of the letter "with a strong pencil that he took out of the bosom of his tunic, pushing something out of it, the way farmers push rotten wood out of a tinderbox, several words in fairly large lettering." He then folded the letter, had water brought to him, washed his face, and pressed the soft covering of the letter against his face, then gave it back to the emissary. "Now the picture was quite different and very like him", and the painter was delighted. Katharina Emmerick "saw" how he at once departed, how his servants stayed with Jesus at the Jordan and had themselves baptized, and "I also saw that the emissary arrived back in Edessa, and the king went out some way through the gardens to meet him and was indescribably moved by the letter and the image." The image of Jesus' face gave her the impression of being "like a parchment stitched onto a colored silken cloth", the curious "folds" of which interested her so much that she had six drawings of it made for Clemens von Brentano, which he specifically included in his text.

The story was becoming ever more obscure. All that seemed certain was that one or several mysterious images may have existed and that the image from Genoa could have nothing to do with these texts. It was quite obvious that no one single object that I had ever heard about or ever seen could correspond to all these texts that stood in contradiction to each other. Yet in the great iconoclast controversy, in which above all Emperor Leo III the Isaurian, in the year 730, wanted to destroy all icons so as to "purify" the Christian religious practice, the people who defended images repeatedly advanced as their main argument against all the opponents of images the existence of the Holy Face of Edessa, which was said to have originated from Jesus himself. "The Holy Face" was referred to in 787 at the Second Council of Nicaea for the same reason. For this item, they said, had become evidence for the Incarnation of Christ as no other object had. This "image" showed, they said, that the invisible God had truly become "visible" in Jesus. It was thanks to this image, then, that for the Church God was not only there in his word, but could also be "seen".

At this point in my search, I simply felt tired. I also felt I had become ill, like "King Abgarus, limping with something in his foot", and would have liked to be healed by a little miracle and be healthy again, free of any thought for my aching joints. But my right knee was hurting like anything, so I could hardly turn over in bed; each time I did, it hurt. Then Sister Blandina called me up again and said that I absolutely must read the closing report of the International Scientific Symposium on the Turin Shroud, from March 2000, and in it, in particular, the "Hypotheses as to the Early History of the Turin Shroud", by Karlheinz Dietz, from Würzburg. "I know that well", I said, in torment. "Nevertheless," she said, I ought to read that text over again, since in the meantime I had seen more; her friend Dorothea in Germany had brought it to her attention. It was, she said, most important. I hobbled from the bed to the medicine cabinet, swallowed two tablets with a glass of water, and then hobbled to my little library, where I soon found that volume of articles; it was among the few that had survived the recent relocations. For as long as the pains continued, I might as well read something, even if I could not sleep. That essay ran to forty pages and was furnished with 154 footnotes and a bibliography of 182 items. That was how scholarship was supposed to look. One could hardly make a more thorough approach to a subject. This was another academic pièce de résistance by Professor Dietz, whose education and precise analyses I had come to admire since first I knew him.

It was from him I had learned that in the East, icons are not "painted". They are "written", so they say in the world of Orthodoxy. So that there, icons have always been understood as *texts*. I have never been able to forget how six years earlier, in farewell to Ellen and me, he had unrolled before us in the large vestibule of his house in Würzburg a one-to-one copy, about 4.5 yards long, of the Turin Shroud, and expounded it—like a scribe reading a scroll of Scripture—as the greatest icon in the world. In the essay now in my hand, he had attempted to reconstruct the earliest travels of this Shroud, in accordance with the results of the most recent research. I could now see how much I had forgotten since I first read it. It was, yet again, far more confusing than I had remembered it as being; since for Dietz, the Abgar image in Genoa, for instance, was not identical with the often-mentioned Edessa image or any other well-known portrait of Christ. For him, the only image that could possibly be in question as the "'image of Christ not made by human hand', the so-called *acheiropoietos* of Edessa", was the Turin Shroud. For "many, though not all, of the characteristics of the Edessa image are substantially in agreement with those of the Shroud". The mainstream of the legend of the Abgar image did indeed reduce "the impression to Jesus' face", yet nonetheless, if one stood back objectively the most convincing hypothesis would have to be seen as "the identity, as Ian Wilson has suggested, of the Turin Shroud and the Edessa image".

In this connection, the mysterious Greek designation of the Edessa image as *tetrádiplon* would have to be seen as quite particularly significant. This expression meant that the image had been "folded four times". That was why, along with Ian Wilson, he was of the opinion that it must be a question of "a considerably bigger cloth", which would have had to be folded four times. The most important sources for this assumption, he said, were two manuscripts of the so-called ancient Acts of Thaddeus, which were preserved in Paris and Vienna. It was recounted there that Jesus, once when he had washed his face, was handed a cloth "folded four times" in that way to use as a towel into which he pressed his face. The longer version of the Acts of Thaddeus in Vienna, he said, also emphasized that Ananias, Abgar's messenger, was unable to set down an image of Christ because the latter "again and again changed in appearance and was manifested in a completely different, supernatural semblance".

After thorough analysis, the rare term *tetrádiplon* seemed best translated, he said, as a cloth "folded together four times", or "four times overlaid"; but probably best as a cloth "folded into four layers", or "having four folds in it". "However one twists and turns it, *tetrádiplon* does not simply mean a hand towel or a piece of material the size and shape of a handkerchief, but a large cloth with four folds or perhaps in four layers hung together." Hence, he said, this *tetrádiplon* of the Acts of Thaddeus could have nothing "in common with the small pieces of material of the copies of the Abgar image preserved in Genoa and Rome". By using his philological virtuosity, Dietz explained ("taking the context as a basis") that the texts "do not permit" us to reduce our understanding of their object simply "to the face".

I felt dizzy—perhaps this was also on account of the pain in my knee. The dizziness was not decreased by recalling what scholarly knowledge I myself had earlier written down and circulated: that the Turin Shroud must have been folded in a very complicated way in order to hide it in a special casket in such a way that the face alone looked out through a window. I could have made a drawing in my sleep of the exact system of folds by which that great cloth could easily fit into that mysterious concept. At any rate the Shroud alone, and nothing else, could be understood as being a *tetrádiplon*, wrote

Dietz. That was also why it was understandable that when speaking of the Shroud, many old sources talked only about a face, he said, without mentioning a body. Recent investigations into the "fold creases" in the cloth, he added, had provided only further support to this theory.

It was a complex and complicated essay. As in the Acts of Thaddeus themselves, "here everything flowed together", even sources of varying origin and reliability. What I understood, in the meantime, was merely that around this "Mandylion"—whatever it might be—there were buzzing and fluttering, like bees, wasps, and butterflies around a meadow in springtime, names and concepts like "Thaddeus", "Abgar", Edessa", "towel", "sudarium", "four folds", and an "aqueous print". It had been rediscovered in a niche in the city wall of Edessa in the sixth century; that much seemed clear. Not much else was.

When I woke up, some hours later, my knee was no longer hurting. It was as if it had never hurt me—whether on account of the strong Voltar tablets or what I had read, which was a bit too much, I have no idea: the pain was gone. A week later we met Blandina again in Manoppello, but on the steps outside the sanctuary we first of all had another talk with Father Germano di Pietro, the former Father Guardian of the friary, who had long regarded our visits here with a skeptical eye. "Now, listen, Father Germano," I asked him this time, as soon as I greeted him, "why isn't every thread of the image finally being scientifically investigated?" He laughed. "Why should it be? Why should it be picked to pieces and tormented and taken out of its lovely old case? It has no need to be taken to scientists. Science is coming closer to the Holy Face, day by day. Just you wait. The scientific disciplines are coming toward the cloth at top speed, not the other way round." He laughed again, before seating himself in his car. He had spent many years of his life here before handing over the leadership of the friary, and thus the office of Guardian of the Holy Face, to the gentle Father Carmine Cucinelli in 2004.

Shortly afterward we saw Sister Blandina again, on her knees, up behind the altar, in front of the image, saying her Rosary. "One can see him most clearly while praying", she said, and smiled. I fetched two chairs from the body of the church and sat down next to her with Ellen. "Why ought I to read Dietz's hypotheses about the early history of the Shroud, then?" I asked quietly. "Look at the image", she replied, and lifted up her Rosary again. Light from the late afternoon sun was flooding softly into the church. Blandina had switched off the lights in front of the veil and behind it. Nobody disturbed her at her prayers, and no one disturbed us in our gazing. The light from two windows at the bottom of the nave was shining gently through the face. I pulled my chair somewhat closer to the glass. Sister Blandina was praying in Italian, "*Ave Maria, piena di grazia, il Signore é con te*"—"Hail Mary, full of grace, the Lord is with thee...." The image before my eyes was changing: it shone out, it faded again— every time I moved my head, it changed, again and again, and I was continually moving my head: from left to right, right to left, moving it up, and then back down. "*Tu sei la benedetta fra le donne e benedetto il frutto del tuo seno Gesù*— blessed art thou among women, and blessed is the fruit of thy womb, Jesus." Now the image had taken on yet another appearance. "*Santa Maria, Madre di Dio, prega per noi peccatori*—Holy Mary, Mother of God, pray for us sinners...." Now it was looking supernatural, yet real. I closed my left eye and scanned down the image with my other eye, like an electronic scanner, by the light of a neon tube on one of the pillars at the back. In the radiant illumination of the distant lighting, there was absolutely nothing to be seen on the woven cloth, it was simply white. "... *adesso e nell' ora della nostra morte.*—now and at the hour of our death. Amen."

I kept on gazing. "Just a moment", I said then, and stood up. "Could you please switch all the lights on for a little while?" Blandina turned the switch. "But there is a fold—no, four folds—in the cloth!" I said, and went right up close to the glass. The weave was seamless, yet it was marked by one fold the whole length of it, and three across, like ladders in a stocking, as clear as the lines on your hand. They were so clear and strongly marked that on the forehead they had even occasioned slight damage to the weave, where the horizontal fold crossed the vertical one. There was a fold the length of the cloth, running from top to bottom, over three folds across it from left to right. I took my glasses off, rubbed my eyes, and looked again. I was not imagining it; Ellen could see each detail exactly the same. I closed one eye again and ran my gaze down the woven cloth to admire the "essential feature of mysterious inaccessibility" in the changing light and the way this image indeed "changed in appearance again and again and was manifested in a completely different, supernatural semblance" and withdrew itself from one's understanding and one's ability to form a clear idea of it. Yes, it was changing before my eyes, with every movement of my head. It was an image of many images; no wonder no painter had ever been able to capture it. Yet the four folds were something else; they remained, clear and unambiguous.

The delicate cloth had probably been folded three times, perhaps crosswise the first time, folding the top to the bottom, then crosswise again, and then the left side over the right (or vice versa). All that was mysterious about it was how the folds got into the veil. Why had they remained, like the lines on someone's hand from which old women in the East like to try to read the future?

"Recently, I have often wondered", said Blandina, breaking in on my reflections, "whether it was not simply natural for this cloth to be handed over to Jude Thaddeus by the council of the apostles after Mary's death. Among the apostles, after all, he was the only one who belonged to Jesus' family!"

The "Armenian Gravestone from Edessa in Mesopotamia"
on the Sarcophagus of Saint Thomas the Apostle in the basilica
of Ortona, on the Adriatic coast of Italy

Doubting Thomas

S aint Thomas, when he doubted, was allowed to see and to touch the wounds of the Risen Lord", Blandina had written at the end of her slim volume in 1999. "May many scholars have a similar experience, through taking an intensive interest in the image on the Veil, and proclaim the praise of the Lord." A pious hope. Since then, Sister Blandina Paschalis Schlömer had sewn herself a new habit; now, she no longer wore the black and white of the Trappistines, but brown and white, with a sand-colored veil. Her Abbess does not wish this opinionated fellow sister to appear in public in connection with her activities as a regular Trappistine nun. On Saturday July 17, 2004, we drove out to her and "her" sanctuary again. I had taken two days off, over and above the weekend. Nothing better to do had occurred to us than to drive over again from Rome to Manoppello. "Father Germano was right," I recounted to Ellen on the way, "when he said that all the scientific disciplines are coming closer to the image on the Veil. Nobody ought to be in a hurry to let scientists get their hands on it. Look at my digital camera. Ten years ago, scarcely any professional could have taken my photos of the Holy Face. Or think of my PC, which I've had for no more than sixteen years, or the e-mails I have been sending off in split seconds for just six years now—with entire books as attachments, if necessary, or complete photo albums. And think of the great explosion of opportunities for research in recent years through the Internet. Yes, that is a real information explosion—and already, no one can imagine what the limits to this will be!"

Ellen did not let herself be disturbed by it all. "Where are we going to eat?" she asked. We had just left the long Cucullo Tunnel behind us and were driving down the bold looping curves of the highway, which was carried along the mountainside on giant stilts here in the 1960s. A daring masterpiece of road construction, in the middle of an old earthquake area, and yet marvelously beautiful. To the right, Sulmona appeared in front of us at the western foot of the Majella massif: Ovid's hometown. "Should we invite Blandina out to a little restaurant in Sulmona to celebrate the special day? We have always wanted to go there." We were soon agreed. Immediately, I started feeling hungry. A quick drive to Manoppello, collect Blandina, and back to Sulmona. We were already looking forward to it.

Sister Blandina thought differently. "No", she replied to the invitation, "we will go to Ortona; I have never been there, and I have always wanted to go." Where was that, then? "On the coast, less than forty miles from here." And why? "Because the Apostle Saint Thomas is buried there, and I have always wanted to visit his grave." "You're getting confused, dear Sister", I said. "Thomas is buried in India, after all. He was the only apostle to do missionary work there." No, she insisted on Ortona; and San Tomasso was buried there. "Why not?" said Ellen. "Fish tastes good, too." She was right, as I had to admit. Directly above Blandina's hermitage, the road led up into the mountains behind which the coastal plain opened out toward Ortona. It was marvelously beautiful, yet as so often, we were somewhat late starting off because Blandina had forgotten first one thing and then another, while I sat in front of the house with the engine running. It was already getting too late to reach Ortona before the time when churches usually closed.

There was indeed a Saint Thomas' church, a basilica, even, in the town; the latter had hitherto been unknown to me. There was not a soul in the square in front of the church. Probably all were having their midday meal by now and had occupied every place in all the restaurants. I was in such a hurry, from sheer hunger, that I rammed a dent into our rear bumper, parking the car. The main door of the basilica was still open. Blandina pushed the heavy door wide and disappeared into the darkness. We got out quickly to go reserve the last available places in a little fish restaurant with a view over the sea, which we had spotted through the car window. We need not have been in so much of a hurry; other than a family at the next table, we were the only customers in the old Palazzo Farnese. It smelled wonderful. The sea outside the window could not have been more blue. We studied the menu and ordered water and wine to start with. Two sons, the daughter, and the mother of the family at the next table were deep in a book over their pasta, and the father was reading the paper. Blandina did not come. "I'll go and fetch her", I said to Ellen, and put a piece of bread in my mouth.

The main door of the basilica was still unlocked. Normans had destroyed it in 1080, an inscription told me, and it had been rebuilt in 1127. It was dark inside the high building, and there was no one there. "Sister Blandina?" I called softly. No answer. "Blandina?!" Still no answer. In the apse, there was a stairway that led down to a crypt, where I finally found Blandina kneeling in front of an illuminated sarcophagus beneath the altar. It was of baroque gold work, with an inset medallion of the Apostle on the front of it. Behind it, a broken black stone slab was set into the floor, with a bust in bas-relief in the middle of it. A bearded man with austere, almost Chinese or Mongolian features looked up at me from the paving. To the right and left of his head, the Greek words "Hagios Thomas" were carved into the stone. With his eyes wide open, his right hand reaching reflectively up to his beard and chin, and in his left a staff topped with a small cross, he looked alien, as if he had come from far, far away. Yes, a tablet on the wall of the crypt told us, this was the grave of Saint Thomas. On September 6, 1258, "in the time of Manfred, Prince of Tarentum, a son of the Hohenstaufen Emperor Frederick II", three galleys from Ortona under the command of Captain Leone were said to have brought his bones to port here "in a sacred treasury". They were said to have returned from a military expedition in the Aegean, where they had helped to protect against the Genoese the Venetian monopoly of the trade routes to the Orient, which they dominated. With written authority to plunder all the Genoese islands, to that end, they had also captured Chios, where the natives had shown the Admiral a holy building in which the Apostle was buried, having been brought back there from India. "As was the custom in those days", Leone had the bones brought onto his galleys immediately, together with the "Armenian gravestone from Edessa in Mesopotamia, where the bones of the Apostle had lain up to the third century". Edessa? Edessa must once have been a real transfer and forwarding station for Europe and Asia. Ellen came to fetch us.

"What should I eat here, then?" asked Blandina, finally seated at the table; "I have never been in a fish restaurant before." In Trappist monasteries and convents the food is strictly vegetarian, except on solemn feast days, when there are fish or eggs to eat. "How about spaghetti alle cozze?" I suggested. "That is almost always good at the seaside." "What is that?" "Spaghetti with mussels." "But how do you eat them, then? I have never eaten anything like that." "I'll show you." We lifted our glasses to Saint Thomas and, then again, when the spaghetti came. "Oh, how lovely!" exclaimed Blandina, when she saw the plate in front of her. I took the first mussel out of its shell for her and turned to my own plate. But Blandina, most of all, was looking at the shells in delight, this time as an icon painter. "Do you think I could take them away with me? I would like to be able to mix colors in them!" "Of course." When the waiter was out of sight, Blandina quickly wrapped up her empty mussel shells in the *Saint Thomas Messenger*, the diocesan newspaper, which she had picked up at the entrance to the church. As we were going back to the car, I thought about my mother, who came back from her first airplane flight with a handbag full of shrink-wrapped Libby's' milk for the coffee and sugar packets, which she had gathered together in the plane.

Two days later I saw Blandina again, when we were just about to walk out to the car to drive back to Rome. She beamed at me through her spectacle lenses. "Something quite splendid has happened!" she said. "You do know that I have been wondering for a long time about what material the Holy Face is imprinted on. Together with my friend Dorothea, I have now found an entirely new set of clues to follow. I have written a report on it."

She gave me five sheets, printed out from her computer in a large typeface that imitated handwriting. I put these away; we said goodbye in friendly fashion, and I sat down in front of the steering wheel. My desk at home was full of work. Two days later, I came upon Blandina's sheets again as I was searching my inside pockets for some notes I had mislaid. I started to read, standing up; then I sat down. "July 20, 2004: event of today", she had headed her report. Word for word, it runs like this:

I was washing up. I was finally intending to clean the mussels, which after being rinsed had been soaking in the last of the dishwater since Sunday. Then the telephone went. Dorothea Link! She was reporting on her researches on the samples of silk I had sent some time ago, the finest silk organza. I had been able to see with my magnifying glass that the quality of the threads had a greater similarity to those woven in the Veil than other woven material available to us made of cotton or linen: the threads were smoother. Frau Link confirmed this observation. She was now convinced, she said, that in the weave of the Veil we were at any rate dealing with material similar to silk, and not with linen. I objected that the ancient Egyptian byssus-cloth had likewise been extremely fine and smooth and that there, however, it had always been a question of linen threads. "No", she said, "I found in the dictionary the information that for the ancient byssus-weaving, linen, silk, or mussel-anchor silk was used!" That was something new to me! The question of the weave of the Veil has already been concerning us for nearly three years now. The transparency of the threads and the extremely smooth surface have always inclined us to doubt the use of linen for weaving it. Silk, however, had been excluded as a possibility by several people investigating the Veil.

All that went back and forth between us. When Frau Link now referred to "mussel silk"—I was hearing the word for the first time in my life I said, "Oh, how interesting! I am just washing some mussels!" Yet where was the silk supposed to be? There is a little graft, by which the soft body of the mussel is connected to the silvery shell. But it seemed so small to me! "No," said Frau Link, "that's what it said: anchor-silk, a weave of anchor-silk!" For three years, she has been voicing her suspicion that the threads in the weave of the Veil do not have the structure of plant fibers but look more as if they had been blown out of a jet. That was the conclusion she drew from her observation of the woven material, enormously enlarged on a computer screen. "I'll call you again later!" I said, when I thought about the mussel silk, and rushed to my washed mussels to dry them. These magical beings were supposed to produce something like silk, then? But where? I dried each half carefully. For mixing colors, the shells had to be clean. Despite all my care in washing them, I could feel a good number of uneven bits on the backs of them. I started to rub them, to get rid of what I took to be the remains of food. They put up a tough resistance. And when I tried to use my fingers to help, I found in my hands the finest soft threads, which would not come away from the shells: "Anchor silk!" shot into my mind, "Mussel anchor-silk!" I noticed it was possible to stretch the threads. They seemed really strong, and apparently they would be found in great abundance on every mussel. They seemed to grow and form a tangled net. Under a magnifying glass, I saw that they were also gleaming and somewhat transparent, exactly like the threads in the microscopic pictures of the weave taken by Professor Fanti. I tested some with fire to see if they were animal fibers; they shriveled up into little bluish-black balls, as may be seen in the weave in the pupils of the eyes in the face on the Veil—similarly, in the pictures taken by Professor Fanti from Padua.

The threads seemed to be microscopically thin "mini-tubes" of some transparent material. The color of the threads I investigated today was between white and a pale ochre tone, sometimes going into yellowish. The mussels had already withstood cooking and, through my measures to cleanse them, an acid bath—it was no wonder they were no longer white. Yet in all their characteristics, even the color tones, they reminded me vividly of the material from which the Veil is made. Might one of the women who were present at the burial of our Lord—the most holy Virgin, or Mary Magdalen—have possessed a thin veil of that kind and have covered the face of the Lord with it, as a final tribute? I recently read, concerning Mary Magdalen, that at the first anointing of his feet she wore a veil, one that did in fact cover her hair, it said, "but basically concealed nothing", it was so thin. I looked at the mussels with their silken gleam and their most delicate lines, and the Veil appeared before me in its iridescent properties, its shading of colors comparable only to nature, the delicate threads and the knots in the weave, even the "burned" pupils—and it seemed to me as if we had come an enormous pace closer to the truth about the material. It only remains now to undertake precise investigations into mussel-silk threads and, possibly, a tiny test on one of the threads of the material in the Veil, for comparison. The Lord of creation knew quite well what kind of threads would be needed for a miraculous image like that represented by the Veil. And human love made it available to him! In any case, the Veil is not only clear evidence of the merciful divine-human love of our Redeemer; it is likewise a sign of a human love that was shown to him. Manoppello, July 20, 2004, Sister Blandina Paschalis Schlömer.

I scanned through the report rapidly again, stood up, and went out onto the balcony. "*Ho visto il Signore, Halleluja!*" the Gospel reading in Saint Anna church had said this morning: "I have seen the Lord." It was the twenty-second of July. The churches of Rome were celebrating the feast of Saint Mary Magdalen, the sinner whom Jesus had loved more than all others. The one who stood beside the Cross, when there was no Thomas or Peter there any longer. The one who was present at his burial, where likewise there is no mention of any apostle other than John, and, finally, the one who was first to see him alive again, having run to his tomb in the gray of morning so as to anoint him one last time as soon as day had dawned and to weep for him and once more cover him with kisses. "They have taken him away!" she had sobbed, when she gave the alarm to the apostles. I called Ellen to tell her about Blandina's news.

Mary Magdalen at the foot of the Cross: detail from the Isenheim
Altarpiece by Matthias Grünewald in Colmar, between
1510 and 1515

Mary Magdalen

I had not heretofore heard anything so conclusive concerning the material. Was that not—if it should prove correct—the key to so many questions?—a material woven in filaments of mother-of-pearl, or at least in some kind of mother-of-pearl substance? What could better explain the shimmering gleam of the Veil, explain its transparency or its holographic effect? I soon found out, from the Internet, that byssus was fire-resistant, like asbestos, and the word was derived from the Aramaic root "bus". It was referred to on the Rosetta Stone, with the help of which Jean-François Champollion was able to decipher Egyptian hieroglyphics. It had been found in the graves of pharaohs, and there was evidence concerning it in Syria, Canaan, Mesopotamia, Greece, and the very oldest treasury registers: a legendary, fantastic woven material, "spun gold". It said in one place that Jason's Golden Fleece was made of byssus. Elsewhere, you read that the curtain in the Jerusalem Temple was made of purple and byssus. In the Bible it was prescribed as being obligatory for the carpet in the holy of holies and for the "ephod", the priestly garment worn by the high priest. There was no more costly material in the ancient world. According to the Apocalypse, this was the material for the "garment of the bride of the Lamb", I was told by the theologian Klaus Berger from

Heidelberg: for the bridal dress of the Church. I had never known or heard anything of all this.

Poets and scholars had described the transparent golden sheen of byssus, "as fine as gossamer". Whenever young girls wove the strands into their hair, that hidden gleam must have made them irresistible for young men. Rostock University, on the Baltic, had set up a long article about it on the Internet—for indeed, byssus was harvested from the sea and from the anchor fibers of mussels. The threads came from the "secretion, containing stuff like the white of an egg, of the byssus-jet at the base of the creature, which on contact with the water stiffens to firm threads", I learned from a Frau Norma Schmitz. Today there were only a few pieces of this material preserved in museums, because manufacturing it was prohibitively expensive, she said.

The threads of one family of mussels found in the Mediterranean are particularly suitable because of their length for being worked into mussel silk. Examples from the 'fine anchor-mussel' (*Pinna nobilis*), the largest mussel in the Mediterranean, grow as much as a yard long. They hang upright with the tip of the thread in the sediment, at a depth of 2.5 to 5 fathoms, and anchor themselves on the sandy bottom with their byssus. The threads are very fine, tough, and resistant. Depending on the type of sediment and the age of the creatures, they may be anything from colorless to dark brown. Byssus is neither soluble nor flammable and is resistant to alcohol and ether, acid solutions and leaches. The mussels used to be harvested in calm, clear water, either by diving or from a boat, by using long metal spikes or special tongs. The amount gathered was very small: one creature produced only one or two grams. For a little over two pounds of raw byssus, up to a thousand mussels might be needed. Out of that, less than half or maybe nearly three quarters of a pound of mussel silk might be made. After harvesting, the threads were washed, dried, and combed several times; the more you combed them, the more brightly they gleamed. It was only through being soaked in lemon juice, however, that they acquired the typical golden-brown color that made mussel silk so famous. No further dyeing was needed—nor was it possible, since no dye would take on the threads.

In contrast to linen or silk, the threads of byssus were transparent in a uniquely iridescent fashion. This was one of the times when I started to smoke again. Had the Camuliana legend not already recounted that the image "not made by human hands" was supposedly recovered "out of the water"? The mussel was an old metaphor for Mary. Above the colonnades of Saint Peter's Square, all the saints stood in mussel shells, as I had noticed a number of times up there, when papal Masses were being transmitted to the press platform. What was holy—the pearl—came out of the mussel. Years ago, on the Mount of Olives at Jerusalem, a Franciscan had shown me a Byzantine mosaic from the third century that represented Christ, in the middle, as a pierced pearl.

"Thus you were decked with gold and silver; and your clothing was of byssus, fine linen, and embroidered cloth; you ate fine flour and honey and oil. You grew exceedingly beautiful and came to regal estate", was quoted from the Book of Ezekiel on the computer screen when I entered the combination "byssus magdalena" for a Google search. The article from which this came was a meditation by Emil Spath, in which he drew a comparison between the prophet's lamentation over "Jerusalem, the faithless spouse, who had committed adultery on every street corner", and a detail of the Isenheim altar at Colmar, in Alsace, showing Mary Magdalen at the foot of the Cross: only her, without the world-famous Crucified One who had turned blue, in front of whom she had sunk to her knees. In her, according to the author, the "faithless wife who became a whore" had once more become a bride. As portrayed by the master Matthias Grünewald, in Colmar, she had become a unique metaphor for "converted Israel". That was why the painter allowed us to recognize clearly, under—and not over!—the arms of her dress, the heavy gold bridal bangles, which God gave to Jerusalem at the very first. Mary Magdalen was in torment, half out of her mind, having wept till she could weep no more, her mouth twisted and half-open, her arms upstretched to the dead Christ, and her fingers knotted and clasped together in agony.—From her head, however, a transparent veil fell down over her forehead and her eyes, one that let every eyelash on her eyelids be seen, like the Veil above the altar at Manoppello.

"Who else", remarked Ellen, "would actually have left this Veil behind in Christ's tomb, if it does come from that tomb?" Yes: Who else, among those who were noted as having been present at the hasty burial of Jesus? It was recorded of Joseph of Arimathea that he asked Pilate for Jesus' body and bought a large piece of pure linen for the funeral. Would this costly piece of material not have been particularly mentioned there if it had been he who provided it? It would not have come from the Roman legionaries who organized the execution; they themselves had thrown dice for the victim's robe. And Mary? According to everything that has been handed down about her, I would see Jesus' Mother clothed rather in wool or linen, not so much in satin, silk, and jewelry. For Mary Magdalen, the case would have been different. In her former calling, in which an enticing beauty was part of the business, I could imagine her wardrobe, likewise, having been quite different. The ladies on the Elbestraße in Frankfurt hardly had to scrimp and save for their expensive fox furs. It must have been rather similar in the little port of Magdala on the Sea of Galilee. If it was a question of anyone among the women accompanying Jesus having a veil of byssus, then it would have been Mary of Magdala. Who would want to contradict Sister Blandina there? Who, other than that Mary would finally have given her beloved, in his tomb, her most expensive cloth as a farewell present—the veil of the Magdalen!

The subject would not leave me in peace. Mussel silk, I discovered, was in ancient times harvested and woven in two cities in particular: Alexandria, on the Egyptian coast, and Antioch, near that of Syria. Later, the harvesting of it also spread to other places on the Mediterranean, such as Taranto in southern Italy, which was at one time a great center of this craft. Since then, it had come to an end everywhere—except on Sant'Antioco, a small island southwest of Sardinia, where to this day mussel silk is extracted in small quantities; perhaps we may hear in the name of the island a last echo of the great ancient city of Antioch. This island, it said, was "the last thread in the cloth of the sea".

On July 26, I suggested to my editors in Berlin that I make a quick voyage of discovery to Sardinia in pursuit of the last threads of the Golden Fleece! But the idea fell into the summer slump. It was even possible to discover through Google that the very last byssus-weaver on earth was living on Sant'Antioco. That was why, it said, Signora Chiara Vigo had played the most prominent part at an big exhibition about the "golden threads from the bottom of the sea", early in 2004, at the Museum of Culture in Basel. "Everything dies twice: once in its own death, irreversible and concrete", said the motto of the exhibition, "but then later, through that other death in the consciousness of others." So far as it was at all possible, I would try with all my powers to postpone a while the second death of the culture of this fascinating and forgotten material. In the meantime, however, Sister Blandina was quicker than I was, yet again. "Gentile Signora Vigo", she started her letter to Sardinia on August 3, 2004. In the letter she gave an account of the "Holy Face" and of her latest discovery, enclosing relevant photos and asking Signora Vigo whether we might perhaps count on her advice as an expert. On the evening of August 6—the day when in Manoppello they always commemorated the Transfiguration of Christ on Mount Tabor, with drums and trumpets—she found a reply on her answering machine that all the evidence she had sent suggested that the Veil appeared indeed like byssus, although Signora Vigo naturally could not anticipate the results of an examination made in person. Blandina listened to this message again and again. It was not long before she had brought Signor de Luca, the Mayor of Manoppello, to invite Chiara Vigo to take a free flight to the mainland from Sardinia, at the expense of the community. She could stay in Suor Blandina's hermitage. Ellen and I had promised to bring her from the airport to the sanctuary.

September 1, 2004 was a crisp late-summer morning, with a cooling breeze from the nearby sea, when Ellen stopped the car in the prohibited area in front of terminal A of the Leonardo da Vinci airport at Fiumincino, where she was going to wait for me. The airport was still half-asleep. The display board in the terminal showed

7:35 as the Alitalia plane AZ 1570 from Cagliari touched down on the runway outside. At 7:24, in the far-off little town of Beslan, in northern Osseto, a group of armed terrorists with explosives fastened around them had stormed School no. 1, just after teachers, children, and parents had come crowding in for the first school day after the long vacation. The pictures that came flashing across our screens over the days that followed were horrifying. Over three hundred hostages murdered. For many reporters in the world, recording apocalyptic horrors had become their daily bread, especially these days. On that morning, however, I did not listen to the radio—nor did I switch it on later, on the freeway. Instead of that, the thought that went through my mind yet again in the arrival area was that reporters had it easy—as the constant lack of evidence faced by Professor Pfeiffer came into my head. And the anxiety, probably shared by all professors, that someone, sometime, would be able to show that they had made some little mistake—or a big one. Reporters never had to prove anything. On the contrary, they had their own sufferings and distortions, but they were not judges, advocates, or professors and teachers. If they dared to do so—if they were not trying to play at being professor, teacher, judge, or lawyer—then they could merely report and recount the things and events they had observed all day long, in darkness or light, from nearby or far off. The more voices telling it, the better. The more contradictory, the more vivid and truthful.

As Chiara Vigo walked through the barrier, I put straight back in my pocket the piece of paper on which I had written her name in large letters, with a felt-tip pen, to greet her. Her fingernails were like spindles. Pier Paolo

Pasolini could have given her a leading role in any of his films. "Among our people, byssus is a holy material", she said in the car, "and absolutely cannot be sold." What did that mean, "among our people"? Was the island not simply part of Sardinia? "Oh, no", she responded with a husky laugh. She came from the people of the *Maestri* and spoke Sardinian, Italian—and Aramaic. Right away, she broke into a song that the fishermen sang when they were returning to port. The population believed they were descended from Chaldaeans, Aramaeans, and Phoenicians, she said, and trace their descent back to Princess Berenice, the daughter of King Herod and beloved of Emperor Titus, who captured Jerusalem. "Berenice?" I was starting to ask, "Berenice?" when she suddenly held up to the morning light a little bundle of raw, unspun mussel silk, finer than angels' hair. The gold of the seas! In her hand, it shone bronze in the sunlight. Immediately, Ellen took a wrong turn, so that we found ourselves, unintentionally, not on the bypass, but in the midst of Rome's morning rush hour. She laughed still more hoarsely. She was in Rome again, she told us, for the first time in thirty years. That time, she had been trying to escape from Sant'Antioco and from her handicraft. There she had been, sitting in a bus, looking forlornly at the thousands of foreign houses in the great city, when a gypsy woman sat down opposite her, looked at her, and immediately started talking to her. What was she doing here? What was she running away from? She should go back again straightaway, back home, where she had come from, where she would become world famous before she was fifty. When would she be fifty, then, I asked impolitely. Next year, on February 1, 2005. Simply hearing her laugh was a pleasure. Similarly, it was a pleasure merely to look at the little bunch of byssus in her hand, in the morning light. And it was just the same with her stories; they gushed out as if from a spring. Every year, in May, she dove for the golden threads two-and-a-half fathoms down to the seabed, by the light of the full moon, so that after harvesting them, she could comb them and spin them and weave them into tiny precious articles. We went flying along the freeway to Manoppello. The mayor was waiting for us in the town hall; that very day, he had received the solemn attestation from President Ciampi that old Manoppello had been elevated to the status of a city.

Sister Blandina was waiting for us on the Tarigni Hill, in front of the church. As we came down the central aisle, leaving behind the cheap fake organ at the back of the church, in the direct light the window cross behind it showed through the milky rectangle of the *Volto Santo* above the tabernacle. Chiara Vigo genuflected in front of the altar, then gazed up and was silent. She genuflected again after we had mounted the steps behind the altar and were standing in front of the image. She had never ever seen a veil so finely woven as this, she said. "He has the eyes of a lamb", she said at first, yet, "and of a lion", and crossed herself. "*O Dio!* He is the Lord of Heaven and earth." Then, "That is byssus", she said, once, twice, and a third time; then she was silent and gazed and was still silent and gazed for longer. "That is byssus." It can in fact be dyed, but only with natural purple, she had told us earlier in the car, and she was the only person who still knew how to do it and thus produce various shades of red or green. "But byssus cannot be painted on. That is impossible. Nor is it possible to weave it as finely as this. All the rest is possible."

Chiara Vigo stayed five days. She was truly the only surviving weaver of byssus in the whole world. Yet how did she arrive at the definite conclusion, without any chemical tests, that the woven material of the *Volto Santo* consisted of byssus? I wanted to know. "Because as far as I am concerned it has the essential characteristics of that material, which are not to be found in any other material in the world", she replied with her marine laugh. "I have known it since my childhood: this is the only woven material that lets bright light pass straight through it, that turns to shades of bronze in shadow and coppery-gold when it is lit. Those are the typical peculiarities of byssus. They are the same peculiarities as this *Volto Santo* possesses. I get cold shivers down my back when I see it. Of course, it will have to be investigated properly, but that is what I can say about it."

In Blandina's house she had seen right away, in the microscopic enlargements, a silvery glitter that showed typical salt deposits; and she had by now spent hours in front of the image on the Veil. She knew that these salt deposits would prevent the material from being painted. Why? "Simply try to paint on mother-of-pearl—and then you won't ask again. It is just not possible." She passed hours in front of the Veil. The rest of the time in Manoppello, she sat with Blandina and combed her raw byssus, over and over again, and put it to soak in various things. In a bath of lemon juice, she had told us earlier, it became golden; in a bath of cows' urine, it turned rather paler, more white. She had never yet sold one single piece of it, she said; it simply cannot be sold, whatever the offer. She makes a gift of it, she said, according to her own free decision: "Byssus is a holy material", she said; "it belongs to God alone." "That's similar to how it is with icons", said Blandina, next to the hearth. "Strictly speaking, icons are not things that can be bought and sold. The person who receives one makes a donation, according to his means. That is how it should be, anyway."

When she had finished combing out the bronze byssus, after their meal, Chiara Vigo stretched it out with one hand and, with age-old movements, twisted some ten or twenty of these angel hairs into a thread with the spindle she had brought with her; then she first made a gift to our daughter Christina, winding some round her wrist. Soon she stretched fifteen warp threads lengthwise on a little weaving frame she had also brought. She intended using a little hand shuttle to manufacture a small piece of material for comparison. Yet she knew for sure, she said, that she had never seen such fine threads or such delicate weaving. She would never be able to achieve that, "nor will anybody else". During the breaks, she sat on the veranda like the principal of a flamenco troupe in her sleeveless patterned dress and shared her cigarettes with me—or sang us once more the song the fishermen of Sant'Antioco sang when putting out to sea in the gray of morning.

During the night, before I came to fetch her for the journey home, she had tied and knotted a Rosary of byssus for me so that I could pray more easily and better. "With this, your report about this discovery will become a song. Think simply that you must dive into crystal-clear water to get it and bring it up from deep down below."

How far back did it go in her family, this craft of which she was now the sole inheritor, I wanted to know, I told her on the freeway, shortly before we reached the airport. "*O Dio!*" she laughed yet again. "Unimaginably far back—and the line always ran through the mothers. I learned it from my grandmother, and she had it in turn from her grandmother." She knew of ten generations before herself, together with all the circumstances of their lives. "Eight women, among my mothers and grandmothers, were called Maddalena. A neighboring island, where there was once a center of byssus harvesting, is called Santa Maddalena."

A Chamberlain from Ethiopia and the Cabbalist from the Sea of Galilee

Back at my desk again, the first thing I did was to transfer the new photos onto my computer. I looked again at Chiara's Greco-Canaanite features, the aura of her skeptical eyes, her archaic gestures, her fingernails, the music in the way she expressed herself, and her mimicry. I looked at her again weaving, saw the little bunch of combed-out byssus in the wooden box on the wall in front of Blandina's little house, and enlarged the bronze gleam of them in the sunshine on the computer. Then I ran before me in a series the seven photos I had taken as Chiara held her sample of weaving in front of the Holy Face in the sanctuary. In comparison with the threads of the Veil, her threads, which I had watched her spinning, were as thick as strands of wool, and the structure of the weave as coarse as a fishing net. Chiara Vigo knew that. "I shall bring an entire congress of weavers here from Turin", she had sworn in front of the *Volto Santo*. "No one has seen such a fabric, and no one can imitate it."

On one plane or another, the photos were indistinct, and it had been difficult to bring the depth of focus into line with the distance between her sample and the cloth itself. Yet here on the screen, they all showed something I had hardly noticed back in Manoppello. The color tone of the sample on all the photos, whether they were distinct

The Bēta Giyorgis Church at Lalibela, Ethiopia

or blurred, exactly matched the color tone of the Holy Face, which was so difficult to describe. This color, impossible to catch precisely, which was constantly disappearing before one's gaze—bronze, gold, transparent, gray, chestnut, umber, brown—here it seemed to be always exactly the same in both pieces of material. On the Veil, however, this color-tone of the mussel silk was not to be found everywhere, but only in the very darkest patches: in the hair, the eyes, and the open mouth.

This dark tone must have been the original color of the cloth, if it was mussel silk, and not the pale tone.

This was not white linen.

A new mystery. It occupied me for weeks. If the Veil should really be made of byssus—which this very color yet again made most likely—then how could the pale areas of the Face ever have been painted on it? And what did we mean by "painted"? That, too, was in fact impossible with byssus. Yet was not this new mystery even greater? How can a pale image be put onto a dark material? That question took us straight to the heart of the persistent rejection of the image by many clever men and women, who had hitherto proudly and steadfastly refused even to look at the Veil. For their main objection was always simple and convincing: all that was painted. Anyone who said that it was impossible to paint on this material must simply be cranks, they said—and that several notorious cranks had already collected around the image. Every photo, they said, actually showed the fine brushstrokes. For that reason alone, it was hardly worth even taking a close look at it (and close up, everyone would in any case necessarily see that without exception, the "brushstrokes" disappeared in direct light). It was too fine, they said, not to have been painted. The eyes, the eyelashes (only visible in enlargement), the tear ducts, the hairs of the beard, the teeth(!)—all of these were quite simply too delicately drawn—and, in addition, were artfully left unfinished!—not to betray the hand of an artist, in fact a master, who was extremely well informed about the iconography of the ancient world, especially in comparison with earlier pictures and icons; this object could not possibly, therefore, be an original model but was at most a copy of other copies of some unknown original—or, indeed, of the original on the Turin Shroud.

If, however, in the first place there were no traces of pigment visible, even under a microscope; and secondly, it was absolutely impossible to paint on mussel silk; and then, thirdly and lastly, it was obvious even to any layman that it was impossible to put a pale picture onto a dark, gossamer-fine woven material—then only one answer was possible, as it became clear to me one evening. If the color was not painted, not put onto the material, then—in the very opposite way—it must have been taken away.

Then the dark must not have been put onto the pale, but the pale had been taken away from the dark. At that thought, I was reminded of a place where I had never yet been and that I had nonetheless been wanting to visit for many years of my life, after having read a first article about it, as a youth, in a yellowing copy of a Swiss cultural journal. Later, as a reporter for the old color supplement of the *Frankfurter Allgemeiner Zeitung*, I had really intended to go there, but it never came about. There was only a book of photographs that I had bought in preparation for the journey and that I still took with me each time we moved. This book told about a legendary place in the Ethiopian highlands, where the ancient

Christian culture went back to Philip the Deacon and a chamberlain of Queen Kandake, whom Philip had baptized between Jerusalem and Gaza, a few months, or a few years, after the Resurrection of Christ. In this culture, therefore, the emperors and kings counted themselves—until their reign died out a few decades ago—a part of the house of King David of Jerusalem. "Lion of Judah" was just one of their ancient titles. That is why, sometime in the Middle Ages, they wanted to build for themselves, in East Africa, a city of Jerusalem— that city which, as pious pilgrims to the Holy Land, they had always admired, with all its churches that they revered there and all those important sites and places where Jesus had walked in his lifetime. The location where they intended to build this second Jerusalem presented them at any rate with a critical problem. There in the highlands there was no stone for building this city, and certainly not the white stone of Jerusalem.

Then a unique idea occurred to the advisors and architects of the priests and kings. They had their workers excavate square or cruciform pits in the relatively soft tufa stone until these pits were deep enough for them to have, there before them at the bottom of those pits, great monolithic blocks of stone. And in those very blocks, which did not rise above the level of the plateau, they had their stonemasons chisel their way in and then carve out complete church interiors, with doors, windows, steps, altars, and artistic friezes—everything a church might need—and all cut out of a single block. They simply cut away and never added anything: not a single stone. This was the sculptor's principle: creating something new simply by taking away. It was the principle formulated by Michelangelo, when he set free the *Pietà* from the block of marble with his chisel. He simply took everything away that was covering the perfected sculpture—the Mother with her dead Son on her lap: the Son with centrally parted hair, slightly open mouth, his teeth visible, and a slight beard, as on the Veil at Manoppello. In Ethiopia, however, all the churches in the priestly city of Lalibela were created as sculptures in this very same way; through simply taking stone away, they became a cultural marvel of the whole world. Only now, now that I was old and in front of this image in the Italian Abruzzis, I no longer wanted to go there. For was this Face not the equal even of the marvels of the priestly city of Lalibela? And did not the white and pale parts, here too, have to be where something had been taken away from the golden brown of the mussel silk? Did the Face not have to have been bleached away out of the original color tone?

Over two thousand miles away from Lalibela, high above the northern shore of the Sea of Galilee, lay another ancient town, which had a similar story to tell. Safed was one of the very few places that, after the Jews had been scattered by the Romans, continued to have a Jewish community through the next two thousand years. Jesus himself must have had this place before his eyes as "a city on a hill". After the Jews had been expelled from Spain in 1492, however, Safed had truly become a new center of Jewish teaching. This was the era, in the sixteenth century, when a cabbalist by the name of Isaac Luria had some thoughts, up there, on the question of whether there could be any freedom at all for man if God was supposed to be omnipotent. Did his omnipotence not send all else to the wall, penning it in and removing its freedom? Were we not, then, merely helpless grains of dust—lacking any freedom whatever, alongside this omnipotent God? Time and again, considering this question, Isaac Luria would have turned his gaze out of his study to sweep over the silver lake, shimmering down below in the distance. And some time or other, as he gazed down there, this answer came back to him about God's being and the way he acted: God's act of creation was only to be understood as an act of extreme restraint—it was not possible in any other way. In creating the world, God restricted himself and withdrew—in order to offer his creatures room in which to live and air to breathe. In order to grant the world, and the people in it, space to have their own existence, their own freedom of choice, through his self-restraint.

God thought differently from the way we do. "My thoughts are not your thoughts", he had his prophet say, thousands of years ago. The cabbalist from Safed called this principle of God's self-curtailment "Zim-Zum" in Hebrew. In the last century, the philosopher Hans Jonas, from Mönchengladbach, took this little discovery made by Isaac Luria, from the Sea of Galilee, and during his exile in America developed it further into his new and complex philosophy of responsibility. Could not this idea be of help once more in our new century, too, in explaining the origins of this unique image of Christ in Manoppello? Explaining that it, too—from a technical point of view—was like visible evidence of God's self-restraint? As if God intended to leave behind on this Veil a clear document, like a fingerprint, of his creative power; and one that points toward how he created? That he created by giving us space and room to breathe; by restraining himself. God did not bring pressure to bear or leave an obvious impression. He created something new, in the way that Jesus breathed on the apostles when, after his Resurrection, when the doors were all barred, he suddenly stood among them again—among Peter, Philip, John, James, and Jude Thaddeus; and later, also, stood in front of Thomas.

"Are you finally going to put that light out?" said Ellen, in bed. It was by now very late.

Padre Pio and Padre Domenico

The little Albanian's accordion, which normally in summer just would not stop whimpering away down in the street, had long ago fallen silent. The first of the autumn storms was sweeping through the streets of Rome. I turned over in bed. Time had speeded up, like the wind that was chasing past the shaking window. Life was making ever more enormous leaps forward. It was only that spring that I had "discovered" the Veronica. Yet it was on a journey to Padre Pio's grave in March, as part of my work, that I had seen the image properly for the first time, in company with Sister Blandina, whom I now felt as if I had known for a long time. On the journey to the resting place of Italy's greatest saint of the twentieth century, I had come to know the Holy Face and a talkative Trappistine nun. And now Padre Pio himself seemed to be taking a hand in the story—that mysterious man whose effect on people was woven into countless conversations and memories in the south of Italy.

For it was not to be merely one week before the editors in Berlin printed my report on the sensational discovery of the mussel silk by Chiara Vigo; I thought that report was the revelation of my life and that it enhanced the reputation of my newspaper. A second week dragged by, as if the discovery had never been made; as if I had never written my report about it. Every day, I looked for

Padre Pio: a photo of a photo from around 1960
in San Giovanni Rotondo

indications of how suitable today would be for publishing it—every day, in vain. Day by day, the editorial conference saw as more important: the preview of a new film about Hitler; an official journey by the German minister of the interior; fashion week in New York; some school pupils meeting the members of the German Philharmonic; a football scandal in Naples; a sex scandal in Hong Kong, and so on. Each day, a different sensation pushed my report—on the Face of God!—out of the paper's features page.

By the third week, I was becoming resigned. "The era for reports like this is past", I told Ellen. In Germany, at least, the age of Christianity, in which reports about the origins of our culture could still arouse interest, seemed to be past. Or, I had been somehow unable to explain it properly to my colleagues. Yes, I was getting old. Soon, younger Italian colleagues were sure to get wind of the story and shout it from the rooftops in their own fashion. I had been flogging myself to pieces for nothing and had spent many nights rummaging around in books without result. It was time for other adventures.

Thus by Thursday, September 23, 2004, I was no longer expecting anything at all, when in the morning, at the newsstand beside the colonnades, I took a *Welt* from the newspaper rack to leaf through it and see what was supposed to be the great news for that day. Germany's "Eastern Development Program" was making progress, I learned on the front page, with six photos of the federal reconstruction minister in Berlin. Yet then—on page ten—in a close-up that took almost half a page, "the True Face of Jesus" from Manoppello in the Abruzzis was looking at me: a photo I had taken on my last birthday, with a report occupying an entire page, as well-placed in the newspaper as it possibly could be. The sun was shining brightly; doves were fluttering on high above the newsstand. The head of department, Wolfgang Büscher, had come back from his holidays to editorial headquarters especially to make my report ready for printing. That was the last piece of work we did together before he left the paper and the company for a new period of traveling through the world and then joined another paper, as I later found out.

Beside the *Welt* in the newspaper rack, however, a large portrait of the Capuchin Padre Pio was gazing at me from the front page of the *Osservatore Romano*, looking as if he were winking at me. Today was the anniversary of his death; since his canonization in 2002, the Roman Church celebrates the feast day of this mystical Father on September 23. "The *Volto Santo* in Manoppello is certainly the greatest miracle we have", he had once confided to one of his fellow brothers in 1963. He said that, never having either seen the image himself nor visited it—at least, not in the same way as ordinary mortals. That, too, was something I found out about only later.

Now, however, my Italian colleagues were receiving the news about the *Volto Santo* with appropriate patriotism. No one could say that the cloth had previously been unknown. Time and again, it had been in the headlines— and then time and again forgotten again, at least in the rest of Italy, beyond the Adriatic. For centuries, it had been celebrated in many poems and songs. The Church had never denied that this image was a valuable relic. In 1718, Pope Clement XI accorded a "plenary absolution" from all temporal punishment for sins to everyone who made the pilgrimage to this sanctuary. Time and again, bishops had stood reverently before it, and cardinals had made private pilgrimages to it, as in recent years did Cardinal Sodano, the Cardinal Secretary of State, Cardinal Tettamanzi, Cardinal Martini, and Cardinal Laghi, to name just those four—all of whom had been here before my journey with Cardinal Meisner. "*Ho visto Gesù!*" the shaken former prime minister Giulio Andreotti wrote in the guestbook, "I have seen Jesus!" In the seventies of the last century, a certain Professor Bruno Sammaciccia had made passionate efforts to spread the fame of this unique relic in several publications. He was followed in the eighties by a Father Antonio Serramonesca, using a wealth of sources and after a great deal of preliminary work, which he had published in the sixties. In the nineties there were Father Pfeiffer and Professor Resch in Innsbruck, on behalf of Germany and Austria. Starting the next day, almost without exception, my colleagues in Italy were calling the *Volto Santo* almost a *Seconda Sindone*—a second Shroud. At once there were articles in all the larger newspapers in Italy, and many of the smaller ones, about the discovery of mussel silk. There followed more lavish reports in illustrated magazines, together with TV programs to which Chiara Vigo was invited from Sardinia, and Father Pfeiffer from Rome. Soon, my report was appearing in translation in two American magazines. On January 6, 2005, it appeared for the first time in Moscow and, shortly afterward, in French. On December 30, a large group of Greeks and Russians appeared in Manoppello, and a little later a family from Shanghai who spoke only Chinese and who genuflected before the image with shining eyes.

During my vacation, therefore, I retired to the Capuchin friary in Manoppello, as the guest of Father Carmine Cucinelli, the new Guardian, to research and prepare for this book. One Sunday the doorbell rang because a visitor wanted to speak to me. The stocky man with a short black beard and friendly eyes introduced himself as Antonio Bini; he had a degree in economics and came from neighboring Pescara, and he had been engaged in research on the Holy Face and promoting its fame for many years and had now heard and read about my article. As his real reference, however, he pulled out of his briefcase his baptism certificate, which attested to his having been baptized on January 6, 1953, on the feast of the Epiphany of Christ, in the parish of San Donato, in San Giovanni Rotondo (in the province of Foggia) by a certain "Revd. Fr. Pio di Pietralcina, Capuchin". Saint Padre Pio himself had baptized him.

Nonetheless, a pile of books he had brought for me, together with a whole series of reports, told a quite different story; not only about the legendary Padre Pio, but also about a little brother whom Pio had had here in Manoppello—a certain *Padre Domenico da Cese del Volto Santo*. He was a great barrel of a man well over six feet tall, with a long beard and sky-blue eyes that swept as high as heaven, who also had to be seen as an important advocate of veneration of the Holy Face in the last century—long before Sister Blandina had even heard of it for the first time. "Why have you come all this way to me?" Padre Pio had once said to one woman who revered him and had come on pilgrimage from the Abruzzis to see him in the Gargano mountains. "After all, you do have Padre Domenico."—Domenico's grave in his birthplace of Cese, near Avezzano in a valley high up in the Abruzzis, was also a place of pilgrimage, like that of Padre Pio, as Antonio Bini informed me, before looking up for me a particular page in a book, on which this Padre

Domenico, on Sunday, September 22, 1968, "came into the church from the friary at about six in the morning to unlock the main door; and on his way back, found Padre Pio on his knees in the front row of the choir stalls, down below the *Volto Santo*, with his head propped on his hands".

The legendary saint had at that time long been famous throughout Italy for his capacity for "bilocation"—that is to say, for the firmly attested presence of his person in two quite different places. Both of them, Pio and Domenico, were likewise famous for their stigmata, the marks of the wounds of Christ, which they bore in their hands, their feet, and their chest. "I no longer have confidence in myself. Pray for me", replied the friar, on that September morning thirty-six years before, when Domenico spoke to him and asked what he was doing there. "And I'll see you in paradise!" "Praise be to Jesus Christ", responded Domenico, dumbfounded. About twenty hours later, Pio died some 125 miles away in his cell, which he had not left for a long time.

"It was like in ancient Rome," said Antonio Bini with a shy smile, "before the theft of the relic. Pio had come to visit the relic one more time before he died, just as the poet Petrarch tells us in one of his sonnets about an old man who set out on one last pilgrimage to the Veil of Veronica in Saint Peter's, because—so we are told—'the longing commanded him to contemplate here the portrait of him whom he hoped soon to see in heaven'.—Padre Pio, in his last night on earth, had become like this pilgrim. This was also his last miraculous bilocation before he died: to visit this image of Christ—even though he himself had personally had so many visions of Christ."

Father Domenico himself, on the other hand, did not die until September 17, 1978, in hardly less remarkable circumstances. A so-called *bambino*, a "cinquecento", a Fiat 500—in short, what was at that time probably the smallest car in the world—had knocked this giant down in Turin and fatally injured him. He even consoled the young driver involved, who came several times to visit him in the hospital: "Do not let it make you unhappy. I am old, and it makes no difference if I die. But you are young. Live in the fear of God, then, and prepare yourself well for your marriage!" The burden of a good reputation was the cross that many saints had to bear: so wrote the Bishop of Aquila shortly afterward in his obituary; and that was how it had been for Father Domenico. "He was extraordinarily zealous in promoting the cult of the Holy Face in the shrine at Manoppello. And at the end, it was this very reverence for the Face of the Lord which brought him to Turin, to visit the Holy Shroud—where Sister Death was then waiting for him and received him in her sudden embrace."

At that time, the friary at Manoppello had already been his new home for fourteen years. He had been born on March 27, 1905, as Emidio Petrarca, and he would have been a hundred years old exactly on Easter Day in 2005. Yet during his childhood, it looked almost as though he would never have a chance to be ten years old. In high-spirited fashion, like a little lad announcing that there would be no school tomorrow, he called out loud in his class on January 12, 1915, "There's going to be an earthquake tonight!" The next morning, at half-past seven exactly, the area round Avezzano suffered the worst earthquake in human memory, just as he was at Mass with his father. The church collapsed and buried them both under the rubble. An unknown man, his face streaked with blood, rescued first him and then his father from the debris. After that, Domenico did not see him again for many decades, until in October 1964, he went on a pilgrimage to Manoppello. "That's him!" cried Father Domenico, when he stood in front of the mussel-silk cloth and gazed for the first time with yearning at the Holy Face. "That's the man who had rescued me in 1915! That's his face!" Therefore, fifty years after being rescued, he had himself transferred to Manoppello by his superiors in the order, so as to spend the rest of his life simply serving the image of the man who rescued him, whose immaterial beauty he compared, when talking to pilgrims or in the friary, to the coloring and outlines of "butterfly wings", as friendly Father Lino, who had taken over Domenico's post after the latter's death, albeit without his belief in the authenticity of the *Volto Santo*, recalled at Manoppello. Not until years later was it discovered that in butterflies' wings we do in fact see color effects without any pigmentation—simply through the breaking down and overlapping of light waves, as in a rainbow.

"Domenico was not exempt from controversy", said Father Emilio, shortly after Dottore Bini's visit to me in the Capuchins' friary. "Among many of the brothers, he was even seen as a kind of wizard with sinister powers, on account of his remarkably successful healings. But ordinary people, from a long way around, revered him as a saint and sage and loved him." I was now sitting with Father Emilio, Father Carmine, and Father Lino in the choir stalls, early in the morning—sitting on Padre Pio's last seat—to add to the number of the three steadfast men in their morning office. Father Domenico must also have knelt here and sat here, and the dark brown of the seating does not look as if it had been replaced since then. Some months before, Father Pfeiffer from Rome had drawn my attention to an oil portrait of the colossal priest, which was gathering dust in the poignant museum over the sanctuary, in the midst of the haphazard collection of exhibits: a charismatic bear of a man, with sky-blue eyes, a long, snow-white beard over his brown habit, and pressing to his heart with the great paw of his right hand, as delicately as a love letter, a copy of the Holy Face. At that time, he must probably have looked a little like Father Emilio, next to me in the pew, who had spent decades of his life as a missionary with the highland Indians of Columbia and now bestowed passionate care on the friary's garden.

Apart from the light of two reading lamps behind us, it was still dark in the church; Father Carmine had unlocked the main door at six o'clock, just as Father Domenico had done on September 22, 1968. We were sitting here in time with the rhythm of the decades and the centuries, with the prayers of the millennia. "My soul thirsts for God, for the living God", it said today in the psalms, "When shall I come and behold the face of God?" Sitting down, I could recognize only the eyes of the *Volto Santo* over the top of the balustrade. Only when I stood up could I see the entire face up there, the face in whose gaze Padre Pio and Padre Domenico had already immersed themselves here, in the hope that in the next world this pair of eyes would sometime come to meet them in the face of the merciful Judge.

After the early office of Lauds, I stayed sitting in the choir stalls for a little, while Father Carmine and Father Emilio were in the sacristy preparing to celebrate Mass and vesting. Oswaldo, the bearded sacristan, had arrived, as one could hear by the squeaking of his trainers at every step. He was probably already lighting the candles on the altar, on the other side of the balustrade, beneath the *Volto Santo*. Neon lights flickered on. Was I dreaming? Was I awake? In the cold, I pulled my coat over my shoulders. "In a certain sense, Christianity has become the soul of the modern world", went through my head as the lamps were lit. Starting from Europe, this modern world had covered the whole world and illuminated it, for good and for evil. No television set was ever switched on or off in Peking without its having been planned and developed in Europe, after Christianity had burst asunder for the world of the West the circle of taboos that had held the ancient world in its clasp. Yet the soul of Europe, and of Christianity, was still the Church of the apostles. The essence and being of this Church was still to be found in the sacraments and the Gospels. In some sense, then, one might imagine the structure, the web of essential relations, of the modern globalized world as being like a Russian matryoshka-doll, in which there is always one more still farther in. That was going through my head, as if I were once again having to prepare a history lesson, as I had many years ago in Frankfurt-am-Main. At the point where we could go no farther in taking things apart in trying to understand this world, we came up against belief in the Resurrection of the Son of God who had been put to death, concerning which the Apostle Paul indeed had said that without this, our faith would be nothing but empty words.

If, however, we looked once more, closely and in detail, at the heart of the oldest and most important testimonies to this faith, then we encountered, right at their heart—after the discovery of the empty grave by Mary Magdalen—a simple text of just a few lines from the first century in which, in the account by John the

Evangelist, he talked especially about two men and two cloths. "The disciple whom Jesus loved", it said there, came to the tomb after running through the gray of morning, "and stooping to look in, he saw the linen cloths lying there, but he did not go in. Then Simon Peter came, following him, and went into the tomb; he saw the linen cloths lying, and the napkin, which had been on his head, not lying with the linen cloths but rolled up in a place by itself. Then the other disciple, who reached the tomb first, also went in, and he saw and believed." That was the heart of it.

The linen cloths John was talking about there were certainly nothing other—and that had long been something we might take as certain, considering all indications—than the Shroud of fine linen that was venerated in Turin as a relic of the Passion of Christ. The napkin that was talked about, however—there was never any doubt of this, either for Saint Padre Pio or for the Blessed Padre Domenico—could not have been anything but the piece of mussel silk up there in that frame. "That is the heart of the world", these two men must have thought.

Yet the gossamer weave of the cloth could not seriously have soaked up any more "sweat" or blood than a nylon stocking. A "sweat cloth" of Christ, literally so called—and neither of these men could have known anything of this—certainly more than three times as long as the *Volto Santo* of Manoppello, was known, however, and there were good witnesses to it, yet not in Italy, but in Oviedo in Asturias, the mountainous province in northern Spain. Many pilgrims still knew about it in the Middle Ages. In modern times, however, outside of Spain this relic had been almost entirely forgotten until just a few decades earlier.

Holy Blood

We noticed on our last investigative journey that in the autumn it got light much later in Oviedo than it did in Rome. At eight o'clock, it was still utterly dark. Rain had been soaking the green valleys all around the city. It had now stopped, but the red stone streets were still gleaming in the light of the streetlamps, as Ellen waited with me in the left-hand doorway of the San Salvador Cathedral, and I pulled my coat together. The former royal capital lay in a valley near the end of the pilgrim way of Saint James to Santiago; it was now blanketed in Celtic mist. We had driven along beside the sea for half a day to get here, with the steep, towering Picos de Europa on our left and in the corner of our eye on our right the spray from the Bay of Biscay. Only two weeks before, Ryanair had set up flights between Rome and Santander. It was enough, this time, to take one day's leave to be able to travel there and back over the weekend, to the place where I once had gone on my first journey abroad as a youngster—then, it had taken many weeks. This time, however, it was a journey back into the depths of history more than a journey abroad. For the fact that here in Oviedo, too, a *Sagrado Rostro*—in English, a "Holy Face"—or "Holy Sudarium" (*Santo Sudario*) was preserved, and had been since the eighth century, was known to everyone who had taken interest in the Turin Shroud in the last few years.

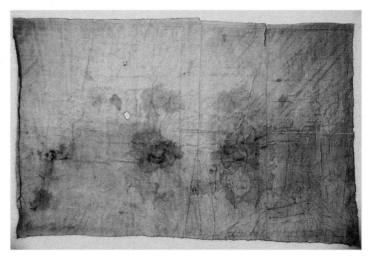

The sudarium of Oviedo from the cathedral of San Salvador in Asturias, Spain

The *Cámera Santa* was the oldest treasury in Spain. The cloth that was preserved here did not bear any image, however, but merely stains of blood and water. Furthermore, it had been well researched, and in recent decades there had also been intensive academic exchanges between the Spanish and researchers from Turin. A comparison of the results on each side had shown that the traces on the two cloths corresponded to each other in a striking fashion, not only with the same blood group, AB, from a dead man—although these were nonetheless quite different items. They were in some mysterious way compatible and complementary; that is to say, both had certain things in common to tell us concerning the death of a man cruelly crucified, and each of the two could tell us something more on its own account. That was why I had been wanting to come here for years. This time, I had to come.

For perhaps it was this way, I pondered: that there was indeed a kerchief with which a woman had wiped the blood off the face of the badly scourged man on his way to execution—even if the Gospels told us nothing about it—and that the collective memory had stored that away in one of its traditions. And then at some time or other, however, this authentic memory was transferred to the inexplicable "True Face", so as to be able to have, after all, something like a plausible explanation for its inexplicable origin. Did it perhaps in that way become the sixth station in the way of the Cross, which welded together two different cloths into one single event, in an allegorical amalgam?

Only one thing was now clear: the Veil of Manoppello could never have been a kerchief, used for mopping sweat. It was far too thin, too fine, for that. Neither blood nor sweat could ever have been mopped up or wiped away with it; and certainly, no woman would ever have tried to do so with this material. Was the cloth in Oviedo, then, in fact the thing to which the old Veil of Veronica owed its name and its legend?

What exactly I wanted to do in Oviedo I did not know. There was no prospect of being able actually to look at the cloth. It was, rather, an old journalist's reflex—simply having to be there. Having to be in the place about which one was going to give a report, on which one had to report. "I am hoping for everything and expecting nothing", I e-mailed from Rome to an unknown Jesús María in Oviedo, who was expecting our visit there. A friend in Rome had suggested the man's name to me.

It must have been just the same half-and-half state, between darkness and light, in which the Magdalen hurried to the tomb, and then John and Peter. Twilight lay upon the empty square. The gothic cathedral was just being opened by a caretaker. A cold wind from the Atlantic was finding its way into our coats. We had made the whole journey especially for the sake of this moment. Yesterday, I had found a note left for me at the reception desk, saying we should wait here at a quarter to eight. Three times a year, the sudarium was shown to people in the cathedral, each time only briefly for the ceremony of blessing at the end of the liturgy: on Good Friday, the feast of the Triumph of the Cross in September, and again eight days later, on the feast of Saint Matthew, Evangelist and Apostle. Three times—no more. Apart from that, no one ever got to see it. Then, however, the church was bursting at the seams, every time. Pilgrims came from all over the world, simply for the sake of the blessing. Not long ago, a cardinal from Poland had tried in vain to get permission to see the sudarium once apart from those times.

Now I could see Jesús coming across the square to the entrance of the cathedral in the gray of morning with another man beside him, whom he introduced as Pedro. They greeted us briefly, went into the dark cathedral with us, and then disappeared into the sacristy; they came back out together with a cathedral canon, who shook hands with us. Together, they led the way for us to the right-hand side of the cathedral, opened a door there, and shut it behind us. We climbed up into an ancient tower and, from there, back down into the *Cámera Santa*. Jesús had told us yesterday, in a bar, how in 1934 some anarchists had tried, using an enormous charge of dynamite, to blow the treasury right into the air out of the crypt below us. The ceilings were blown away, both of them; but with an updraft effect, all the important treasures remained undamaged.

Now, I could hardly believe my eyes. Pedro had opened the heavy barred door; he had gone around behind a treasure chest to a great gold-plated wooden frame, put the key into the lock of a glass door in that, and from behind it he hauled out a large cardboard box with a photo of the cloth on it, which could normally be seen behind the glass; he opened a double wooden door, drew back a red satin curtain embroidered in gold, and suddenly we were standing before the sudarium of Christ, the *Santo Sudario*. It was as if I were still asleep and dreaming. Jesús and the canon stood back. I stared at the woven material and the stains and lifted up a tassel of the curtain, which Pedro pulled back so that its shadow would not spoil the picture. The picture? There was no picture, no image. There was nothing but a bloodstained cloth, about the size of a handkerchief, sand-colored, the color of the desert. It was like an audience with the pope. We could look at it for the length of an Our Father, said Don Benito, the cathedral canon, and then it would have to be locked up again. The three of them withdrew behind us. There was nothing between us and the cloth—and the Holy Blood. I gazed, unbelieving.

"Lifeblood", from wounds in the back of the head, had soaked into the cloth from the man's hair, and "the blood of a dying man" had gushed forth from his mouth and nose. It ran up to the top of his forehead, as his head fell down onto his chest, Jesús had told us. He had been crowned with thorns. The way he died had been typical for a death by crucifixion. I had brought my camera with me from Rome, but it was impossible even to think of photographing that cloth. It had the dull bronze color of an old piece of material and had been crumpled up, from the look of it; on it there were rust-colored stains: the Holy Blood. It glimmered slightly in the shadows, in various different tones of brown. No glass prevented our seeing it clearly, nothing at all. I could have kissed it and did not do so. I could have touched it and did not; could have laid my forehead against the bloodstains and did not. Yet I noticed all that only much later, in the rain outside in Oviedo. Right then, the precious relic was simply surrounded by an aura of untouchability, of incomprehensibility. The Holy Grail had been described, from ancient times, as a "vessel" that caught the Holy Blood of Christ. Here was that same Blood, right in front of me, a couple of handbreadths before my eyes—for the time of a good long Our Father. Everything was forgotten before that cloth.

Then it was all over. Pedro was locking up the reliquary again. I looked at Ellen and looked unbelievingly at the neon lights on the floor that had illuminated the ancient piece of material from below. Together, we looked into a cabinet next to it, at the five acacia thorns that were stuck into the sudarium when it first came to Oviedo; then at the great treasure chest, with the silver strapping King Alfonso had put on it. On the front of it, it quoted in Kufic Arabic script the Revelation of Saint John; on the lid, in Latin lettering, the "*SUDARIO*" was listed among the relics that were kept in this chest from 1113 onward. I could not quite take it all in. This was all a dream, which only flew away when I was having a drink with my fish in one of the many *bodegas* of Oviedo.

"Simply lean right back now, like in the cinema", Blandina had said in a text message she sent after me from Manoppello. "Be quite calm now, like someone watching a film in a cinema. The one who is doing something here is the Lord!" I could use this advice. For in fact what Jesús, and the books and reports of investigations that I had bought in Oviedo, told me about that cloth was in the first instance unambiguous only on one point. It was quite certainly not, as I had imagined, a kerchief with which some woman had perhaps really wiped the blood off the face of the badly scourged man on his way to execution—even if people may perhaps had believed that in earlier centuries. People very probably had in fact regarded this blood-smeared cloth as being that—what else should it be, if they related it to the Passion of Christ, as the tradition had been handed down to them?! In reality, however, it was—as was discovered, as late as 1989, through meticulous work on it—an item that documented and retold to us the exact sequence of events in the death of someone by crucifixion, with more precision than did the Turin Shroud—more precisely than any other document, including the Gospels.

When the man to whose face this cloth had been pressed gave up his life in one last outcry, so this material said, his body (which had been hanging by its wrists fastened up on the Cross) sagged down like a wet sack. The ribs and the lungs had been driven in by this fall, squeezed together and pumped right out, while at the same time the head fell forward, with the chin on the chest and the right cheek inclining onto the shoulder; and from the mouth had gushed forth a great effusion of "death blood": a mixture of serous water and blood that, in the course of the process of dying, had collected in the lungs—and which was clearly differentiated from the blood running from any normal wound. As this man was dying, an edema must have formed in the lungs. When he died, he had spouted blood from his mouth and nose. There was such an enormous gush of it that the hand of some nearby pious Jew—for Romans were not so squeamish in such matters—must have quickly seized this cloth and pressed it against the face and the mouth of the dead man. He had wrapped it over again, doubled, because the dead man had been bleeding so freely, and then wrapped it around the back of the man's head before tying the whole cloth in place. It was not long enough to cover up the whole head; it was about 33″ long and 19 or 20″ wide. At the back of the head, however, it covered a few more small wounds that might have been made by nails or thorns, from which, before death, some "lifeblood" must have run out, as doctors had established. They must still have been bleeding an hour before being touched by the cloth. The nose had been broken. Some blood in the beard and the hair gathered at the back of the neck also left their traces on the cloth.

The dead man must have hung on the Cross for about another hour after that. After three-quarters of an hour, someone had tried again to stop the flow of blood from the nose, which was coming through the cloth, with their hand. Finally, the dead man lay horizontally and was carried a little way away; at this, blood started coming out of his nose again. Someone again had tried to stop the bleeding and, in doing so, left their fingerprints. It must have been taken off again in the tomb, we are told. Until just a few years ago, nobody at all could possibly have known all this; until a few years ago, this had been seen as simply a bloodstained, very old, and most revered relic.

The way the threads in the cloth at Oviedo were wound suggested that it had been made in the ancient world, in the Syro-Palestinian area. The criminologist Max Frei, from Zurich, found on the cloth, besides the staining, traces of pollen from a kind of thistle that flowered in the spring around Jerusalem; and other traces of blood that would have been especially typical for North Africa and southern Spain—this, after he had, some years earlier, been able to reconstruct the travels of the Turin Shroud, with the help of similar traces, from Jerusalem by way of Edessa, Constantinople, and Lirey in France, to Turin. His findings concerning the sudarium in Oviedo, however, merely corresponded yet again with a multitude of old Spanish sources, which had always assumed that this relic, along with others, in the face of the attacks by Islam in its early years, had been brought by way of North Africa to safety in northern Spain—where, at that time, in a marvelous fashion, the bones of James the Apostle had suddenly turned up, after having been in the Sinai Peninsula.

"Isn't it getting to be crowded in that tomb?" asked Ellen in the airplane, on the way back to Rome. "Is there not one cloth too many among those we know already? John talks about two cloths in Jerusalem: the linen wrapping and the face cloth. Yet in Turin, Manoppello, and Oviedo there are three cloths—to mention only those three." I looked out of the window at the lights of Barcelona below us. I did not know. There was only one thing I could no longer doubt at all: that all three of them were, in a shattering way, authentic. I had no theory about them that might collapse: I simply did not know in what way they belonged together. It seemed overwhelmingly obvious that the bloodstained cloth in Oviedo belonged with a dead man and came from a tomb. That it "had been on his head", as John said, was not probable. It was wrapped around him, in fact. Whether it was then "rolled up in a place by itself", who would venture to answer that? But perhaps all the contradictions rested indeed on the difficulties of translating from the Greek, which I could not solve in any case; and certainly not if I thoroughly immersed myself in the relevant specialist literature. Whether, then, the Veil at Manoppello perhaps did not originate from Christ's tomb—that I no longer knew; nobody knew. Nor was I expecting that anybody would ever be able to answer that question in any convincing fashion—certainly not Sister Blandina, to whom I handed over my collection of books and documents from Oviedo, together with the corresponding photos, at the first opportunity. I could see no possibility of even simply reading through all that.

Some weeks later she called me: it was urgent that I should come. I had no time. Then I should come as soon as possible, she said; she was completely shattered. In the meantime, she had had some photos the size of the original made, in Germany, from the material I had brought back. I simply must look at those! What? I should see for myself, but I had to come soon! Another of her "super-impositions"? I asked. I should see for myself. And then soon after that, I really did and can still see it in front of me, and was more moved by it than I had ever been by any of her experiments with the Turin Shroud. She had indeed once more made out some points of reference on the two very different cloths, and she showed me a transparency of the Manoppello Face that she had fixed with Scotch tape over the bloody imprint of the face from Oviedo, so that they corresponded in a distressing way and could be folded. It was more shocking than any of her previous work and seemed to me a stronger piece of evidence than all the pictures produced by a whole variety of researchers concerning the Oviedo cloth.

Here, the blood was suddenly spouting forth, not from an imaginative approximation, a reconstruction sketched of the face of the executed man—the books from Oviedo were full of those—but in a great gush from the real face of the man: out of the half-open mouth of the friendly face I had by now been gazing at so many mornings and evenings. It spread out onto the left cheek, into the roots of the beard beneath which, in Manoppello, the skin still keeps a delicate shade of pink under direct light; and then, as the head tipped forward and downward, it ran up the cheeks to left and right, along the ridge of the nose to the forehead, running exactly and clearly between the two inner ends of his eyebrows, until the bleeding came to a stop up there in a triangle. The way they matched, one on top of the other, was frighteningly exact. "I have calmed down a little now," said Blandina, "but I did get terribly excited when I made that discovery and found the right positioning."

"But I have read that it was taken off before the burial," I said, "so that this cloth probably is the cloth rolled up together in a place by itself that John talks about."

"The Shroud researchers in Oviedo tell it like that. Yet according to what I see here, it must have been different from that. There are too many ways they completely and exactly correspond. Hence, for me, it looks like this: as if this sudarium had stayed on the face in the tomb, too—but beneath the Shroud! The researches in Oviedo have shown that it was only laid upon the face and not used for wiping it clean—the bloodstains are not smeared. And that is how I see it, too. It was held against his face immediately after death and then bound in place. Nobody took this cloth away again afterward; it would have remained under the Shroud. Why should the cloth be taken away in the tomb? It was the custom in Israel to cover the faces of the dead. Lazarus, after being raised from death, also came out of the tomb with bandages wound around him and a 'cloth' wrapped over his face. That was why Jesus asked the people standing around to take them off him. It is certain that in Jesus' case, too, we are dealing with a Jewish style of burial, in which various 'cloths' were used.

"In Cahors, in southern France, for example, a kind of cap is still venerated as a relic and, according to tradition there, was likewise supposed to have been used for Jesus' funeral—and it shows traces of blood on the inside, so I have read; in the weave of the material, aloes have been detected. At Jewish funerals, such caps were called *pathil*. They were used to keep the lower jaw closed. There is evidence of this cap being in Cahors since 1239 and in Constantinople before that—where of course it was called a *soudarion*. There is no contradiction at all for me in all this. On the contrary, I can see more and more clearly how all these items seem to complement each other and build up a picture, like in a jigsaw puzzle. Someone would have fastened the Oviedo cloth around the head with the cap from Cahors, before the whole body was wrapped in cloths soaked with aloes and myrrh. After that, it was probably made secure with some kind of string. That is what we can deduce, at any rate, for the cloths that lay over the face: they all show various criss-cross lines, with a little vertical creasing—the kind that appears when you tie up some material. The traces are very delicate, but they can certainly be made out. And that is why, on the Turin Shroud, in which the body was wrapped from below and which was then brought over the head and wrapped round the front of the body, the bloodied hair on the head cannot even be seen at all, but simply the forehead and the back of the head. This point has often been made, very much as a criticism. There is no imprint at all from the scalp itself on the Turin Shroud. Yet this was the part covered by cap!

"Since this observation has been consistently confirmed for me, I more and more imagine that Jesus—especially with the Oviedo cloth—had been truly wrapped and secured in his 'packaging', so far as the necessary haste permitted. He must have slipped out of this multi-layered wrapping on Easter morning, like a baby bird from an egg—yet without cracking the shell. Or should we, perhaps, imagine the Resurrection with Jesus giving a groan as he takes the bandages off his eyes, then slowly and wearily setting down first one leg from the burial-shelf and then the other, yawning deeply and finally making his bed in the tomb, folding the sudarium and carefully placing it in the corner? That picture is quite absurd. I think it would have been quite different at Jesus' Resurrection. He would have been wrapped up in bandages like every dead Jew of his era; we have to imagine as being among these the various pieces of material that we call 'shrouds' and perhaps other ones, too. The body of the Lord was covered in these cloths as in a cocoon. And he would have risen from amid all these cloths like a sparrow taking off—with the difference that his 'cocoon' remained intact. And that was not the only difference. For after that, he also went right through walls without their falling down. The Resurrection consisted in his softly opening his eyes; it was a moment accompanied by tremendous amazement."

Blandina went into her next room and came back with a sheet of paper on which she had drawn her Jesus, with strong strokes, in an—admittedly transparent—cocoon: there was the face on a large rectangular cloth, with a cap, a rectangular veil from the hair down to the chin, and a kind of bandage wrapped round it all. She had written in the top left corner, "The four 'shrouds', or rather the three 'sudaria'," and underneath on the left, "Sequence (from top to bottom): 1, Manoppello; 2, Turin; 3, Cahors; 4, Oviedo."

"Where, according to this scheme, is the blood cloth from Oviedo supposed to have lain in the tomb?" I asked her, giving her back the sheet.

"That sudarium would have been lying under the shroud, which had been folded up, in the place where the head originally lay; it would have become hard with the dried, crusted blood—where else? Along with the fallen shroud and the veil or handkerchief of mussel silk that had lain over the top of it, it would have been seen as one thing. Two days after Jesus' death, the cloth from

Oviedo was a piece of material hardened with dried blood and serum. After the disappearance of the body on Easter morning, it would have clearly marked the place where the head had been, like an stiffened, invisible carrier substance. Along with the cap from Cahors, it would have lain beneath the sheet in some kind of rounded shape, like crumpled-up paper. By the time John and Peter arrived, the other cloths or bandages, and also the soft shroud, had sunk down flat on the burial-shelf. That is why it says twice in the original Greek text that these cloths were *lying* there—in contrast to the sudarium, which stood out *as if it were inflated* in the place where the head had been."

"Well, which sudarium was it? You have just said that the real sudarium, from Oviedo, lay *hidden* beneath the shroud."

"Yes, but there was still this veil from Manoppello."

"Well then, why does John call the cloth a *soudárion*? This veil can never have been a cloth that someone used to soak up sweat. It is much too fine, after all, to absorb a single drop of water."

"That's right; but here it occupied the place of a sudarium. It would certainly have lain right on top, as the final delicate cloth, as the outermost covering, directly over the face. And that is why there is not a single drop of blood to be seen on it. On top here, it had no need to soak up anything more—neither sweat nor blood. Here, this expensive item was merely a final mark of honor for the dead Lord, a last loving farewell."

"From whom? From Mary Magdalen?"

"That might be so. I have always thought of the Mother of God, of Mary—before I found out about the mussel silk. Yet how can anyone know for sure now?"

So there were more cloths in the grave, I remarked, even though John only talked about two?

"It is quite certain there were more! Nor is it true that John talks only about two. He does once mention the 'sudarium' explicitly and separately, because it had a special significance for him on account of the image it held. And what else would he have called it? He talks about all the other cloths, however, in the plural, using the Greek term *othonia*. John has a very limited vocabulary, but one very deliberately chosen. Other passages simply talk about bandages and not about a large cloth or sheet. Where an ancient Jewish burial was concerned, plenty of material was certainly used, in any case. In Kornelimünster, near Aachen, yet another 'sudarium of the Lord' is preserved, which is supposed to have been made of Alexandrian byssus. As long ago as in the time of Hārūn ar-Raschīd, it came from the Patriarch of Jerusalem to the court of Charlemagne, and he made a gift of it to a Benedictine abbey there in 814. It is also as fine as a spider's web, so it is said, and enormously large and has no image or any traces of blood—and, naturally, it has never been investigated in connection with the other jigsaw pieces of the burial relics. Perhaps that, too, was there; or perhaps it was used only to wrap all these relics later, for a time. So that even if the evangelist had talked only about two cloths, we can proceed on the assumption that there were many of them; that was simply what was normal. He would then have mentioned those two in particular, because they were special. Because something special had happened to them. Because on two of the cloths, an image had been left behind!"

"And why do the evangelists not mention the image on the Veil one single time? After all, John says that when he saw the 'sudarium', 'He saw and believed!' Yet he does not talk about an image."

"The evangelists could not write everything down. The fact that they mentioned the cloths at all was, first of all, the main evidence that no grave robbers had carried Jesus off, as was alleged at a very early stage. John Chrysostom pointed this out, I believe, as long ago as the fourth century. For robbers would certainly not have first stripped Jesus, in order to bring him out; that makes no sense at all. Robbers would have carried off the dead man in haste, along with all the cloths! Secondly, John was writing his description of the Resurrection still in the midst of the Jewish world, with its strict prohibition of images, in which the first Christian communities already had troubles enough. Hence, John probably was not free to and could not talk about it publicly, it was so holy! For how easy it would have been, in the Jewish world, to slander this image as an idol—and to destroy it. It had to be protected, from the very start. Paul does not talk about Mary, either. Is that supposed to be evidence of a lack of reverence for the bodily Mother of the Messiah, whom he must certainly have known—or, indeed, evidence of Jesus' having had no mother?"

"But just a minute, Sister Blandina, one more time, please! You have now talked about a large package, into which Jesus was tied with several cloths, before he was laid in the tomb—a bundle laced up in the oriental or Jewish fashion. Yet the images on the cloth in Turin and here in Manoppello show the face and the body of a man in a way that could be reproduced only if both the cloths were in a position that had to have been as flat as a photographic plate—or like a film stretched flat inside a camera. If the body was wrapped up in the cloths, however, as you say, then the images would have to have been completely distorted! Then this face in Manoppello, for instance, would have to look like the impression your face would make if you rubbed color all over it and then pressed your face against a towel. That is quite crazy—that would leave an impression that had absolutely nothing in common with the image here. And it would be the same in Turin!"

"Yes, you're right about that. Quite true. The images in Turin and Manoppello are not an impression on the cloth. And they never were. Nor are they traces of photographic emissions or whatever else people may have dreamed up by way of theories or hypotheses in the last few decades. If this were not the case, then the images would really have had to appear completely distorted on the cloths—as distorted as the impression on the Oviedo sudarium. Jesus' being wrapped in a bundle in the tomb seems to me indeed to be a fact, one that is simply more fully confirmed and demonstrated by careful investigations. What that means, however, is that these 'images' in Turin and Manoppello really are inexplicable, and will remain so. That they are, quite simply, miracles. That is probably just the way things are, even if there is hardly anyone who likes to hear this expression nowadays—least of all, perhaps, those theologians whom I have come to know."

She gave a ringing laugh and beamed at me through the reflective lenses of her spectacles.

"God can write straight, even along crooked lines—that is something my father taught me. You can see it here in a way that is truly moving: these cloths were completely twisted and entangled, lopsided and all askew, when God chose them to be the screen on which he would paint pictures of his Passion and Resurrection—in a way that no artist has ever been able to conjure up following his lead, not even on the flattest surfaces in the world. For the main question is not whether this image came into being perhaps in this way, or maybe in that, but that this image—just like the image on the Turin Shroud—after all, in practice, simply cannot exist! Nowhere else in the world are there any images that are, even in the remotest way, similar to these."

It was difficult ever to have the last word in dealing with Sister Blandina—and I did not want to do so, as I looked again at the double picture that she had made, that she had put together and created in her little hermitage, in which the blood on the sudarium of Oviedo was rushing forth from the open mouth of the Holy Face of Manoppello. I seemed to have come to the end of my work; there was probably nothing more to be seen in this connection.

Mount Tabor in Galilee, Israel

Raining Roses on the Mount
of the Transfiguration

I had now known the cloth for years, and in the meanwhile I had also learned nearly all the arguments for and against it. I had pored over books, leafed through catalogues, and studied piles of *bolletini* and countless footnotes. The arguments for and against the genuineness of the image of the Face repeated themselves. There was scarcely any visitor who was not at first put off by the "ugliness" of the Face—and that included Ellen, my most beloved wife, and my best friend, Peter ("hideous"), and even my friend Christian ("horrendous"). And almost all of them were united as to one point, "Not like that!" In a sense I could understand them all.

Fleeting as well as observant visitors were scarcely able to see, at first, the thousand faces, infinitely numerous, in this one image. The ones who saw this, rather, were the handful of women who cleaned the church or came to Mass in the church every morning. It was Rita, from the second pew, or Teresa from the third, or Pia or Sylvia from the fourth, who were more likely to see this—or Oswaldo, the bearded verger with his rough voice, who never missed any service. And the one who in any case saw it best of all was of course Sister Blandina. Probably no one in history—apart from the Madonna, of course—had spent so many hours in front of it as she had in the past few years. Yet, "No!" said Father Lino in the friary, "I have personally seen—and you are welcome to write this down—the way, every morning at four o'clock—at four o'clock!—Father Domenico was already kneeling in prayer in front of the *Volto Santo*. He spent more time in front of it than anyone else!"

"Just come and look from here", said Blandina to me, yet again. "He is so very lovely from here." I put myself in her place and saw an entirely different image. Because I was a head taller, I could see, through the image, the neon lights on the pillars behind, while Blandina, in the same place, did not see them at all. Ten people in front of the cloth were all seeing something different—all through their differing angles of vision. That was why photos obstructed rather than cleared the way here. On the forehead and the temples, and under the right eye, there was a core pale blood-red in the threads, which became visible almost only when there was no direct lighting—or could only be brought out again by using a computer. This Face was asking for icons. It was asking to be translated. Each and every photo of any old master was more true to reality than any photo of this changing image of light. It was impossible to reproduce it in many versions, just as people—up till now—could not be cloned.

One evening in December, Sister Blandina pushed a heavy flashlight into my hand when I was just about to go down from her hermitage to the Capuchin friary in the dark. "No," I said, "I don't need it." "Yes you do," she said. "Out there you can't see an arm's length in front of you." "No," I said, "I'll go by the stars." And I took her flashlight with me. The next morning I brought it for her in front of the Holy Face, where we had agreed to meet. I had once again brought two chairs up there;

we sat and looked at the image; there was no one else in the church, and Blandina had switched the lights off. Outside, it was raining. Then I switched the flashlight on and turned the narrow beam of light onto the forehead and then wandered down to the eyes with it, then to the mouth. The change, going from static lighting to a moving light was amazing. The image did not change in nature but changed its expression and completely transformed what one felt, looking at it. "Oh!" exclaimed Blandina, "Oh, oh!" She, who had already known the image such a long time, had never before seen that. I handed her the flashlight, and then she felt her way over the face with the beam of light, the way Mary Magdalen might have felt the face of Jesus—his living face with her eyes, his dead face with the tips of her fingers. In the tentative, groping light, this gaze was like that of someone who had just walked into this room through the walls. This was how he must have looked at Thomas.

And in a similar way, he met people here twice yearly—when the image shared itself with everyone who came to see it: when it came out of the church in a procession and into the open air.

The longer of the two processions took place on the third Sunday in May, and the shorter on the sixth of August, the feast of the Transfiguration of Christ on Mount Tabor. On both occasions the image of light was exposed to natural light, once in broad daylight and the other time just before twilight: an action that brought it incredibly to life. As early as the evening before the procession in May, Manoppello was unrecognizable. Bus after bus then joined a row of them below the church, in a parking lot that was deserted the rest of the year. From north and south, people had come streaming into the village. The evening before, Manoppello held a rehearsal, when in the waning light of evening the wooden statue of Saint Pancras from the church was carried from the Piazza Garibaldi, in the little town on the opposite slope, across to the shrine, where the next day it would come to "fetch" the image of Christ. When one looked into the church from behind them, all the women had clearly just been to the hairdresser. A brass band from Tarentum accompanied the procession. For as long as it took the procession with Pancras to push its way through the narrow alleyways of the town, rose petals rained down upon it from the upstairs windows of the houses, scattered over it by women, as soon as it left the little town to make its pilgrimage over to the Tarigni Hill. Once there, Pancras was greeted by a thunder of small ceremonial cannons from all the hills around, and fireworks shot into the late afternoon sky. Yet that, as we said, was merely the general rehearsal.

The pilgrim hotel next to the church, *Il Volto Santo*, was bursting at the seams. In the parking lot in front of it, hamburger stands and candy booths had been set up and were urgently needed. Who else could supply meals for the pilgrims? Manoppello was full of elderly married couples, farmers with their wives, and early in the morning, in the bar of the "Holy Face", they were already eating pickled yellow beans and barbecued pork and drinking beer. This time, three of Blandina's blood sisters had traveled here from America, Germany, and Italy. Next door in the church, from early in the morning, one Mass after another was being celebrated—all of them full to capacity. The women, especially, were singing even louder than usual, with an enormous emphasis in their voices. In front of the sanctuary there was a heavy carrying frame, built of wood and painted silver. After the first Mass, eighty-seven-year-old Father Ignazio, in gold brocade vestments, had accompanied the Father Guardian to the enormous monstrance and had led a solemn little procession to the frame from the shrine, past the high altar, through the side aisle of the nave and the central aisle, where the Holy Face was made fast onto this frame for its journey. Women and men pushed to get to the front, to blow kisses to the image, to touch the glass, or lay bunches of flowers before their relic. The church's main doors were wide open.

During the Masses, an ownerless dog had been lolling about in the central aisle, in front of the altar, and no one had disturbed it; it had been turning itself about, scratching itself sociably, and seeing to its bodily hygiene with its nose and tongue. "He's always there", I heard in the bar. "Some people think he's the reincarnation of a Capuchin who still has some ground to make up." Rough voices joined together at the Creed, declaring belief in the "Creator of heaven and earth and of all things visible and invisible". Then the Holy Face on its stretcher was carried in front of the main door by four men, members of a brotherhood wearing red robes, and set down once more; there, from within the church, it gleamed snow-white and transparent against the sky. The worthy mayor was waiting outside, wearing his tricolor sash, in a circle with the other dignitaries, the mayor of Pescara by his side and the heads of other local communities. The brass band was there again and people from the coast and from the mountains—the square in front of the church was black with people. Finally, a group in the midst of which the Pancras statue was swaying moved off at the head of the procession. A group of children in white robes with angels' wings sewn on preceded the group of Capuchins in their brown robes, preparing the way for the Holy Face, singing hymns and swinging smoking thuribles; behind them, two carabinieri in parade uniform, with red cockades on their tricorn hats. Then the *Volto Santo* was carried out of the church.

I was waiting at the left-hand pillar of the doorway. As soon as the Holy Face left the church, it changed to a pale silver-gray against the sky. And from then on, it changed in appearance at every step, at every bend. On this path, the image altered at each corner, at every turn in the way, and every change in one's angle of vision—while still absolutely maintaining its identity. "In what a friendly way he's looking at us", said Ellen at the first bend. "He laughed as he was being carried out of church. did you see it? As if he had been waiting all year for that." "He's not always friendly", said old Signor Blasioli beside us; he had been there when, during the war, the whole of Manoppello was blanketed in fog, when the allies were preparing to attack it during the German retreat. He could still show the places, he had told me, where they had dropped four bombs into the fog, without disturbing a hair on anyone's head or a hair or a feather on any creature or damaging a single house. The Holy Face protected Manoppello from being harmed in any way, he said. "Oh, no, he is not always friendly", repeated old Luigi, "he is always changing, and sometimes he is even severe."

The acacias were in full flower, and their scent wafted beguilingly from right and left of the twisting path of the procession, which very slowly, in four great loops, was coming down the Tarigni Hill to the main road that led up again into the town. Seen against the green of the hill, the face became almost flesh-colored, with green eyes; going over the next bridge, it was once more silver against the sky; and in between times it disappeared— and yet it was continually looking straight at each and every person who was here. Quite tenderly, and quite keenly. When a shadow fell from one side, he sometimes looked like someone who was peeping out of the window from behind a curtain. Two paces farther on, it looked as though he were pulling the curtain to one side himself. In the little town, at every house the image would pass, the women had hung out of the windows their loveliest and most expensive cloths and brocades and damask; and from those windows, as from every balcony, they scattered handfuls of rose petals over the image, which looked like tongues of fire raining down on the pilgrims. The fireworks were there again, in the morning sky, and after that the brass band playing at its very best. Introducing the procession was a brilliant inspiration. For only like that—in natural light—did the image give out its full flavor, freely, like a bottle of perfume being opened. Earlier, the contrast with the rest of the year must have been far stronger still, when the "Holy Face" spent the whole year hidden in a shadowy side chapel in the Capuchin church. Up until Thomas Edison's invention, in that permanent dim twilight, it presumably looked just as dark as the Vatican's Mandylion or the one at Genoa. Yet no lighting scheme, however sophisticated, came anywhere near the intensity of the experience emanating from this Face whenever it was exposed to the sun on its way in the morning light, the full light of day, or the light of evening. That was the true light of this Face.

In the meantime, we had come through the Romanesque lion-portal into the Church of San Nicola. As guest of honor, from Rome, Father Pfeiffer celebrated the solemn Mass, and he preached about paradise, blissful and red-faced, always smiling. He was not indeed yet an honorary citizen of this garden of heaven, but he certainly was—and had been for years already—in Manoppello. He invited us to supper in a country inn outside the little town, where as a matter of course he enjoyed privileged terms, and the simple cooking still gave one some idea of why in earlier times, all papal cooks had had to come from the Abruzzis. "Father Pfeiffer," I said, on the way there, on which we were able to walk quite safely in the middle of the road, on this feast day, "there are a couple of questions I had forgotten about. If it is really true that the one and only true, authentic image of Christ on earth is preserved in this tiny little town in the Abruzzis, if this is true, then are not all your arguments a lot of foolishness that cannot really explain why it should have simply remained unknown for four hundred years? If this is true, then it would have spread like wildfire, long ago! Anything else, after all, is simply incredible. Why, I ask you again, why should anyone believe you when you tell them and not, instead, regard you—or absolutely anyone else who says the same—as being quite simply mad? Why?"

"Why, you ask me? Why should anyone believe the Christian creed, as 1.2 billion Catholics do and about two billion Christians altogether—or at least, they should, if they call themselves Christians. After all, no one has to: 'I believe in God, the Father almighty, maker of heaven and earth, and in Jesus Christ his only Son. . . .' We don't have to believe that, and we are indeed hardly able to. That the 'maker of heaven and earth' should ever have become man, which is what Christians hold to be true, that seems in itself to be quite simply crazy—and that is how the Jews saw this belief, which did after all spring from their midst, from the very beginning, in fact. And that is how they still see it today, together with Muslims and Buddhists and Hindus and pagans and agnostics and atheists. That for Catholics, God has never been far away since that time, but is supposedly entirely and wholly present in a little piece of consecrated bread, which in every Roman church is carefully kept in a golden treasury over the high altar or beside it—the Creator of heaven and earth, shut into matter and locked away! That seemed simply and completely absurd. It defies the mind and understanding! Yet that is the belief of the Roman Church, even if it is de facto shared by fewer and fewer Catholics themselves. For it remains in fact simply incredible.

"Does it not, I now ask you, defy the mind and understanding much less to think that God should in the second place have also left behind an authentic picture and that—in the third place—this image, which in earlier times only the Byzantine emperor, along with the leading clergy, was allowed to see on quite special occasions in the imperial apartments at Constantinople, merely for a few minutes each time and by candlelight—that this same image can nowadays be seen quite openly, in the light of halogen lamps, by anyone who wishes to do so? That it can be viewed, here in the Abruzzis, at any time and for as long as you like? No one has to believe anything. Yet which is the greater miracle, then, and which the lesser one? That is one thing. Another thing, which has nothing at all to do with believing or not believing, is the fact that, where the 'Holy Face' of Manoppello is concerned, it is quite simply the matter of a technical impossibility, which anyone who likes can verify with his own eyes."

Now I gathered momentum again and asked, "Yet let's just assume now—if only for a moment—that this pope, or the next, follows your argument and makes a pilgrimage to Manoppello, like John Paul II made a pilgrimage to Turin in 1998. And let us further assume that, after that, the Veil with the image is made available for every kind of research and investigation. Then let us assume further, that you—either during your lifetime or thereafter—are found to be justified in all, or in most, of your theories and hypotheses. How would that change things for the Church and for the world?"

"There would be a tremendous seismic shock. It is the ultimate yardstick for man, which would then be returning to the Church. It is the original image of every person and of his freedom—entirely human and yet wholly withdrawn from our arbitrary will. Before that gaze, many disputes and many errors would dissolve into nothingness. Before that gaze, any enmity would melt into pity. For the Church has one single head, and that is Christ. He is the Lord; and here is a true image of him. Older than any text! If, then, we also have in common, in material terms, a true image of him, then the reunion of Christendom becomes far easier—with Protestant churches, just as with the Oriental church and the Graeco-Russian Orthodox, among whom icons, from the very beginning, occupied an incomparably higher place than in the West. In the East, the image—even without this original, this mother of all images and all Christ-icons—has always been ranked alongside Holy Scripture; in the East, the image itself has always been seen as Scripture. With this discovery, that will receive yet another unsuspected dimension. For ecumenism, the full discovery and acceptance of the primal icon of the image of Christ will thus have an absolutely revolutionary significance, with tremendous consequences; there can be no doubt whatever about that. Perhaps that is why Manoppello—on the Adriatic coast—lies on the old dividing line, the line of fracture, between Eastern and Western Christendom. Nevertheless, the rediscovery of this image will have another serious effect on the role of the pope, too, and will necessarily do so."

"How is that?"

"Because what used to draw people and pilgrims to Rome in earlier times was the Veronica: that was the true image of Christ. For the past four hundred years, then, the popes have been feeling the lack of the most important item that drew the crowds—that is, the Veronica. The pilgrims did not actually want to see the pope. He was a potentate like any other. And often he was not exactly a role model; he was no better than any other ruler. That, thank God, is very much changed today— and that is the way it will stay and has to stay. As the Successor of Peter—that is, of the apostle on whose weak shoulders the Church was instituted by Jesus himself— the significance of the popes will continue to grow. Their role as deputy, as *Vicarius Christi*, however, will not only be powerfully changed, but it will be taken off their shoulders again altogether. For this role was not one the popes originally played at all; and the way we understand the role of 'vicar' did not originate in the West at all, but in the East, developing from the Byzantine understanding of what the Eastern emperor was. There in Constantinople, in fact, the emperor was always seen as the first *Vicarius Christi*—since the days of Emperor Constantine the Great, since the year 313.

"And that was only possible if in acting in this way he could appeal to an image that somehow fell in his lap. For in the East, only an image could represent the emperor himself, never another person. Whenever the emperor could not come to a province himself, he sent his image— and the image was welcomed at the city gate with torches and candles as if it had been the emperor himself. No other person could deputize for him—only his own image! That image alone was always the emperor's deputy; that started with coins and carried over to the pictures of the president that we still have hanging in governmental offices today. That is where that comes from. And just as the image of the emperor stood in for the emperor, so only the image of Christ can be the true and incorruptible deputy for Christ. The fact that we now have once more before us the image that stands in Christ's place is not merely going to be the cornerstone for ecumenism. It will also bring a seismic shock throughout the Church. I have colleagues who say to me, 'If you were right, this would mean a revolution.' They are unable to recognize what this is and regard it as true for the simple reason that it seems to them too great a thing. That is the difficulty—even though the happiness is far greater still."

Now, my book was finished, I thought, even before we could sit down on the veranda of the inn and think about what we wanted to have to celebrate the day. I would never get to see anything greater than the Pentecostal procession of the Holy Face amid the rose petals and the tongues of fire. God had become man, and it was no construction of theological doctrine that the Face was saying at every turn of the path coming down the hill and going up. But how it shone! Christianity was not the religion of a book. "The miraculous image of

Manoppello is in the world, and the world does not recognize it", said a woman at the next table, who had come with her husband from Hamburg for the procession. "In that respect it is in the deepest sense an image of Christ." On the way, I had also come to know Fabrizio, a young man from Manoppello. He had been collecting every possible kind of information about the Holy Face for twenty years and wanted to tell it all to me. Yet I did not want to discover anything more about its story or to hear or see anything beyond the story about the deputy—nor did I need to. Nothing except this incomparable radiance of the Holy Face, shining gold and bronze in the sunlight and in the shadow of the trees.

Bramante's spiral staircase in the Veronica pillar of Saint Peter's,
leading up to the innermost treasury, on March 13, 2005

In the Inmost Hold of the Vatican

There was hardly anything more to be researched that really interested me. The final arguments had been exchanged; the last locked doors were not going to be opened for me; as for the last mysteries, I was willing to let them remain a mystery—and I would have to. I was not going to see the Vatican's genuine Veronica from Jerusalem—the *Sancta Veronica Ierosolymitana*. For a long time, I had kept hoping for that, as one hopes for the last missing piece to complete a jigsaw puzzle: what I needed in order to complete the picture of my researches into the "true image" of Christ. I had given that up by now, just as I had given up hopes of being allowed to see again the Edessa Mandylion of the popes. By now I knew that there was no prospect of seeing, still less of photographing, the Vatican's "genuine Veronica"—and the basilica's canons would certainly have their reasons for that. I was unable to feel sad about it. The pillar beneath the dome of Saint Peter's would keep its secret long after I was dead. For all I cared, it could.

I had received no answer at all to the last request I had made to the archpriest of the basilica, Cardinal Marchisano. I had consoled myself by rereading, in Ian Wilson's book about the *Holy Faces, Secret Places*, which was both instructive and full of ideas, all about his vain attempts to come face-to-face with this "central image", even for one single time. "A new air of *Glasnost*", he said with resignation in his closing chapter, "is needed to blow through the darker corners of St Peter's and the Apostolic Palace." Yet the canons of Saint Peter's would probably remain, even in the future, the only group of people in Rome who could see the Veronica unhindered. As it had been in the fifteenth century, when King Frederick III had had himself ordained as a canon of Saint Peter's by Pope Nicholas V, simply so as to be able to venerate the Veronica from up close—and after him, King Christian of Denmark.

At the beginning of 2005, I renewed my request one last time in a letter to the cardinal so as to close the file after that. Yet a week later, the file had been reopened. "Quite exceptionally," it said now in a rapid answer from the Vatican in Piedmontese German, "I shall be happy to give you a positive response, even though I have to tell you in advance that the relic that is locked away in the top of the pillar is in very poor condition and is unrecognizable." I could not believe my eyes. I was going to be allowed to see the Veronica without having to have myself ordained as canon? "Waiting to hear of a date when you would like to view the relic", the President of the Fabric of Saint Peter closed his letter to me. The very next Sunday, I followed him—after Vespers in Saint Peter's, at which he always walked as last of the canons in their entrance and recessional processions—with Ellen into the sacristy. By way of a staircase at the back, he had already returned to his palace on the next floor up. The porter told him we were there. After a few minutes, he opened the door, and we greeted one another in friendly fashion. "Right," he said, "then we can see what is the best date we can find." He took out a notebook and leafed back and forth in it. "What about Thursday morning, at ten o'clock?" That suited us absolutely.

"Vital that you take a meter rule!" Sister Blandina told me by text message. "You really must take the measurements of the image." It was a gleaming bright morning on Thursday when we called punctually at Cardinal Marchisano's office in the *Fabbrica di S. Pietro*. The marble of the basilica was shining like snow in the sunlight. I felt I wanted to pinch myself: today was *the* day. My pocket was bulging with the camera, brought along just in case, and with freshly loaded batteries. We had bought a flashlight specifically so as to be able to illuminate even the darkest corner of the secret dungeon of the Vatican. I had the meter rule in my coat pocket. The cardinal invited us into his drawing room. Over the sitting area was hanging a portrait of Christ by Mantegna in a costly baroque frame, with—if I was not mistaken—byssus-colored hair. "No, no," said the cardinal, quietly smiling, as he sat down in front of us, "all the things here are of course merely copies." I looked over his shoulder at two framed pictures of the Turin Shroud, which were hanging on the wall beside the window. He had followed my gaze. "You should write something about those!" he remarked, with all the pride of a local patriot; the Cardinal himself came from near Turin. And it was up there that he had learned his excellent German. "I'd be happy to," I said, "and about those in Oviedo and Cahors. I would love to put together a mosaic of all these relics from the tomb, sometime, and describe what they can now tell us today. That's why I am here, today." He listened intently.

We conversed a little about Germany and Italy, about God and the world, and about how, as a child, he had been astonished by the first blacks he had ever seen, in the streets of Turin, after Mussolini's Abyssinian campaign. He was an educated, sensitive man with an all-round culture. Even I listened to him with fascination. Suddenly he stood up. Had he heard something? Had he, perhaps, heard outside the door the quiet clinking of keys belonging to one of his officials, who was now going to lead us up to the vault inside the pillar and unlock the treasury there for us? I could not hear anything. Yet things were now finally about to happen. Once more, I could have pinched myself. He led the way for us across the hallway, opened the door, and offered to shake our hands. "What?" I asked. "Your Eminence, weren't we going to look at the Veronica relic?" He nodded. "Yes, yes, I know. You will be receiving a letter."

A Swiss guard saluted as we left the Vatican through the arcade beneath the left-hand bell tower. It was chilly and cold. On Saint Peter's Square, the day seemed to have grown even brighter, the marble whiter, and the sky still more polished. I fiddled with the meter rule in my pocket and took photos of the obelisk and Ellen instead of the "true Veronica" in its treasury. Had I done something wrong? Had the Cardinal seen the bulge made by the camera in my pocket? Ought I not to have brought my wife into that realm of males? Did my own appearance along with all these other suspicious signs, simply constitute far too great an offense against the Vatican's unwritten code of behavior? Or had I said something wrong? I did not know, and nothing occurred to Ellen that we ought, perhaps, to have noticed earlier. There was no answer, for all our puzzling over it, and there was no other answer from the Vatican. At first, I was expecting something each day, and then each week . . . and then

I gave it up. I would never ever get to see the Veronica relic.

This book had to be completed, nonetheless. My reader in Berlin was demanding the first samples of material for reading. There was hardly time enough to finish the rest of the manuscript. For my next birthday, I once more took a couple of days' leave and drove with my wife to a little country inn not far from Manoppello, where neither an Internet connection nor a cell-phone signal could keep me from work, so that I could finally write the last chapters. The innkeeper already knew us, and the room was already familiar to us. Ellen picked up a book; I unpacked my laptop, moved the table in front of the window so that I could look out onto the slopes and summits of the Abruzzis, and leaned against the warm radiator. Snow was still lying on the hills in mid-March; it was a cold winter. Yet it could not get at us here. In the lounge below, our table was already laid and had once more been moved in front of the fireplace; a bottle of wine, already opened, would be waiting for us there at midday tomorrow, in front of the glowing logs of olivewood, and the cook, without asking, would bring us some hors d'oeuvres from the kitchen and then a couple of plates with his fabulous pasta, and the main course after that, before asking us whether we had any special preference for our dessert and coffee.

Happy Birthday! Apart from this, I do not make much of it. Yet this time, it had not been a bad year, really not at all. We could happily celebrate that. Oh, life—oh, to be in the world! First, however, I intended to use this evening and tonight to write up what I could still bring forth from my memory and understanding. I set about it straightaway and wrote and wrote and wrote, until I was starting to feel a little cold. No telephone rang to disturb my work. I stood up to warm myself against the radiator. Perhaps I ought to move the table itself closer to the warmth. I put one hand on the radiator; it was luke-warm. I went into the bedroom; it was just the same there. I went downstairs to see the innkeeper; he did not know what to do. However many switches and knobs he pushed and turned downstairs or in our rooms, nothing was any use. There was nothing whatever he could do, unfortunately, to put things right. It was a mishap that might have happened to any homeowner, though at the same time, in the Abruzzis, especially in this winter, it seemed to be a classic case of an intervention from on high. Half an hour later, the radiator was stone cold. It was no warmer in bed; the covers were too thin. The coat I laid over the blankets kept sliding off onto the floor. It was a horrendous night, too cold to sleep, and I was too tired to put on an extra pullover and two pairs of socks. "We have to leave", said Ellen, as it was getting light; "we'll have one look at the *Volto Santo*, for your birthday, and then we must get back to Rome as quickly as possible, in the warm car, to a nice warm bath. Even the hot water has failed here." I was shivering. "Yes, I can't work here. We can't possibly stay—I'm as cold as ice."

In the car, my fingers finally warmed up again. The mountains of Italy, with their coating of snow, glistened in the sun, a feast for one's eyes. By midday I had almost forgotten the well-spread table in front of the fire in our favorite inn and even, in Rome, the warm bath I was going to run for myself. The first day of spring seemed finally to be here. We unpacked our small amount of baggage, and as I was about to plug in my laptop again, I saw by the little red light that was blinking that a phone call had been recorded on my answering machine. I pressed the play button. "Good morning," said an unknown woman's voice on my birthday, "I am calling you from the *Uffizio* of his Eminence Francesco Cardinal Marchisano, the Archpriest of Saint Peter's basilica and President of the Fabric, and in fact I am calling about a date on which you might see the Veil of Veronica. I have just now tried to call you. But perhaps you could call me back." There was a crackling on the line as she gave me her number. "Ask for Signorina René. Buon giorno." I listened again to the call, and then again, and yet again, until I had heard the number clearly and noted it down, then I called straight back. She was no longer in her office, a man's voice said. I would not be able to speak to her until Friday, that is, tomorrow morning; she was not there at all on Saturday. I called the next morning. "Ah," said Signorina René, "I'm glad you have called. I was beginning to think I could not get hold of you in time. You can see the Veronica on Sunday, at four in the afternoon, during the canons' procession. But no photos, please! Please come to the sacristy in Saint Peter's at 4 P.M. and ask there for Signor Mauro; he will explain everything to you."

Ellen and I had actually not been planning to get back until a day later, on Saturday. If we had come back as planned, then Signorina René would not have been able to get hold of me, nor I her. An angel must have turned the heating off in Manoppello, or maybe it was Jude Thaddeus.

On Saturday evening, just like a child before a big outing, I laid out my best suit and necktie. On Sunday morning I gave my shoes and my glasses another polish. I had once more prepared my flashlight, notebooks, and camera with the zoom lens; the meter rule was still in my coat pocket from my last visit to the Vatican. We had been invited to a reception on Sunday morning, over beyond Tiber Island. When we tried to go home, Rome had suddenly been brought to a halt by a marathon, and in the Roman fashion there were no buses or taxis either, and we had to walk back through Trastevere; our meal was further delayed, the soup was too peppery and burned my mouth, we quarreled, and suddenly Ellen cried out, "It cannot be true! Look at the time—it's ten minutes to four o'clock. Run!" I ran—I had forgotten my hat and my scarf, and in the queue to go through the security scan in the colonnade I called up Ellen again to say I had also forgotten my notepads and the telephoto lens. Could she please bring them with her to Vespers in case they might still be useful? Out of breath, I arrived in the sacristy on time to the minute.

Signor Mauro Benzoni was a small, very friendly gentleman who was sacristan of the enormous basilica. How many of them were there? I asked. "One", he smiled. "*I* am the sacristan." He must explain this to me, he said: Today, Passion Sunday, at Vespers, the canons, together with the choir, would first of all go in a great procession to the high altar, which was covered with relics today, and they would solemnly cense these with incense. "What relics are those?" I asked him. "Bones belonging to many of the martyrs and saints of Rome. Today they are joining in the celebration, and today they are also there at the blessing." Then, however, the procession would move slowly back to the main entrance, he continued, while the Litany of All Saints was sung, across the church and back again, before they finally sat down in the choir to sing Vespers; after this, the faithful would be blessed with the Veronica from the balcony. Could I please be waiting at the foot of the Veronica pillar, he said, before this. We would then go up together during Vespers to where he would take the relics out of the treasury. He showed me inside the church the exact spot arranged.

I looked up at the pillar. The balustrade of the loggia up there was draped today with burgundy-red satin, and six large candles were standing on it. I followed the procession with my eyes, spellbound; the crucifix going ahead, then the choristers of the papal choir in white surplices, behind them the canons in violet, lastly the celebrants in sumptuous old copes, and right at the end Cardinal Marchisano in crimson. "*Sancta Maria*", I heard Pablo Colino, the choir conductor, intoning in his smoky voice, as he filled the giant space, singing antiphonally with the people of Rome the Litany of All Saints in Latin. "*Ora pro nobis*! Pray for us!" "*Sancte Michael, Sancte Bartholomae, Sancte Joánnes, Sancte Simon, Sancte Thaddæ, Sancte Thoma, Sancta Maria Magdalena*". It went on for minutes. And time and again, "*Ora pro nobis*, pray for us, pray for us, pray for us." This moving supplication went right through you. From the Cardinal's side, Signor Mauro left the procession and came to me, wearing ordinary clothes, nodded, opened a small door behind me in the balustrade surrounding the base of the pillar, preceded me down four steps on the outside of the pillar, opened another door in the base of the pillar, and switched on the light in a little entrance that led up four steps into a small room inside the pillar, which Bramante had built as the first support for the enormous dome—into the inside of the foundation stone of this millennial basilica.

The room was a spotless white, with plain whitewash, and brightly lit. At the end of the entrance hall, the sacristan picked up an old red damask purse from a stone—it jingled—and stepped onto a narrow, elegantly curved spiral staircase beside it. A loose rope ran up on the right as a banister, and a rope hung down the open middle of this winding spiral as a banister on the left. Signor Mauro turned around: "We'll go up rather slowly; the stairs are tiring. They always remind me of the way up to Golgotha." I tried to count the steps and got mixed up right away, as if my head were spinning. Coming up the last steps, we could already hear again the loud Latin singing of Vespers, still louder up here than down below. Above the spiral stairs, a room opened onto a wide hallway, leading directly onto the loggia of the pillar. This was no dark chamber, no somber dungeon—on the contrary. Everything was very light and free; very clear, and open in front to the immense space inside the basilica. "*Dominus a dextris tuis, / conquassábit in die irae suae reges*", rang out from below; "*De torrénte in via bibet, proptérea exaltabit caput*—The Lord is at your right hand; / he will shatter kings on the day of his wrath. / He will drink from the brook by the way; / therefore he will lift up his head." We seemed to hear the sound of the voices as still purer and more beautiful than down below. Signor Mauro was softly singing along with them.

I had never been in a more beautiful treasury. Over the arched exit to the balcony, a grill had been constructed made entirely of bees, the heraldic symbol of the Barberinis, Pope Urban VIII's family. The hallway was as wide as a small room. Both long walls were painted with what looked like quite real crimson tapestries. The front of the room led out over the balcony to the inside "outdoors" of the enormous space of the basilica, nearly two hundred feet above the floor. The sacristan put his hand into the damask purse embroidered with silver and took out four heavy great keys and a little old instruction book (handwritten, I saw) and with one of the keys unlocked a large grill on the right. "This installation dates from the sixteenth century, and the treasury has been in constant use ever since."

Beyond the grill, he pushed aside a dark-red cloth hanging, inserted two keys into two appropriate keyholes on the left of the next heavy iron door, one at the top and one at the bottom, turned them, and then with the last key, in three other keyholes on the right-hand side, he unlocked with a snap three other locks which must have been connected with a different mechanism. The whole thing must have been perfectly well oiled. After that, he pulled the heavy iron door silently open, around to the left. It was covered with brocade. There was also a brocade curtain in front of the inner part of the treasury, showing the instruments of Christ's Passion in heavy gilt embroidery, with a colored medallion of Christ's face in the middle.

I could not believe my eyes. "May I not take one photo, at least of that?" I asked. Signor Mauro shook his head. No, he said, that was unfortunately not allowed—the privilege of being here was in any case quite exceptional. He was sorry. He took the curtain off a hanging device, holding it between two fingers to left and right, and hung it on a special contrivance on the inside of the open door of the vault. Everything had been considered, and there was provision for everything. The vault was not deep and was hung absolutely all around with gilt-embroidered brocade. I could see the Veronica relic standing in the shadows and, next to it, a cross, but first the sacristan took out a large quartz container, with a lance-head inserted in the top of it. "The point of this has unfortunately been broken off," he said, holding the relic out to me to kiss, "as you can see. It is exactly that small piece which is to be found in Paris." I could hear a humming in my head as I looked at the lance. How small it was, though! "All these reliquaries are from the time of Pope Urban VIII." He took the quartz vessel and carried it to a niche in the wall, on the left beside the vault, which was draped with wine-red damask. From above, a small picture of Christ gazed down out of the damask onto the mysterious ritual objects for which this room was reserved before the blessing. A sumptuous stole lay folded up in the niche and a pair of ancient damask gloves. "The people have already been blessed with this lance, on the second Sunday in Lent, as happens every year. Today they will be blessed with the Veronica relic and with the Cross relic. And then again with the Cross on Good Friday. The stole and gloves are provided for these ceremonies alone." Then he went back three paces with me and fetched the Veronica out of the vault, carried it into the light, and placed it in the niche.

The true Veronica! *La Sancta Veronica Ierosolymitana.* I went down on one knee so as to be able to contemplate it better. I stood up again and moved to the left and to the right. In the presence of all the precious things in this room, I had almost to force myself to look at it, for absolutely nothing could be made out in it. Nothing to attract one's glance or one's curiosity or one's sense of beauty. The contrast with the rest of this unique treasury could not have been greater. The icon was covered with glass. Underneath, some object, which seemed to dissolve.

A patchy dark, dirty, grayish material with no outline. Without any drawing or color. The only contour came from the three-pointed shape of a face cut out in the gold covering, with one point for the beard and two points to left and right, where—on other images of Christ—the hair fell down. This was a covering like that of the Edessa Mandylion, which Ellen and I were able to see shortly afterward in the sacristy of the Sistine Chapel, or like that at Genoa, which we had already seen, after our quarrel—and obviously this was borrowed from these ancient and venerable images. Only on that ground could one regard this object, from any considerable distance, as being a face at all: only on account of the cutaway covering. No trace of a picture was there to be seen, nothing. Nor did anything here seem ancient and venerable. There was no talking about there being any face, or even the notion of a face.

This was in no way compatible with the old reproductions of the Veronica or even with the most critical or malicious of the old reports about the relic. This was no "plain white linen cloth", as Luther was still mockingly describing it. At the top right, the material gave the impression of being eaten away and ruined. Remarkably, a fine wire netting was stretched across the material, underneath the glass. I took out my pocket flashlight and directed the beam onto the material from close up, looking at each little spot; yet one could scarcely make out even that it was woven material. I could make out nothing more with the flashlight than without it. Perhaps a flash might have been able to bring out something more, but taking a photo was hardly thinkable, with Signor Mauro being so friendly. The woven cloth, with its golden cover, was surrounded by a heavy frame with precious stones. To left and right there were two handles. "Try and lift it a moment, and see how heavy it is." I grasped the reliquary on the right and left and reckoned it as being at least eleven pounds, thirteen, fifteen, or even more. "The frame was also donated by Urban VIII; read what it says on the back." The frame had been perfectly preserved. Everything here was irreproachably preserved and conserved. Everything to do with this treasury, and everything in it, was in the very best condition, as if it had only just been completed. Only the image was a ruin. What it had ever been or ever could have been was a mystery.

Here, the nature of things had completely undermined the calculations of the creator of this work of art, supposing that it ever had been a painted picture. Perhaps the materials used or the colors were simply too cheap, supposing that any were ever used. "*A fácie Dómini contremísce terra / a fácie Dei Jacob*" carried up to us from below, the antiphonal plainchant of the Vespers: "Tremble, O earth, at the presence of the Lord / at the presence of the God of Jacob."—"*Qui convértit petram in stagna aquárum, / et sílicem in fontes aquárum.*" It was Psalm 114, and for a while I automatically sang along with it: "Who turns the rock into a pool of water, / the flint into a spring of water." It was so difficult to concentrate on this image. I gazed, and I stared. Time was not pressing—it seemed to have dissolved. Signor Mauro had now also taken the relic of the Holy Cross out of the vault—which seemed to have been built for these three precious things alone: there was no room for more. I did not know where I ought to look altogether; even the view from the balcony was magnificent. Signor Mauro pointed out to me, right and left, the pillars from the Jerusalem Temple. Over the hallway of the treasury was a set of three bells, I found, which were only struck on the occasion of blessings with these three relics.

I took the meter rule out of my coat pocket and measured the image. Signor Mauro looked on and noted the measurements. The area inside the frame, including that with the gold covering (which was in several parts that seemed to be riveted together), measured exactly 32 × 20 cm (12.6″ × 7.9″). The area cut away for the "face", from the top "hair-parting" to the point of the "beard", measured 28.1 cm (11″), and from left to right 13.1 cm (5.2″). Had Canon Rezza perhaps made a mistake, in the year 2000, when he measured 25 × 13 cm (9.8″ × 5.1″)? However that may have been, there was in any case no face there. "But tell me," I asked the friendly sacristan, from whose face a smile was never entirely absent, "why is there actually no photo of this?" "Why is it not allowed to be photographed?" He almost blushed, giving the answer: "So that there will not be any gossip. So that no one should laugh over the fact that the image has disappeared—or that it looks the way it does. That no one should make a jest of that. For you can see how ancient and venerable it is; even if it has faded now, or something like that." He said it so respectfully, in such a refined and hesitant way, as if he were talking about his father or grandfather being ill, and nobody should photograph them in their sickbed, in pain.

He dismissed me before two canons came up to give the blessing from there. Preoccupied, I mechanically counted the steps all the way down the spiral stairs. Sixty-two fine-cut marble steps led downward in a corkscrew spiral. After only twenty steps, I felt I would like to go quickly back up, so as to look at everything again from the beginning, more carefully, and go into it more systematically—I wanted in particular to imprint the Veronica on my memory. How long had I been up there? Before I went up, I had been thinking how much I would have liked to take a photo. I had my camera with me, loaded. A pity, I was now thinking to myself, as I took a quick photo of the staircase, that a picture could not at least be taken simply of the treasury, the lance, the lock. The little corridor; the cupboard ornamented with gold brocade; the curtain. Most of all, though, a photo of the embroidered face of Christ on the brocade of the outer covering and that on the damask of the covering in the niche for the relics. Nevertheless, it was no pity that there could be no photo of the Veronica. For the Veronica in the Vatican was absolutely nothing.

Down below, Vespers was still continuing. The Magnificat had begun: "My soul magnifies the Lord. . . ." After Vespers, the choirmaster announced, another blessing would be given with the ancient "relics". He did not say "Veronica" or "*Volto Santo*"; in politely reserved fashion, he merely described as a "relic" the object that supposedly, as the Face of God, was once the magnet drawing all the world to Rome. It was as if no one here had believed in it for a long time. I hurried back toward the high altar so as to be able to look up better to the loggia behind which I had previously been standing so exaltedly. A sound of bells I had never heard before came out of the pillar; then two canons came out to the edge of the balcony and lifted up the heavy Veronica relic so as to make the sign of the cross, once on high, once to the left and once to the right. Perhaps it took five seconds, perhaps only three. Now I could at last look up through the camera lens. It was too far for a photo that would be any good at all; even with the telephoto lens, one could not make much of it. The light from the feast-day lighting in Saint Peter's was reflected on the silver frame that I myself had lifted up when I was up there before. No one was allowed to bring a telescope in here. From far below and some distance away, you could make out as much as you could up there, right in front of it: nothing.

I now knew that it did not fit into the old empty frame of the Veronica, the one with the broken glass in the treasury—neither the cloth beneath the covering nor the part shown in the cut-away section of the gold. What was once shown in the old, smashed frame of the Veronica could not have been this Veronica from the pillar. The long side of this relic was too long. Nor was *this* Veronica ever transparent; *this* frame, from the beginning, had no two sides for viewing, with two sheets of glass. What could now be seen quite clearly through the camera lens was the marble angel in the background, bringing down the Face of Christ, in profile—with wide-open eyes—from heaven: by the school of Gianlorenzo Bernini. The bells sounded again, and now the canons were coming with the relic from the Cross and giving a blessing with that, too—this time, however, three times: once straight in front and once each to left and right of the balcony. The choir sang *Vexilla Regis* (the royal banner of victory), a hymn from the sixth century. At a stroke, the surging and murmuring of the crowd in Saint Peter's was stilled. A tremendous silence fell over all: amazement. Not even a child was crying—nothing. Some Romans and some pilgrims were kneeling. It was seldom like that in Saint Peter's. The bells sounded again, in the pillar; the magnificent feast-day lighting went out. Ellen found me at last; unfortunately, she had forgotten the notepads.

Outside the main entrance, it was still light. The wide square of Saint Peter's was blocked off; there were no people there. John Paul II was expected to arrive back at the Vatican from the clinic very soon. It was Sunday, March 13, 2005. It was as if the starlings of Rome were already dancing over the colonnades to welcome home the gravely ill Pope for the last time. They were forming in clouds in front of his window, like a veil in innumerable folds. Like a symphony of form and movement, conducted by heaven, of an intermixture and interweaving of feathered flags and veils and streaks, in which no bird ever collided with another. A marvel before one's eyes. I searched desperately through all my pockets for any scraps of paper to jot down the most important impressions with my pen while they were fresh, the things I would so much have liked to photograph before they slipped my memory. One thing above all, I would passionately have liked to take a photo, clearly and in real close-up, of that marvelously embroidered face in the middle of the heavy old brocade curtain with the gold embroidery in the treasury. And the similar embroidery on the damask over the niche. They showed the *Volto Santo* in Manoppello, in all its proportions, with absolute clarity: with its open eyes, this was the face of the true Veronica—in the inmost fastness of the Vatican, as clearly as if on a "wanted" poster.

Yet I could find no paper in any of my pockets. It was fast getting dark. The mosaic of Mary, "Mother of the Church", glimmered softly in the light of the lamps over the colonnades. I took a photo of the gable of the Sistine Chapel in the light of evening, with the obelisk in front of it in sharp outline. Suddenly, sirens were coming nearer and a flashing blue light chased along the outside of the piazza's ring of columns. Carabinieri had kept free a narrow lane through the crowds, with a barrier of gleaming strips of plastic. Cries of "Viva!" and singing greeted the Pope. This time, he was not coming back to the Vatican in his illuminated popemobile; rather, he was huddled on the passenger seat of a minibus. It turned into the empty square of Saint Peter's at high speed. Passion Sunday was drawing to an end. The Pope wanted to be home for Easter. The gleam of floodlights coming on over the pillars suddenly flooded the oval in bright light. No one yet knew that this was John Paul II's last homecoming to Saint Peter's.

Etching of the burial of Christ, Erfurt, 1735

Homecoming and Farewell

From that evening, John Paul II had twenty-one days and nights still to live. The search for the Face of God had long since become the underlying theme of his life. "My heart says to you, 'Your face, Lord, do I seek'," Psalm 27 said—in a cassette to which we had often listened on our journeys on the freeway—in his strong, melodious voice: "'Your face, O Lord, do I seek.' Hide not your face from me."—That was why I had finally written to him on August 6, 2004, "Dear Holy Father", to say to him that I had to tell him about an image of Christ "which is like no picture on earth". I had sent in the same envelope six large-format prints of my digital photos—one dark, one transparent, and various details shown in varying light—and had written, "It is at present in the keeping of the Capuchins of Manoppello in the Abruzzis, in the Diocese of Chieti, where it has been revered by the inhabitants for four hundred years as the *Volto Santo*. Over the centuries, before that, many sources spoke of the same image as 'Veronica' (or *vultus sancti*)—and there is much to suggest that this precious relic disappeared one day, in mysterious fashion, from the Vatican, where it had long been preserved in the Veronica chapel of the old Constantinian Saint Peter's. It fits perfectly into the old frame of the Veronica, which is still preserved in the treasury of Saint Peter's." I then told him a little about the technical impossibilities of this "image" and of its colors with no trace of any pigmentation and about the ways it corresponded to the Turin Shroud. Both of these images on cloth, so far as my own observations went, seemed to exceed the limitations of human technical capacity. "On March 24, I was privileged to be present in the Sala Clementina," I ended my letter, "when you presented your vision of a Europe of man illuminated by the Face of God." Might I not ask him with these few lines, when he was in Cologne, where he had invited the youth of the world to come in the summer of 2005, to show to the young people as well as the old the "Veronica of Manoppello"?—"We want to see Jesus" was, after all, what he himself had chosen as the motto for this World Youth Day, the request some "Greeks" in Jerusalem had once put to the apostles. "In the Veronica, they will see Jesus", was the last thing I wrote. It was a good month before a reply from the apostolic palace, with the papal arms on it, lay in my mailbox.

"What you had to say about the *Volto Santo* of Manoppello has been very carefully noted", a papal monsignor from the secretariat of state wrote to me. "His Holiness has asked me to thank you sincerely for this and for your interest in the universal pastoral service of the Successor of Saint Peter. From his heart, Pope John Paul II asks the intercessions of Our Lady of Guadalupe for God's protection and guidance for you and your family and also great joy in the service of the gospel." Nine days later, my first report about the Holy Face of Manoppello appeared in my newspaper in Berlin. Cardinal Meisner, in Cologne, read it and spoke to me about it at a chance meeting in January 2005, in Saint Bartholomew's Church on Tiber Island. "Yes," I said to him, "this image probably does truly show the Face of God—at least, according to what Catholics believe about that." Some days later, he rang me up one evening from Germany and asked whether we could really drive over together to Manoppello some time as I had offered him. He would be in Rome again in April, and he had kept the whole day free on the fourth for this trip. "Oh, the most popular of the German bishops wants to go on an excursion with you!" my friend Peter from Munich laughed, when he rang me shortly after that.

On the evening of February 1, shortly before eleven o'clock, the windows on the top floor of the apostolic palace, overlooking Saint Peter's Square, were suddenly lit up alarmingly bright, whereas normally, at that hour, the lamps were going out. "The influenza-type infection from which the Holy Father has been suffering for three days has been complicated, this evening, by acute bronchitis and a contraction of the larynx", a first communiqué issued by the Vatican during that night said briefly. "For this reason, it was decided to make an emergency admission to the Agostino Gemelli Polyclinic. This took place on February 1 at 10:50 P.M." The Pontiff's long dying had begun. He had came back again in triumph from the clinic, but then had been readmitted in a great rush for a tracheotomy that had become urgently necessary and that deprived him of the power of speech for the rest of his days. And now he was just coming back home for the last time. In two weeks it would be Easter.

Only a few days after that shocking Easter Sunday on which John Paul II had given his last mute blessing "urbi et orbi" from his window, Cardinal Meisner called us up again to remind me of the date agreed for our trip to Manoppello. The Pope died on the evening of Saturday,

April 2, up there behind that window. Early on Monday morning, at seven o'clock, Cardinal Meisner was standing in front of our house. Really, I urgently needed to get on with my work and report on the events for the editors in Berlin; during those days, the press center was a hive of industry. Italy was shining, as we raced along the freeway toward Manoppello. On the heights of Tagliacozzo, Cardinal Meisner received over his cell phone an invitation to bid farewell to the deceased Pope later that morning in the Sala Clementina of the apostolic palace, in the Vatican, before the body was taken across into Saint Peter's. I stepped on the gas.

Father Carmine and Sister Blandina were waiting for us at the main door and, in the parking lot, two angels in the shape of young men in leather jackets, who wished the Cardinal from Cologne (whom they recognized immediately) strength and God's blessing for the conclave. But he should, please, make sure that the right person was elected as Successor of Peter!

We walked up the central aisle to the front; Cardinal Meisner genuflected before the tabernacle and looked up at the image, stood up, went up the steps behind the altar with us and genuflected again right in front of the image, and gazed up, silently, before sighing, "My Lord and my God!" I went back down the steps to go and open the main door, so that the Veil would become transparent in the direct light, and looked at the time. The time available for a visit to the Holy Face had never been shorter. As I was closing that half of the door again, Father Carmine brought us the key of the treasury, so as to open the reliquary for a private examination. I was anxious lest the Cardinal should stumble as he was coming down the steps with the heavy silver monstrance; Ellen, Sister

Blandina, Father Carmine, and I walked behind him in a little procession. Meisner brought the image on the Veil into Father Carmine's office and then, at my wish, out into the courtyard again, for a photo I wanted to take in daylight. I had never been so close to the image, near enough to kiss it, and yet I was much too excited to understand what was happening to us. Almost all the photos I took were blurred. "The face is the monstrance of the heart. In the *Volto Santo*, the heart of God becomes visible. *Pax vobis!*" wrote the Cardinal in the visitors' book of the friary, and he said to Father Carmine, "He does not merely look us in the face; he looks into our hearts. Yet not with the gaze of someone who gives orders, or that of a strict judge; it is the gaze of a brother, that of a friend. It is the gaze of the Good Shepherd." Then he smiled: "In Cologne, in a certain sense we celebrate Christmas all year round, with the relics of the Three Kings. With this Veil, you always have Easter here. Do not ever doubt that it is genuine!" Two pilgrims from Canada were already waiting in front of the empty reliquary when we returned with the Holy Face, the Cardinal once more leading the way. He gave me the monstrance so that I could put it back in its mounting, and then Father Carmine locked the glass reliquary again. We fetched three chairs and put them up by the window, prayed the "luminous" mysteries of the Rosary, and went out to the car again to go flying back to Rome, to the bier of his dead Polish friend. It was like a time machine bringing us back, right across the country. Toward noon, we turned into the Vatican again, just before Saint Peter's Square; the Swiss guard saluted.

By way of back stairs I had never seen before, we were ushered into the presence of the dead Pope. All the pain had disappeared from his face. The facial muscles, so long cramped by Parkinson's disease, had relaxed. He was no longer ill; he was no younger, yet now he was once more lovely to see. He simply seemed now to have become still more serious than on the previous Wednesday, when I had last seen him at his window. His hair was covered with a simple miter, and he was wearing a red chasuble, with red shoes on his feet: ready to set off. His bishop's crosier, with which he had circled the earth so many times, was lying in the crook of his left arm: this time for his last journey. I gazed at the nose that had become pointed and at his large ears with their many convolutions. I had never in my life been so close to the Pontifex Maximus—and for such a long time. A Rosary had been twisted around his fingers, so that he seemed to be praying it with us, one last time. The Paschal candle was flickering beside his head. In the pew opposite, on the left of the catafalque on which the dead Pope was lying, an archbishop was desperately trying to silence his cell phone, which was ringing in the midst of the antiphonal prayer. Cardinal Gantin, from Benin, was kneeling beside him; the old man had come from Africa especially to see the Pope and was now directing his half-blind eyes toward him. I let my eyes wander over the frescoes on the ceiling of this sumptuous room: yes, it was here, in the Sala Clementina, where it almost hurt one to hear him. Here it was, last March, that he had tortured himself with the effort on behalf of his vision and his testament for Europe, on behalf of his "dream" that he wanted to "entrust to coming generations": "a Europe of man, illuminated by the Face of God."

I looked at him once more when we got up again after half an hour. When he was elected, in the autumn of 1978, we had intended to name our fourth son after him early in the following year—the son who then turned out to be our first daughter, Maria Magdalena. An hour later, our second daughter, Christina, called me up and said that Cardinal Meisner had just said to her in an interview for an American magazine, "Today, I have seen the risen Lord of Easter!"

"In the time of the iconoclast controversy, the Church defended images," Archimandrite Zeno had been saying for years in Russia, "and today, the images are coming back to defend the Church." During those spring days in 2005, that was obvious—the images were absolutely storming back. Some, I could touch and even kiss, while others were flashing past before my eyes and raining down on the whole earth. They went flashing out from Rome into countless rooms and other places or went fluttering across Saint Peter's Square in the newspapers of yesterday and today, as the wind blew them around before my feet.

Three days after we had taken our farewell from the Pope—after which millions more people would crowd past his bier—I was shaken by seeing in the *Corriere della Sera*, the picture of another quite different farewell, the last "adieu" of Stanislas Dziwisz, John Paul II's private secretary and most intimate friend for many decades. This photo showed one of the last moments before the body was locked in darkness. To the left of the open coffin of plain cypress wood in which the Pope had been laid in crimson and white stood Piero Marini, the Master of Ceremonies, in episcopal purple, with an unmoved countenance. From the right, Archbishop Dziwisz, likewise in purple, in a gesture of infinite melancholy, had laid his arm, which hid his own face, over the edge of the coffin, with his open hand drooping down; he was slack with sorrow, an old man who had lost his father. Yet as a last gesture of love, he had just laid a "kerchief" of the finest white silk over the face of his Holy Father, hiding his face now, above the folded hands, from the gaze of every observer. This was a custom of unknown origin, the text accompanying the picture said. Nonetheless, it was in fact a new ritual in a papal funeral, which John Paul II himself had introduced in an instruction that had hitherto been kept secret, as Archbishop Marini had announced to the public three days earlier. "His eyes, / which are withdrawn from our view, / shall behold your beauty," a prayer said, written for this last concealing of his face by this Pope who was a visionary and a poet.

Ten days later, I listened to Cardinal Ratzinger in Saint Peter's, when before the cardinals went into conclave in the Sistine Chapel he spoke of the fact that God had revealed "his Face to us". The more than life-size Veronica in marble was looking over his shoulder on the crossing pillar beneath the dome; I had been permitted to visit the inside of it only a month before. Unmoving, the allegorical figure of the "true image" held up the fluttering sudarium on which the Face of Christ had left its impress—yet this time, over the head of the severely aggrieved Dean of the College of Cardinals. Countless editorial teams would choose this very image, from among the wealth of images of the event, as their front-page picture for the next day, April 13, 2005.

Hands Transformed

This was the day on the evening of which, in the Sistine Chapel, Joseph Cardinal Ratzinger was elected the new pope by a large majority of the 115 cardinals assembled there. It was not the first evening, however, on which the new Pope Benedict XVI had come into contact with the Face of Christ—of course not. For the incredible heart of the Catholic faith—of which he had previously been the guardian for decades—was indeed the fact that the Creator of heaven and earth became man: not a sacred cow, not a gray goose or a mountain baboon, not an oak or any other sacred tree. God took on a quite particular human face (resembling only the face of his mother). That is the belief of Christians. Christ is the image of the invisible God, said Saint Ambrose. That was why the fact that the one and only God could be depicted had from the beginning been an essential difference between the Christian world, both in the East and the West, and all other religions and cultures. In contrast to *Yahweh* and to *Allah*, Christians had an image of their God. Everyone, from the humblest peasant to the emperor, from the wisest scribe to the dimmest fool, could gaze upon him and recognize him.

Very few scribes in our own day, probably, had reflected upon the Face of Christ as intensively as had the former head of the Congregation for the Doctrine of the Faith.

Detail from the Entrance to the Holy Sepulcher in the
Church of the Holy Sepulcher, Jerusalem

A few years before he had even had to endure being criticized by his fellow cardinals for the declaration *Dominus Iesus* (Jesus, the Lord) because in it, he quite simply reminded people once more of the fundamental belief of Christians. For years now, he had not been able to get the Face on the Turin Shroud out of his thoughts. After the beginning of the new millennium, Joseph Cardinal Ratzinger gave the opening lecture at an international congress about "The Face of Faces—The Hidden and Transfigured Face of Christ", at the pontifical Urbaniana University. In the Middle Ages, the Cardinal told everyone, the God who entered our history had become *le Beau Dieu*, the "fair God" whom the masons chiseled out of the stone at the entrances to cathedrals. I had already seen hundreds of portraits like that, and yet the idea had not really taken hold of me until a good year earlier, when my eldest brother Karl Joseph died in Berlin.

We had come to his funeral from Jerusalem on the first available flight, a night flight, and I could not be really sad, because Father Goesche, the parish priest who accompanied my big brother to his grave on that bright winter's day, had also over the past few weeks kept him company on his journey back into the house of our parents' faith—after a long deviation by way of all five continents and many cultures, during which he had nevertheless taken with him, everywhere, a photo of the Face on the Turin Shroud. Wherever I went to visit him, that picture always hung in his room. That was why one could not, perhaps, in his case really talk about a conversion in the usual sense. It was in particular the parish priest himself who was still truly radiant as he talked about his last conversations with my brother in his funeral oration in the chapel of the Olympic stadium.

"Believe me, Father, he said to me only a few days ago," he beamed, and struggled for words, "I have seen the whole world, the Taj Mahal in India, the pyramids in Egypt, the cathedrals in Champagne, and the Dome of the Rock in Jerusalem. I have always and everywhere searched for the most precious and most valuable things in the world, from the Sufis to the wisdom of ancient China, in many foreign religions and cultures. I have read hundreds and thousands of books. Yet nowhere and in no text—not even in the Bible—have I found this face again! That is the only thing I want to see again." Father Goesche was almost laughing.

A few weeks later, we saw each other again in Rome, where he was trying to gain Joseph Cardinal Ratzinger's support for setting up a papal institute for fostering the old liturgy, which Padre Pio celebrated in southern Italy right up to his death, in neo-pagan Berlin. Obviously, their conversations had been successful; the Cardinal had opened for him all the doors he needed. Shortly afterward, we met in a Chinese restaurant near Santa Maria in Trastevere. As it turned out, Father Goesche had been a student of Professor Pfeiffer's and in his student days had many times undertaken the pilgrimage to Manoppello. That is why he quickly became more fiery than the chilies on our plates when Ellen asked him about the prohibition of images in the Bible: "Is not every image contrary to this prohibition? Are the Jews and Muslims not right, then, with their opposition to Christians?" The passionate parish priest almost choked: "For heaven's sake, no! God only demanded this important renunciation so as to be able himself to grant a much more wonderful fulfillment than humans can imagine. Right away, in the first and most important commandment, he leaves this exemption open because he wanted no one but himself to be able to fulfill it. It was similar, after all, with his demand that ancient Israel would have no king. Yet everyone had kings! That was a cruel requirement for the Israelites. Why should they not have a king? For this reason alone: that God himself intended to be their king!" Dr. Goesche took a sip of his drink: "That was also how it was with his demand that no one be allowed to make themselves an image of him—or, consequently, any of men, who are made in his image. He wanted no one but himself to grant this image—in a way more impossible to conceive than any artist could even imagine."

"Yet Jesus' Face is not even mentioned by a single evangelist", said Ellen. I came to her support: "Yes, only once, in the Transfiguration on a mountain."

"That is correct. Yes, basically it is only described in that one passage. Yet how? Matthew writes that it 'shone like the sun', whereas Luke says, 'As he was praying, the appearance of his countenance was altered.' Is that what we call a description? And not one of the four evangelists describes his appearance, either; yet about fifty times, his gaze is referred to. At Nazareth, he suddenly turns round, on the edge of a precipice down which they were going to throw him, and *looks* at the crowd persecuting him—and they suddenly separate before him, like the Red Sea did before Moses. In Mark, it says that in the synagogue, another time, he told a man with a withered hand to stand out in the middle. Then he asked those standing around, 'Is it lawful on the sabbath to do good or to do harm, to save life or to kill?' When they were silent, 'he *looked* at them one after another', it continues, 'with anger, grieved at their hardness of heart, and said to the man, "Stretch out your hand." ' He did that, and his hand was sound again. Following that moment, the Pharisees went out and made the decision to have Jesus killed. That is how it was with his gaze. Mark tells how he once directed this gaze 'lovingly' on a rich young man, who he wished would follow him. Then the young man went away sorrowful because he preferred to stay with his great possessions.—That was how it was with his eyes."

The last time we met, in Berlin, my brother had said he very much hoped to be able to visit me in Rome. Now, it was as if he had sent Father Goesche. Soon, he had brought us by way of Jesus' gaze to the subject of the two faces in Turin and Manoppello, and we were getting each other excited—and because the best answers come only from good questions, I recalled again the fundamental objection to this special image of Christ in the Abruzzis. "Is it important at all", both Isolde, my friend Peter's wife, and Stephan, our son-in-law, had each independently asked a little while back, "when we have after all got the whole Bible?" No, I had replied to them right away. If the cloth did not exist, or if the image is a forgery or a copy, then it is not at all important—and no one need even look at it. "But if this historical record in the form of an image does exist, then it is extremely important, especially for our own era. The Word become flesh! And you are asking if an image of this is unimportant? If this image is authentic and comes from the empty tomb in Jerusalem, then in a way—along with the Shroud—it is the first and oldest page in all four Gospels! Then, it is not merely the image of all images, but also the text of all texts, the word of all words—in a unique complete semantic package!"

"Why 'a complete semantic package'? What is that supposed to mean?"

"It is supposed to mean, in what this image signifies in all that it expresses. 'A picture says more than a thousand words', Kurt Tucholsky noted in Berlin, as long ago as 1926. This has become a platitude. Today, however, the whole thing can be said much more exactly and rationally. For nothing makes the distinction between an image and a written text so clear as a computer does. No numerical system makes any basic distinction whatever between texts and images; for a PC, they are both simply quantities of data. Yet there is still a considerable difference, because any image file normally contains far more information than any text file! Each modern digital photo has on average about four times as many bytes as a whole book. Speaking in a purely technical sense, it stores four times as much information. And every holographic image takes even more.—But the image in Manoppello is neither a photo nor a hologram. It is a miracle!"

We sent for another small bottle of rice wine and were soon outbidding each other in the most lovely speculations. For would not history have turned out quite differently if the human spirit had been able to concentrate for the past four hundred years on solving the riddle of this image as much as it had on solving other riddles? What would not the minds of theologians like Albert Schweitzer, Dietrich Bonhoeffer, Karl Rahner, or Hans Urs von Balthasar have been able to say about this historical image-document and to discover in it if they had been able to give their attention to it as they had to other texts? Or how would the world have turned out if Martin Luther had taken this image of the Word become flesh just as seriously as other words (in printer's ink)? It would have turned into a different world, that much was certain. A different history would have passed across the face of Europe, one less ideological and less infatuated with words, less alienated. A more humane history, more pictorial and vivid, simpler and more obvious. For we did not set up a letter from our parents on our desk, but a picture of them—there was no question about that. Or a picture of our children, one of our wife, our husband, or our beloved—quite irrespective of what marvelous letters they may have written us. That was why we could only now recognize which path theology had taken, following the loss of this image—the first page of the Gospels. Thus it was that Christendom had come to have a theology that was faceless—ultimately, to have a theology without God.

"Yes," I said finally, "if we really want to take seriously again the idea that images and writing are to be taken in the same way as texts, then it can only have fatal consequences when this image vanishes from before our eyes as the object of our contemplation and interpretation. For since Luther, the motto of the Reformers, '*Solo Scriptura!*', has indeed actually become the watchword of the whole of Christendom. Only 'Scripture alone' should still count. Hence, when the image of Christ was stolen, it was as if one wing had been broken off, which together with the other texts of the Bible could have borne us up on high to the entire knowledge of truth. Since then, Christendom has been spinning down, fluttering, to the earth. If one wheel of a two-wheeled cart gets stuck, then the thing will, almost inevitably, simply turn in a circle. And is that not what we have already been able to observe so long in theology just as in philosophy? Is this cart not digging itself slowly, like a corkscrew, into the ground?"

Ellen was looking at me as if, with my similes, I were flying off at a tangent myself, out of control—behind the cart with the jammed wheel. Yet it was clear, at any rate, that we ought not to keep the discovery of the image in Manoppello from Cardinal Ratzinger, our neighbor, whom I often used to see beneath my window. Who, if not he, ought to take another look at this "text"? Was he not the greatest "scribe" or "scholar" of our age? He had, besides, given me the ultimate keyword some months before, in a debate about the Resurrection of Christ from the dead at which I had been in the audience. "According to the larger part of modern scientific thinking, religion is a part of the realm of subjectivity: in that area, everyone can experience and feel whatever he likes", he had said then. "But the world of what is material, the objective world, obeys other laws, and God has no business with that." A God of that kind, however, was not God, but merely an element of psychology and of empty promises, he remarked. That was why he had to contradict this belief absolutely. He had to oppose this error, he said, as much on account of his own insight as on that of his office: "No, matter belongs to God; and it is precisely because our subtle Gnosticism can no longer endure this that it is a central point!" exclaimed Joseph Ratzinger; and he elucidated the question at issue with a story from the history of German theology. "When Harnack, at the Berlin theology faculty, remarked in a conciliating way to his orthodox counterpart, Adolf Schlatter, that they were actually in complete agreement, except for one small matter that divided them, and that was the question of miracles, Schlatter responded energetically, 'No we are divided on the question of God, for what is at stake in the question of miracles is in fact whether God is God or merely a part of the realm of subjectivity.' "

I read this passionate statement of the case several times. It was a quiet but fiery *"J'accuse!"* directed against the aberrations of a theology with no God, or against the idea proposed by some modern theologians of a God "who has no hands (except for human hands)". If, however, it were really so, according to the teaching of the Church over which he watched—if the question of miracles really did raise the question of God!—then was it not also, with respect to the miraculous image of Manoppello, first and last a matter of the question of God's being God?—and that he did in fact become man and even left behind a witness to this, which all the scholastic wisdom of mankind could not have imagined? Must not this image—which obviously is not simply a miracle, but which also does not withdraw from us and may be watched and even touched—must it not, symbolically, raise yet again for our own day the question of God? I knew that in large parts of the Church, it had been a long time since miracles were believed in, even by many priests and bishops, even in Rome—not even everyone in the Vatican believed in them. That belief in miracles had to be denounced as magic or explained away in technical terms had long been familiar to me. Miracles do not compel people or compel them to do anything. They do not even compel anyone to believe. They compelled me, however, as a reporter, to give an account of them.

That was why, in June 2004, three months before my letter to the Pope, I had burned a first selection of my photos from Manoppello onto a CD, so that I could hand them to my neighbor and give Cardinal Ratzinger full information about the discovery. For ought not this image to be rediscovered, above all, by the popes, and not merely by journalists? This was the question I had put to John

Paul II's closest colleague. He gazed at the pictures, fascinated. But how gently and mildly his *Dominus Iesus* was gazing at us, with such restraint! Even he had probably never been looked at so mercifully by the "king of the Jews" to whom he had assigned the rights over his life. Some weeks later, just as Cardinal Meisner had done in Cologne, Cardinal Ratzinger read in the newspaper in Rome my first report about the Holy Face in the Abruzzis. Who could have assessed the significance of the discovery concerning mussel silk with greater understanding? The way that this letter that had now reached us in Manoppello from the empty tomb in Jerusalem was "written" on a material on which one could neither write nor paint! Only a few days later, just as I was carrying a couple of full garbage bags to the trash containers, I met the Cardinal down in the Via del Mascherino one sunny autumn afternoon. "Herr Badde", he said from some distance away, in his high melodious voice. He smiled at me shyly and held his hand out, while I still had both hands full. Despite my delight, it was a little embarrassing, although he only wanted to thank me sincerely for my newspaper report. I stammered a little and turned red, and it was after this meeting that I sent him what was for now my most recent letter.

For Chiara Vigo had sent me a bunch of raw, uncombed mussel silk, and since then this had lain in a jewel case on my desk like a small treasure: the gold of the sea, softer than cashmere wool, finer than angels' hair, material for "holy weaving", like that Chiara Vigo had learned from her mother and grandmother. Now, I took it out of the box, held it in the sun again at the window, where it once more gleamed like copper, and then put it into an envelope for Cardinal Ratzinger. Could he not have this shown to the Pope, I put the question to him, to console him in his serious illness—and as a final inducement maybe to see this image for himself during his lifetime? Perhaps he would only be able to hold up the holy material in the sunshine before the sick Holy Father's eyes, since the latter had after all spent all his life in a search of the Face of God: material for the Paschal raiment of the "Bride of the Lamb".

Whether he ever succeeded in doing this, I did not know. I was of course bound to think of it again before the cardinals went into conclave, when the Dean of the College of Cardinals spoke in his sermon of Christ having revealed to us "his face and his whole heart". In the meanwhile, I was gazing at the giant figure by Francesco Mochi from 1646, behind the small man beneath the baldachin in the middle of Saint Peter's, the figure holding up over his head the image on a veil, the image of Christ. I did not know whether Joseph Ratzinger had been able to hand on my final gift to John Paul II. Since he became Benedict XVI on April 19, however, my bunch of mussel silk had after all come into the hands of the Holy Father. At the touch of the lock of angels' hair—the last threads of the Golden Fleece—the hands of Joseph Cardinal Ratzinger had been transformed into the hands of Benedict XVI.

The Disarmed Face

On the morning of that same day in February 2004 when I stumbled down the Via della Conciliazione, in front of Saint Peter's, into Father Pfeiffer's lecture on the "Holy Face", I had signed an agreement with a publisher in Zurich for a new edition of a book that had already been accompanying me around the world for a decade. This was the prayer of a Jew dying in the burning ghetto of Warsaw, which Zvi Kolitz from Lithuania had put down on paper in three days in 1946, in a hotel room in Buenos Aires. God had "hidden his face", it said at the heart of it. One could not otherwise explain the cruelty and the depths into which humanity had plunged the Jewish people and itself. This powerful song of anger and defiance ended, however, in a yet more powerful prophetic love song.

At the time, he had written that ending first of all, Zvi Kolitz had told me at our first meeting, in New York in January 1993. From that starting point, he had unrolled the entire story backward, he said, and then written it from the beginning. The ending, however, with which the story had actually begun, went like this in Yiddish: "*Gott vun Isroel, ich bin antlofen aher, kedej ich soll Dir kennen umgestert dienen.*—God of Israel, I have come all this way so that I may serve you in peace: to do your commandments and to sanctify your name. Yet you do all

311

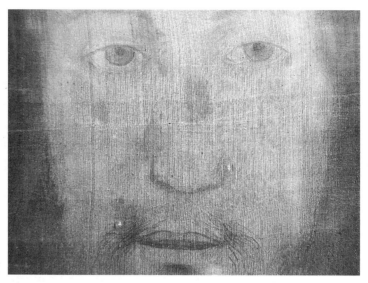

Detail of the image on the Veil at Manoppello

you can to stop me believing in you. If it seems to you, however, that with all these tribulations you will succeed in turning me from the way of righteousness, then I tell you, my God and the God of my fathers, that it will be no use. I will always love you, always, you alone—in spite of yourself! I am dying as I have lived, in a rock-solid faith in you. The God of the dead, the God of retribution, the God of truth and of the law shall be praised forevermore: the God who will soon unveil his face again before the world and who with his almighty voice shakes it to its foundations! 'Hear, O Israel: the Lord our God is one Lord.—Into your hands, O Lord, I commit my spirit!'"

Something similar had happened to me. I too had heard and seen the end of the book—the very last word—right at the beginning, in the autumn of 1999, when along with our daughter Maria Magdalena I stood for the first time before the image in Manoppello, with not the least idea of what was waiting for me in the years that followed—and most certainly without the faintest idea of writing this book and report. And now it was already three years since Zvi Kolitz had died. Yet I could still hear his voice in my ear; more than ever whenever I read these lines from his text of the century, saying that God "will soon unveil his face again before the world". And on that particular evening, too, when I had to sign the new contract, I could not avoid thinking of him and of those words. "Good heavens!" I thought, while Father Pfeiffer, with his projector clicking against the humming of the air-conditioning, conjured up shocking details of the "Holy Face" on the screen, "Good heavens, am I going to have to write another long story about the way God has been unveiling his face for Christians for two thousand years?"

I had of course believed this—but only in the way that most Catholics probably believed it, above all theologians: one did not have to take the Creed too literally. That evening, confronted by those pictures, that seemed scarcely possible any longer. "Good heavens," I thought, "I am not an author, I have other tasks to do here in Rome and a different job, and I do not have the strength left to write a book: I am going to become a grandfather this summer. I am already four years older than my father lived to be, living on borrowed time; and I ought to go swimming or get some other kind of exercise and take better care of my health and spend less time in front of the computer screen." I simply wanted to be able finally to get away for a holiday, like my colleagues, going for long walks and swimming, a journey to Sicily, to Greece, or whatever. Or simply go for a walk along the Tiber sometime, thinking of nothing in particular . . . "And yet," I thought further, "should I not once more—if only for my friend Zvi's sake—write about the way that God has after all unveiled his Face, if I have already some knowledge of that Face and its story? If only in gratitude? He will in any case know better than either of us can explain", I mused.

As I was discovering its vanished history and publishing it again for the first time, my youngest brother, Klaus, died. Now, three months earlier, my oldest brother, Karl Joseph, had died. I had hardly made Sister Blandina's acquaintance when my second-oldest brother, Wolfgang—who had called me when I was with her—suddenly died. Time was running out. I was surrounded by more and more dead people. Ought I not to write quickly what I had learned—and the fact that there was a life after death, with a gentle judge who had already shown his face?

Should I not, then, like Zvi Kolitz, make a great effort to depict once more how one day, perhaps—even if I, as I hoped, was no longer here to see it, the world's no longer knowing which way to turn to escape from its own horrors that it had itself made—perhaps a pope would arise in a time of our greatest need and take the true image of Christ out of its glass and carry it to Turin, to lay it upon the face of the image of the dead Christ, as gently as Mary Magdalen—the way that Leo the Great, in the time of the great emigrations, had once gone out with the image of Christ to meet the Huns before the gates of Rome and moved them to conversion? How the two images not made by human hands would thus come together once more and would be overlaid and joined together—those images that had been separated ever since John saw "the napkin" in the empty tomb "not lying with the linen cloths but rolled up in a place by itself"? What then? Would anyone on earth still believe that God had unveiled his Face? That the Creator of heaven and earth had become man—and had been crucified by men— and risen from the dead? Would the foundations of the earth really be shaken then—those foundations whose thunder my old friend Zvi could already hear in 1946? Or, would they already have been shaken when one last frightful war flared up around the holy city of Jerusalem? I could hear again, in Latin, the psalm, "*A fácie Dómini contremísce terra!*—the earth trembles at the presence of the Lord!" Was this the earthquake Father Pfeiffer was talking about?

I was not trembling. But was I perhaps overexcited by the magnitude of this discovery? For his coming would probably never be like that. And why should it? He had indeed already come. He was already here. The lost Face was not lost. The standard yardstick for Christians had not disappeared. There was no second image in the world that could be set side-by-side with this Veil of mother-of-pearl threads, beside this image of the Word become flesh. Together with the Shroud, it was older than any copy of the New Testament, free from any copyist's errors, and finer than the finest papyrus. More precious than the most precious parchment. No pictorial witness corresponded so closely to all the sources and the witnesses that, from ancient days onward, time and again talked about this true image of Christ "not made by human hands". Yet how small and transparent it was, and how little it had been read! How vulnerable and unprotected, compared with the security in Genoa; compared with the steel safe in Turin; compared with the treasury of the Veronica pillar in Rome! Only three steadfast Capuchins were watching over it, Father Carmine, Father Emilio, and Father Lino, together with Oswaldo, the sacristan with the squeaking trainers, and the Archangel Michael.

"The true Veronica", said Father Ignazio Scurti, who loved this Face so dearly, before he died at a ripe old age and was laid to rest by his brothers in a funeral vault in the churchyard next to the friary at Manoppello, "the true Veil is the eucharistic Host, and you will find the true Face of God only in the face of your neighbor." Now, a candle flickered in front of the smooth cement sealing of his tomb in the churchyard beside a pot of cyclamens, long since withered. The round snow-white eucharistic Host of the very thin, flour wafer was "the most brilliant image" that could ever occur to men for God, as Heinrich Pfeiffer had said to me. The Host, he said, was that "veil of bread" behind which God lay hidden, as Thomas Aquinas, the great "Doctor Angelicus" had said back in the Middle Ages.

We gazed at this very same Host every Friday evening in our parish of Saint Anna, after John Paul II, in the last great provision of his term of office, declared a "eucharistic year" from October 2004 to October 2005. We sat in one of the pews and simply gazed at the white round of bread, seeing how it shone in an antique golden monstrance, with the light of two oil lamps burning to left and right on the altar. Incense drifting in the church. We who came to this "adoration" in the parish church of the Vatican, and then afterward were blessed by Father Gioele with the "most sacred Host", were not numerous; sometimes a handful of men and women, sometimes two handfuls. Two weeks ago, the sacristan began to put on the high altar, in addition to the radiant bouquets of flowers as decoration in front of the monstrance with the consecrated Host, a simple little arrangement of hay. "Look at that! A *manipulus*, a sheaf of wheat", whispered Ellen last Friday, elbowing me, "you must take note of that. That has to go in the book!" I pulled the notepad and ballpoint pen from my shirt pocket. What the verger had put up there to remind us of the origins of the Host reminded me very strongly of the coat-of-arms of Manoppello, with its stylized sheaf of wheat.

Now I was once more leaning my head against the glass of the shrine in the Abruzzis. I was no longer trying to look into this pair of eyes questioningly, searchingly, testing. Now, he was looking at me. Finally, for me, too, "the buzzing in my head" was stilled. He was gazing at us, not we at him. My cell phone sounded briefly; I had forgotten to turn it off. Blandina had sent another text message, I saw, as the screen lit up: "His eyes are more lovely than wine, and his teeth whiter than milk!" It was as if I could hear her laughing as I scrolled down the words on the screen: "With these words, Jacob blessed his son Judah and all his tribe, in Genesis, the first book of the Bible, in the early days of the history of salvation. That is why his milk-white teeth can be seen here! They have to be visible for us to see that this is right. For whom should this clause hold more true than for HIM, if this blessing holds true for the tribe of Judah?" I switched the cell phone off and looked up again to the one who was gazing at us here. Looking at the teeth. One could not say that they were whiter than milk ... but it was well said. The pupils were dark, like a dark red wine. That was right. I gazed at the nose, the forehead, and the little lock of hair with the individual hairs. "Everything passes away, save only the face of God", it said in the twenty-eighth surah of the Qur'an from Mecca. "A disarmed face", said the Jewish philosopher Emmanuel Lévinas once, in Paris, "can disarm the other person." Here before me were both of these: the living Face of the God of the living, disarmed—both visible and invisible. The Lord of the visible and invisible world, in whom Christians used to believe. "Your Face is our home!" wrote Thérèse of Lisieux, the great little saint from the end of the nineteenth century, although she had never seen this cloth. "It is the Lord!" said John to Peter in the boat, when he saw the outlines of this Face shine out in the gray of morning, beside a fire of coals on the shore of the Sea of Galilee. "My Lord and my God!" exclaimed doubting Thomas, when Jesus suddenly stood before him, barely ten days after his execution, in bodily form—not as a ghost—with the lance-wound still open. It was simply no longer bleeding. Most of them did not at once recognize him after the Resurrection. His appearance was as reticent as this mussel-silk cloth.

Now whether the cloth lay as a "second shroud" beside the Shroud in Christ's tomb and along with the sudarium from Oviedo and the cap from Cahors, I did not know. It was so marvelous that even this marvel was perfectly possible and was even very probable. That was what I believed, but I did not know. Nobody knew: not even Suor Blandina Paschalis, the nun before the Holy Face, who had vowed herself to silence and yet could not keep any news to herself—and certainly not this. Even Father Pfieffer did not know, he who was convinced that "the discovery of this image is going to trigger a revolution in the history of ideas." That was quite possible. Yet the path the image took to get here, down through the centuries, would probably always be full of mysteries. Whether it was stolen in Rome in 1608 or as early as 1527 in the "sacco di Roma" was no longer so easy to elucidate. Many of the facts could not be aligned. How it came here or exactly when, no one could say. In any case, the fifth centenary of the arrival of the *Volto Santo* was being celebrated in Manoppello in 2006. It was right that it should be. For this was at any rate a year in which it was going to come before the whole world once more. Many contradictions that we could see now would one day fall together; many questions would have to be put anew. Amid all these questions and answers, there was one thing that was toweringly obvious: that was the existence of this wholly mysterious object here in Manoppello.

Nor was there any more doubt that this was probably the most precious piece of material on earth. It did not depend on books or demonstrations, but was quite independent wholly in and of itself. No book would ever be able to exhaust its significance. Hence, the most important voice in the buzz of discussion around this image was not that of any beholder, any legend, or Greek or Latin source, no professor or article—it was the soft voice of this man himself. He was breathing out; he was giving us his breath—to each beholder individually. That was the overpoweringly meaningful voice of this historical witness. And faced with this voice and this gaze, it was also clear that there was in Jesus' life only one single period of time for this likeness of his face. That was not when he washed his face for King Abgar; it was not after the scourging or at the Transfiguration on Mount Tabor; nor was it when he sweated blood in the garden of Gethsemane or on his way to Calvary, when perhaps a woman may have mopped up his blood. This face had been given many wounds—yet here, they were all already healed. This was no longer a "bloody head sore wounded". The wounds were freshly healed. The broken nose had been set straight; even the horrible wound on his eye, which still showed on the Shroud of Turin, was gone. This was the face that was healed. All the blood had been washed away and all tears. If there was a relic of the Resurrection, then here it was. A greeting from the other side, from the kingdom of redemption.

Thus all the old names had been misleading—it was not the Veronica, at any rate not merely that; not the Mandylion (or not only); not the Abgar image, as described by the legend; and not the sudarium. It was not an image from Edessa or even the Kamuliana about which other legends spoke. It was possible that it had once been in Memphis, in Egypt, where the pilgrim from Piacenza described an image on cloth of this type. Yet all the names and all the legends were always only fresh attempts to explain, to grasp the nature of this inexplicable object.

This Veil of mussel silk was not a picture at all. It was the most precious pearl from the depths of the sea. Yet even if it were merely plain linen, if it were as coarse as a potato sack, and not as fine as a spider's web and sparrows' wings: this was a word that gleamed radiant in the sunshine. This was a word that did not permit itself to be distorted. It was at rest here, amid all the concepts and all the disputes. This was the appearance of the Messiah, of the Holy One of Israel. This mussel-silk cloth was a work of the Holy Spirit. It spoke to each and every one in his own language; here, the Spirit made the Son of Man just as visible as the Son did the Father. His eyes were already bathed in eternity; he was just opening them. He was this moment opening his lips for his first new word in his mother tongue: "*Abba!* Daddy!"

A Memorial of the displaying of the Shroud (with the Sudarium)
in Pinerolo, Piedmont, in 1578

A Final Supplement

The Veil of Manoppello is the sudarium of Christ. This is the mysterious second cloth from the tomb of the crucified Christ that John the Evangelist discovered about forty hours after the death of Jesus in his empty tomb—together with another linen sheet, which is today preserved in Turin.

Christ's tomb was not empty on the first Easter morning. There was nobody in it—that is true. Christ was no longer lying there. Yet in the decisive passage (Jn 20:5–7), it says of the other disciple, the one Jesus loved, that "stooping to look in, he saw the linen cloths lying there, but he did not go in. Then Simon Peter came, following him, and went into the tomb; he saw the linen cloths lying, and the napkin, which had been on his head, not lying with the linen cloths but rolled up in a place by itself." So the tomb was not *empty*. And it is unthinkable that John should have bothered himself with irrelevant details at this point.

That is why Turin and Manoppello belong together in a unique way. These two cloths, so very different from each other, both show miraculous images, and that is particularly important. They are both incredible. Every attempt to explain them in some other way and to derive their origin from some kind of physical or chemical—that is, natural—reaction to an event that gave rise to them, following various models of thought, is misleading and almost completely prevents our understanding them. For in fact these miraculous images reflect nothing less than the miracle of the absolutely inexplicable Resurrection of Jesus Christ from the dead. They are not photos or paintings; they are themselves marvelous new creations by God. The two images are as inexplicable as life itself.

The two pieces of material bear two quite different images of Christ. And these two pictorial witnesses are free of anything that contradicts a single word of the Gospels. "The mystery of faith", we say in the Catholic Church, every time, following the divine transubstantiation of bread and wine into the Body and Blood of Christ: "We proclaim your death O Lord, and we celebrate your Resurrection." The two cloths tell of this mystery.

It has therefore taken us a some time to comprehend this, even approximately. This process is not yet completed. New pieces of knowledge are still being brought to bear on it as well as many strong arguments that make it probable that the Veil of Manoppello disappeared from Saint Peter's in Rome as early as 1527—in the 'Sacco di Roma'—and not later, around 1606, for instance. More important, however, are the new developments and knowledge relating to the future of this, the most precious relic in the world, in which God really is going to reveal his merciful Face by means of this little piece of material to all who dwell upon the earth.

Less than a year after I had held in my hands the first copy of this book, fresh from the printer (on September 23, 2005), Pope Benedict XVI, on September 1, 2006, visited the shrine of the Holy Face in Manoppello by helicopter. This was the first journey of his pontificate inside Italy upon which he himself had decided. This was a turning point in the story of the Holy Face, after which there was no turning back.

That is why there will be many more books, in the future, about this miraculous image. All those reports, however, will never make this book obsolete, where I have faithfully recorded the way in which this true image, which was revered for so long in Rome, found its way back in miraculous fashion—centuries after its disappearance—into public awareness; and this will probably always be seen as the most extensively documented presentation. Hence even in the second edition of the book, early in 2006, I had to insert a new first chapter into the original text, like the new façade to a building, in which I recounted the most recent development that came about after the Pope had announced he was soon going to visit the image himself.

And that is why, now that the book is soon going to appear in both North and South America, I wish to add a new supplement of three quite different texts to the twenty-three chapters of the old book. These tell the readers, as if in three different spheres, a little about the developments triggered by Benedict XVI with his visit to the sudarium in Manoppello.

First there is my news report of September 1, 2006, "Jesus and Peter", which I wrote for the daily paper *Die Welt* during the Pope's visit to Manoppello; I am their Italian correspondent. This piece—as is usual in connection with such events—was written under great pressure of time and in the face of various technical problems, which most like to bother reporters on occasions of this kind. The first computer gave out, and then a second, then I finally found a third; then the telephone was not working, and after that the Internet. Nonetheless, following that marvelous morning on which I had been able to observe the Pope from up close during his encounter with the Divine Face, I did get my report finished somehow in my race against time, soaked in sweat and half-dazed, and was able to copy it off onto the USB flash drive of a friend from Poland; from that, I was able to send the article off to Berlin at the last moment by Father Carmine's Internet connection, next door to the sacristy of the basilica.

The second text of this supplement, "Peter on Mount Tabor", is an interview that Werner Schiederer, a member of the editorial team on the periodical *Kirche heute* (The Church today) had asked me to do a good week later. After I said I would be ready to answer questions like these in more peaceful circumstances and at a greater distance, he had a catalogue of suitable questions sent to me by Erich Maria Fink, who collaborates with him on this magazine and is also pastor of the "Queen of Peace" parish community in Russia, in Berezniki in the Urals, on the Siberian border. I have never seen him.

Finally, I produced the third text of the new extension to this book, "The Face of the King", for the paperback edition of the book in Germany, while I was on a journey through China in July 2007, in a hotel room in Peking on my laptop—after I had been able to see for myself, over the previous days, how perhaps no country on earth is so much waiting to discover the person of Jesus and his merciful Face as great China, both ancient and new.

With this, the final reconstruction of the edifice of proclamation of the news about the Face of God being in a basilica on a hill behind a little town in the Abruzzis, overlooking the Adriatic coast of Italy, should—provisionally—be complete.

Rome, June 29, 2009.

Jesus and Peter

People's voices in the valleys and gorges around Manoppello wake me at about three in the morning, when usually it is the barking of the dogs that starts up and sometimes in winter the howling of wolves. Today, the dogs are silent. The pilgrims are coming, while it is still the middle of the night. About five o'clock, the clatter of the footsteps around the country hotel reminds one of those days, following the death of John Paul II, when the stream of mourners in the streets of Rome was growing into a cosmic love parade.

Today, Benedict XVI is coming on a "cosmic excursion" into the Abruzzis to contemplate, in the little shrine up the hill from the hotel, the human face that Dante, back in the year 1320, recognized as the Face of God—in the midst of a threefold circle of light and love—the Face that "moves the sun and the stars". Today, the visit by Peter's Successor is moving the Abruzzis. Yet by no means everyone is allowed to come. The capacity of the little village for receiving guests is far too limited; the narrow streets and roads would be blocked for miles around. The infrastructure, in these forgotten hills and valleys at the foot of the Majella massif, is completely unequal to this event.

Only eight thousand tickets have been given out to selected participants to welcome the Pope on the square in front of the Capuchins' little church, an average of one for each family in the area. Most will have to follow the proceedings on television or on the giant screen down on the Tiburtina. In the church of the "Holy Face", the only people allowed in at all today will be priests, monks, and nuns.

The sky, however, stretched out over Manoppello, is such a perfect blue that it is as if this day had been planned in paradise. In this little place, a Veil of the "Holy Face" has been preserved for centuries, which Sister Blandina Paschalis Schlömer recognized years ago as being the sudarium from Jerusalem that John the Evangelist mentions in his account of the Resurrection of Christ.

That is why years ago, this passionately committed Trappistine nun moved from Germany into a little hermitage in the Abruzzis, just up a footpath from the "Holy Face". The people of Manoppello have her stubbornness to thank for the fact that the Pope is coming today to see this little corner of Italy, as wondrous as it is isolated.

Her discovery has long since set off violent arguments in Rome. No pope would be able to decide all the questions that have since been raised concerning the authenticity of the image. Hence, there has been decided resistance to this "private" pilgrimage by the Pope, right up into the higher echelons of the Curia. But Benedict XVI has firmly continued to insist on seeing the image for himself; a multitude of pieces of circumstantial evidence make it probable that we are dealing with the same "true image" that was kept in Saint Peter's in Rome from 708 onward.

There is not a word to be heard of all these debates today in Manoppello. Sister Blandina has stitched a large yellow-and-white flag, so that the Vatican's colors are fluttering from the roof of her hermitage to welcome the Pope's helicopter.

He is happy to see "all these faces", he calls out to the people of Manoppello, turning round in the open doorway of the church to the crowd of people that has gathered outside. Then he walks forward, with those accompanying him, into the church (where the Veil, above the tabernacle at the high altar, is shining milkily at him in a monstrance), greets all the groups of people by name, and genuflects in front of the tabernacle to the Holy of holies to be found in every Catholic church; he lowers his gaze and prays, closes his eyes a while, and then finally opens them and looks up to the little Veil. Everything is in slow motion. A camera is whirring somewhere. Someone coughs at the back of church. Then at last he stands up, goes to turn left, then goes to the right. Archbishop Forte leads him up the steps behind the altar. The glass door of the reliquary, which normally protects the marvelous image from pilgrims or robbers, is wide open.

At the top, the Pope merely clasps his hands and gazes. The fingers of his hands are intertwined. He does not move. He is serious, as he was at Auschwitz; absorbed, as his predecessor was at Golgotha; silent, his eyes wide open, gazing, for a minute, two minutes, three, four—an eternity. A choir of seminarians are singing a song by little Thérèse of Lisieux, the Saint "of the Holy Face", that extols the beauty of Jesus' Face, which "has captivated my heart"—over and over again: "*O Volto Santo di Gesù. . . .*"

The Pope gazes. Are his lips moving? A crimson mozetta is draped over his shoulders. He is silent, standing upright and alert. Finally, he crosses himself and walks carefully down the steps and back to the altar; then he begins to speak.

"During my pause for prayer just now, I was thinking of the first two Apostles who ... followed Jesus to the bank of the Jordan River ... and asked ... 'Rabbi, where are you staying?' And he said to them, 'Come and see.' That very same day, the two who were following Jesus had an unforgettable experience which prompted them to say: 'We have found the Messiah.' " Suddenly, he says, they had discovered the true identity of the man they had previously thought of as a simple "master" or "rabbi". And nonetheless, we wonder how long they would have had to follow him before his unfathomable Face would be truly revealed to them? "He who has seen me has seen the Father", they had heard him say in the end, he says. They truly realized this, however, when they met the risen Christ and the "Spirit enlightened their minds and their hearts". Anyone living in this holy tradition, living "in God, already on this earth, attracted and transformed by the dazzling brightness of his Face", he tells us, would always recognize his Face "especially [in] the poorest and neediest." That was the teaching of the saints, he said, who had thrown ever new light upon the Face of Christ.

Sister Blandina is staring at him stunned. Countless times, she has laid the transparency of this Holy Face over the face on the Shroud of Turin and over the most noble portraits of Christ in the history of art. She would wish for nothing more than that the Pope might bless the crowd and the world with the monstrance of the Holy Face. Yet he is now laying the transparency of the Holy Face over the faces of all men.

"May the Lord ever help you to recognize his Face, so as thus to see the Father. United in prayer and in our common search for his Face. Benedict pp. XVI.

September 1, 2006", the Pope wrote afterward for the Capuchins in their house register in the sacristy, after dismissing everyone with the blessing of ancient Israel, "The Lord bless you and keep you. The Lord make his face to shine upon you.... The Lord lift up his countenance upon you, and give you peace...."

"The Pope was enthusiastic!" exclaimed Archbishop Forte in German, in the press of crowds outside the church door, when the Pope was already up in the sky and he himself was being dragged away again to a press conference. The Pope's comment on the Holy Face had been above all "his silent prayer", he afterward told the world's press.

All that now remain, scattered among the empty water bottles in the streets, are a few of the song sheets that Archbishop Forte had printed for today. His friend Luciano Primavera designed them. The cover shows, in the form of a red-chalk sketch, how this day will be remembered in history's library of images; it might be a dream of Sister Blandina's. Here, Benedict XVI is lifting up the Veil with its image over his head with both hands to bless the world. Jesus and Peter are both smiling, calm and relaxed.

Manoppello, September 1, 2006

Peter on Mount Tabor

Erich Maria Fink: We can imagine that September 1, 2006, was a great day for you, Herr Badde. Pope Benedict XVI was visiting the veil-icon of Manoppello. You had, through your publications, substantially contributed to bringing about this pilgrimage. Months ago, you gave us news about it for the first time, after the Pope had promised to pay it a visit soon. Now—if we may put it like this—he was keeping his word. What does this event mean for you and for your activity as a journalist?

Paul Badde: As a journalist and author, one can expect nothing more from one's work. It is a gift, being able to move one's readers. Being able to move the Successor of Peter, however, was sheer grace. Thus, that day became a Tabor experience in my life—with the incredible transfiguration of God's Face on the ancient Veil in Manoppello through the Pope's visit. This was a triumph for the Madonna, who always points us only toward her Son, who was cut off from her sight. If this had been depicted in earlier times, artists would have surrounded it with clouds of angels and hosts of saints.

You even met the Pope personally in Manoppello. Are you able to share something of that with us and tell us what this meeting may have been like for you?

For all those present, it was like a kind of dream experience, as fleeting as it was inconceivable. For when

Benedict XVI received Sister Blandina, Father Pfeiffer, Father Resch, my Italian colleague Saviero Gaeta, and myself in the sacristy of the shrine, he was still wearing the liturgical papal stole. Thus it was not at all a private meeting with the Pope; rather, it was truly an encounter with Peter. It was an incredible acknowledgment of our work.

What impression did you have of the moments the Pope spent in front of the "Face of God"?

He reminded me very much, in his seriousness and his emotional shock, of those moments in Auschwitz when he stood in front of the starvation block where Maximilian Kolbe had been and before that appalling wall for victims of the firing squad. What had been incomprehensible there was right in front of his eyes, here. He had "had" to come to Auschwitz, he said at the time, and that was indeed quite clear. He urgently "wanted" to come here, however, to Manoppello. Within Italy, which has more than a thousand shrines, this was the first journey he had decided on for himself. And one could see that. That is why photos showing him with Father Carmine and Archbishop Forte before the Face of Christ, taken from behind, remind us rather of old depictions of the shepherds adoring the Child—pictures in which the Child in the crib is shining out like a cosmic lamp, whose light is reflected in the incredulous, loving amazement of the shepherds' faces. Here too, there were three shepherds, among whom was the chief shepherd, open-mouthed with amazement.

What in your opinion were the particular emphases given by the Pope through his visit and especially in his address?

The most important emphasis was set by his arrival as such, by which in a few minutes Benedict XVI made this Holy Face, from an unknown corner in the Abruzzis, world famous. BBC World showed the pictures—basically, all the large television broadcasters. It was a "point of no return" in the history of this image. In his address, the Pope was able to go into the process of recognizing the Face of God in the Face of Jesus in a marvelous way. He did this through the example of the apostles, who, like Philip, had recognized Jesus as the Messiah immediately, and yet still had to be asked, three years later, "Do you still not know me?" What the Pope began then, he is quite clearly carrying out more and more. We can already see how the "human Face of God" is becoming the trademark of his pontificate.

In the run-up to the papal visit to Manoppello, you talked about the way this pilgrimage heralded a change of paradigm in the history of European thought. What were you trying to say there?

The rediscovery of the old "true image" of Christendom can only have as its consequence a gradual but complete revaluation of images by the whole of Christendom, by all churches and denominations; for centuries now, images have to some extent "fallen into the hands of thieves". The enormous documentary and scriptural content of images has been lastingly discredited thereby. Outside the Church, this has led to a general schizophrenia of perception between images and writing, which—to take a harmless instance—anyone may observe by looking at a Marlboro billboard, with those giant healthy cowboys, and then underneath the legally obligatory warning that smoking is dangerous for your health. Yet the reason this schizophrenia is so fatal is because it was to the Christians in particular, rather than to any of the other monotheistic religions, that the "true image" was entrusted as one of their most precious treasures. This image maintains a resistance against that ideologizing from which the Church in the West, especially, has been suffering dreadfully for decades. The Pope standing silent before the Holy Face is the most outstanding indication of this we have yet had.

Was there any resistance within the Church to the Pope's pilgrimage to Manoppello?

Yes, there was strong resistance against this journey, both within the Vatican and outside it, from every conceivable direction and for every conceivable reason. That is why I could almost write another book about it, constituting the next part of the "Divine Comedy" we may frequently observe in the story of this discovery. The Pope, however, overcame all resistance in decisive fashion by declaring that he had decided to make this journey—a word of power! The journey to Manoppello was a particularly courageous step in the context of his ministry so far.

In an article, you quote Archbishop Forte, the responsible ordinary from Chieti. He is convinced "with moral certainty" that the "Holy Face" of Manoppello comes from Christ's empty tomb. Is this certainty of the Archbishop attributable to your influence?

Much rather—as in my case and that of Sister Blandina and others who are involved in this story—to the influence of the Madonna, to be quite honest. What is remarkable, however, is that Archbishop Forte has experienced an extremely rapid development in his assessment of this precious thing that has been entrusted to him and to the Capuchins at Manoppello. In an interview two years ago, when he had just made the acquaintance of the image, he was still inclined to be skeptical—although he told me even then that it "closely unites pain and light within it, in a way only love can do". In the meantime however, together with the Capuchin Father Carmine Cucinelli, the Guardian of the shrine, he has obviously accepted the image just as bravely, as intelligently, and as comprehensively as we are told that Saint Joseph accepted the child that Mary was expecting.

"Then Simon Peter came and saw the napkin, which had been on his head!" Archbishop Forte had this sentence from John's account of the Resurrection inscribed in Greek along the edge of an icon of Christ, which he presented as a gift to the Successor of Peter. Did you have any share in deciding the form of this gift to the Pope?

No, that was entirely on Archbishop Forte's own initiative, when he placed the order for this large icon with Sister Blandina. Right down to the relevant quotation from the Gospel of John, it was entirely his choice. I had in any case suggested to Sister Blandina in the autumn of 2005 that she might "write" a little icon in postcard format for the Holy Father. And she did that at the time. She sent this "letter" to the Pope on December 1, 2005, together with the invitation to come to Manoppello, please, to have a look at the mussel-silk cloth.

Through your involvement as a journalist, you have played a special part in bringing recognition of the results of the research of the German Professor Heinrich Pfeiffer of the Gregorian University. Years ago, he had shown how the image on the Veil at Manoppello corresponds with the so-called Shroud of Turin and had at the same time discovered all the characteristics with which the most priceless relic of Saint Peter's, Rome, is portrayed in ancient sources. Do you take it that the original image disappeared in the confusion of the "Sacco di Roma" and finally made its way to Manoppello?

We must take note, for the sake of the truth, that in Germany Sister Blandina was the first to stumble on the story of the discovery, after reading an article about it by the Italian journalist Renzo Allegri. Following this, she developed and refined the technique of 'superimposition', superimposing the two images from Manoppello and Turin, and thereby finally inspired Professor Pfeiffer to work toward his discovery that the Veil in Manoppello was identical with the so-called "Veil of Veronica" from Rome. Recently it has been the Italian journalist Saverio Gaeta who has compiled a host of arguments for the original's probably having disappeared during the Sacco di Roma, in 1527.

You write, for instance, "The loss was brilliantly hushed up." There are people who reproach you for having criticized the Church too much when she could not defend herself. Could you comment on this?

Compared with the kind of thriller one might have been able to construct from this story, my book is as pious as a hymnbook. There are still many details in it that are incredible, which must make some people's hair stand on

337

end. Yet I have not invented these things but simply found things out—in part, from the age of Machiavelli, so teeming with rogues both great and small; no one today has to feel he must excuse himself for those things. What seems to me much more important, however, is to keep before our eyes the immeasurable gain represented by the rediscovery of the "true image". As against that, the loss of the old fake is merely a further gain, not any kind of new damage. The Veronica relic in the Vatican can only be understood as a substitute, to put it politely. John Paul II had it brought to him in the palace, back in 2000, and after seeing it decided that they could not expect any of the faithful to look at it. Unfortunately, at that time he knew nothing of the image in Manoppello; but later he gave me reiterated and detailed encouragement in my research.

You assume that the first pillar beneath the dome of Saint Peter's, which was constructed by the popes from Julius II up to Urban VIII as a treasury to hold the so-called "sudarium of Veronica", was actually intended for the cloth that is now found in Manoppello. Is it not misleading to some extent if in the history of art and in cultural history we talk, with the oversized figure of Saint Veronica in the background, about her sudarium? Ought not this history to be rewritten and the distinction more clearly marked?

Yes, like many other details in this history that demand a purification of our collective memory. The Pope's visit will surely open many doors for this very soon.

Even before Benedict XVI arrived in Manoppello, you were offering an interpretation of his journey with the words, "He is now opening a new chapter in the story of the Veronica's return, in which people will talk about the 'true image' in a way they have not done for four hundred years." Were you here intending to express the hope that the image would return to Saint Peter's as soon as possible? Do you regard the return of this image as one of the primary goals of your overall commitment concerning the image on the Veil at Manoppello?

No, certainly not. It would be just as right to send the image back to Jerusalem, to Mount Zion, where the Mother of God probably last had it as she lay dying. Or perhaps to Istanbul, where it was before it came to Rome. I could only imagine its returning to Rome if the people of Manoppello—who have so marvelously protected it for the past four hundred years—were to bring it back themselves. But that is not very probable.

Do you see yourself as the one who prepared the way for the Face of God to come home, seeing it as seeking in Peter the one who should contemplate it?

Yes, I would like to think that—but standing on the shoulders of many others. It is an incomprehensible gift to have been used as an instrument in this marvelous story. For first of all, it really is a homecoming, with the Face that was hidden so long, vanished from knowledge, coming back into the Church and into Christendom. In the age of globalization, however, it is also at the same time the first arrival of this "human Face of God" before the eyes of the whole of mankind.

Berezniki (Urals) / Rome; September 20, 2006

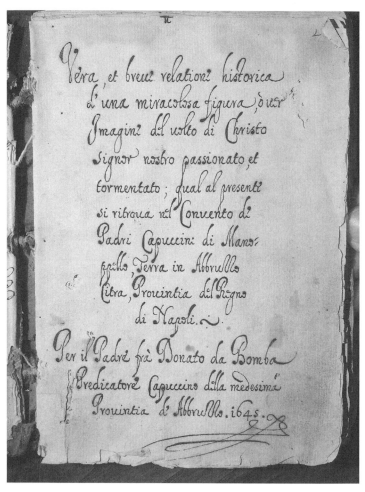

Vera, et breue relatione historica
d'una miracolosa figura, ouer
Imagine del uolto di Christo
Signor nostro passionato, et
tormentato; qual al presente
si ritroua nel Convento di
Padri Capuccini di Mano=
ppello, Terra in Abbruzzo
Citra, Prouintia del Regno
di Napoli.

Per il Padre frà Donato da Bomba
Predicatore Capuccino della medesima
Prouintia d'Abbruzzo. 1645.

First page of the 'Relatione Historica' by Donata da Bomba.
Manoppello, 1645

The Face of the King

There can be no closing chapter for this book. Shortly after the Pope had read *God's Face*, he decided to make a pilgrimage to Manoppello. So that on September 1, 2006, Benedict XVI was the first pope for four hundred years to spend time in conversation with the Face that for so long had been reckoned the most precious treasure in Christendom. Television stations catapulted the image to every corner of the earth. This was a "point of no return", and Archbishop Bruno Forte exclaimed to the Pontifex Maximus, in greeting him, that the Face of Christ was the "polestar" of Christianity.

To express what the Incarnation was, said Benedict XVI, six days later in Rome, "we can certainly say that God gave himself a human face, the Face of Jesus, and consequently, from now on, if we truly want to know the Face of God, all we have to do is to contemplate the Face of Jesus! In his Face we truly see who God is and what he looks like!" Two weeks later, he raised the little church outside Manoppello in the Abruzzis to the status of papal basilica.

Yet even the Resurrection of Christ raises the issue of the delicate Face in Manoppello as no book can. As early as the second century, some texts seemed to be talking about this Veil. The "Song of the Pearl" in the Acts of Thomas, which came from Edessa, talked, for instance, about a "shining image on Chinese material with red chalk" that was "like a mirror-image of me. I saw it in myself, and I saw myself in him." Dante, too, in Rome in the thirteenth century, talked in a very similar way about this image.

"It is simply there", wrote Ulrich Moskopp, an artist from Cologne, who came to see the image as a pilgrim. What was beautiful about it, he said, was "the absence of human creative ingenuity. This is true love. The image is truth. Set free from all hatred and attachment. Here, the struggle is at an end. Here is peace." This is an image that is never emptied. And now the stream of pilgrims from all over the world is still swelling, and they find ever more lovely things to say about the mystery of this miraculous image.

It now reminds me, however, of those words from Shakespeare's *King Lear*, where the old Lear is sitting in misery, having been kicked out by his daughters. Out of doors there is a storm; it is raining. That is how Kent finds him, and, not recognizing him, he says he wants to enter his service. "Dost thou know me, fellow?" Lear asks him. Can he not see his miserable poverty? Everyone has left him. Then Kent replies, "No, sir; but you have that in your countenance which I would fain call master."

"This is it", said the philosopher Robert Spaemann about this scene. "This is a proof that is not of the same kind as mathematical proofs. It is something that is humanly clear, a demonstration not to be outdone by any other kind. If the incredible event of the Incarnation of God is indeed a reality, then I cannot be choosy about the rest. That is to say, that reason does not merely teach me to calculate the probabilities. Reason also teaches me that, sometimes, what is wholly improbable really comes about."

That is why there will never be a closing chapter, a closing paragraph to this book. Everything about this image is improbable. Perhaps the next chapter will be written in Chinese. The Face itself, however, will always have the last word. All the sayings in the Gospels remain in force until the Last Day; then, however, even they may pass away. Only the Face of God remains. He does not wear a mask. His Face remains forever: the Face of the King and of love.

Paul Badde
Peking; July 12, 2007

SELECT BIBLIOGRAPHY

Version of the Bible used:
The Holy Bible. Revised Standard Version. Second Catholic Edition. San Francisco: Ignatius Press, 2006.

Almenar, Jorge-Manuel Rodriguez. *El Sudario de Oviedo*. Valencia, 2000.

Antonelli, Luciano. *Festa Santissimo Volto Santo di S. Anna*. Toronto, 1987.

Bacile, Rosario. *Il Volto Santo di Gesù e Fra Innocenzo: Storia, Tradizione, Devozione*. Chiusa Sclafani, 1993.

Balthasar, Hans Urs von. *New Elucidations*. Translated by Sister Mary Theresilde Skerry. San Francisco: Ignatius Press, 1986.

Belting, Hans. *Bild und Kult: Eine Geschichte des Bildes vor dem Zeitalter der Kunst*. Munich, 1990.

Bennett, Janice. *Sacred Blood, Sacred Image: The Sudarium of Oviedo*. Littleton, Col., 2001.

Berger, Klaus. *Ist Gott Person?* Gütersloh, 2004.

———. *Jesus*. Munich, 2004.

Bini, Antonio, and Giovanna Ruscitti. *Il Volto Santo di Manoppello: Storia, Fede e Legenda*. Pescara, 2004. (Unpublished.)

Bisso Marino—Fili d'oro dal fondo del mare—Muschelseide—Goldene Fäden vom Meeresgrund. Catalogue for the exhibition of the same name, edited by Felicitas Maeder, Ambros Hänggi, and Dominik Wunderlin for the Basel Museum of Natural History, Hamburg, 2004.

Bomba, Donato da. *Vera, et breve relatione historica d'una miraculosa figura, o vero Immagine del volto di Cristo signor nostro passionato, et tormentato; qual al presenti si ritrova nel Convento di Padri Cappuccini di Manoppello, Terra in Abbruzzo Citra, Provincia del Regno di Napoli. Per il Padre fra Donato da Bomba Predicatore Cappuccino della medesima Provincia d'Abbruzzo.* Manoppello, 1645.

Bulst, Werner, and Heinrich Pfeiffer. *Das Turiner Grabtuch und das Christusbild.* 2 vols. Frankfurt am Main, 1987 and 1991.

Corsignani, Pietro Antonio. *Reggia Marsican ovvero Memorie Topografiche storiche di varie colonie e siti antichi e moderni delle province dei Marsi e di Valeria.* Naples, 1738.

Cozzi, Luigi. *Un Fiore della Marsica—Padre Domenico da Cese.* Pescara, 2005.

Dante Alighieri: *La Divina Commedia.*

Dobschütz, Ernst von. *Christusbilder: Untersuchungen zur christlichen Legende (Die Gruppe des Bildes von Kamuliana).* Vol. 3. Texte und Untersuchungen zur Geschichte der Altchristlichen Literatur, new series, 18. Leipzig, 1899.

Emmerick, Anna Katharina. *Der Gotteskreis*, as noted down by Clemens Brentano. Munich, 1966.

Felmy, Karl Heinz. *Das Buch der Christus-Ikonen.* Freiburg, Basel, and Vienna, 2004.

Fernández, Enrique López. *El Santo Sudario de Oviedo.* Granda-Siero, 2004.

Le Fort, Gertrud von, *Das Schweißtuch der Veronika. Part 1: Der römische Brunnen.* Munich, 1928; 1948.

Frugoni, Arsenio. *Pellegrini a Roma nel 1300—Cronache del primo Giubileo.* Casale Monferrato, 1999.

Gaeta, Saverio. *Il Volto del Risorto.* Rome, Milan, and Bergamo, 2005.

Gerster, Georg. *Kirchen im Fels—Entdeckungen in Äthiopien.* Zurich, 1968.

Le Goff, Jacques. *Le Dieu du Moyen Âge: entretiens avec Jean-Luc Pouthier.* Paris, 2003.

Guardini, Romano. *The Lord.* Introduction by Joseph Cardinal Ratzinger. Translated by Elinor Castendyk Briefs. Washington, D.C.: Regnevy, 1996.

Henrich, Matthias. *Rede des Erzdiakons Gregorios zur Übertragung des Abdruckbildes Christi von Edessa nach Konstantinopel im 10. Jahrhundert.* Edited, translated, and collated from the Codex Vat. Graec. 511, folios 143–50v, tenth century. Early 1999, privately printed, in ring-binder with no place indicated.

Hesemann, Michael. *Die stummen Zeugen von Golgatha: Die faszinierende Geschichte der Passionsreliquien Christi.* Munich, 2000.

Hinz, Paulus. *Deus Homo: Das Christusbild von seinen Ursprüngen bis zur Gegenwart.* 2 vols. Berlin, 1973 and 1981.

Janvier, Abbé. *Die Verehrung des heiligen Antlitzes zu St. Peter im Vatikan und an anderen berühmten Orten.* Tours, 1889.

Jan Paweł II: *Tryptyk rzymski.* Kraków, 2003. In a personal German adaptation in rhyme by Gerhard Gnauck: Warsaw, 2005.

John Paul II. *Novo Millenio Ineunte: Apostolic Letter at the Close of the Great Jubilee of the Year 2000.* Vatican City, 2001.

Kemper, Max Eugen. *Das Mandylion von Edessa.* Vatican City, 2000.

Kolitz, Zvi. *Jossel Rakovers Wendung zu Gott.* Zürich, 2004. (*Yosl Rakover Talks to God.* New York, 1999).

Link, Dorothea. *Ein Mysterium enthüllt sein wahres Antlitz: Der Schleier von Manoppello (Volto Santo).* Parts I and II. Privately printed, Enkirch, 2005.

Luther, Martin. *Wider das Papstthum zu Rom vom Teufel gestiftet, 1545.* In *Luthers Werke.* Weimar, 1928.

Manoppello, Fr. Eugenio da. *Preziosa Memoria: Narrativa della Venuta del Volto Santo in Manoppello.* Manoppello, 1865.

Martini, Carlo Maria. *La trasformazione di Cristo e del cristiano alla luce del Tabor.* Milan, 2004.

Morello, Giovanni, and Gerhard Wolf, eds. *Il Volto di Cristo.* Catalogue to the Exhibition in the Palazzo delle Esposizioni of the Biblioteca Apostolica Vaticana. Rome and Milan, 2000.

Da Montichhio, Bernhardino Lucantonio. *Monografia Della Prodigiosa Immagine del Volto Santo di N.S.G.C.* Manoppello, 1910.

Müller, Manfred. *Die biblischen Heiligtümer von Kornelimünster.* Kornelimünster, 1986.

Persili, Antonio. *Sulle Tracce del Cristo Risorto (con Petri e Giovanni Testimoni oculari).* Tivoli, 1988.

Placentinus, Anonymous. *Itinera Hierosolymitana.* CSEL 39, nec Paulus Geyer. Vienna, 1898.

Ratzinger, Joseph. *God and the World: A Conversation with Peter Seewald.* Translated by Henry Taylor. San Francisco: Ignatius Press, 2002.

————. *Il volto di Cristo (Das Antlitz Christi in der Heiligen Schrift).* Vatican City, 2005.

————. "Jungfrauengeburt und leeres Grab." *Deutsche Tagespost,* November 11, 2004 (Würzburg).

————. *Via Crucis.* Vatican City, 2005.

Resch, Andreas. *Das Antlitz Christi.* Innsbruck, 2005.

Rezza, Darius. "Segnor mio Jesù Cristo, Dio verace, or fu si fatta la sembianza vostra?" *30 Giorni* 18: no. 3 (Rome, 2000).

Sammaciccia, Bruno. *Il Volto Santo di Gesù a Manoppello*. Pescara, 1978.

_____. *P. Domenico Del Volto Santo Cappuccino*. Pescara, 1979.

Scannerini, Silvano, and Piero Savarino, eds. *The Turin Shroud: Past, Present and Future*. International Scientific Symposium, Turin, March 2–5. Turin, 2000.

Schlömer, Blandina Paschalis, O.C.S.O. *Der Schleier von Manoppello und das Grabtuch von Turin*. Innsbruck, 1999.

Schmidt, Josef. *Das Gewand der Engel*. Bonn, 1999.

Serramonacesca, Antonio da. *Il Volto Santo di Manoppello e Il Santuario*. Pescara, 1966.

Tussio, P. Fr. Filippo da. *Del Volto Santo: Memorie Storiche Raccolte Interno Alla Prodigiosa Immagine del Passionato Volto di Gesù Cristo Signor Nostro che si venera nella Chiesa de PP. Cappuccini di Manoppello negli Abruzzi in Diocesi di Chieti*. Aquila, 1875.

Valtorta, Maria. *L'Evangelo come mi è stato rivelato*. Vol. 10. Isola del Liri, 1998.

Weber, Francis J. *The Veil of Veronica: A Personal Memoir*. Mission Hills, Calif., 2004.

Wilson, Ian. *Holy Faces, Secret Places*. London, 1991.

Wolf, Gerhard. *Schleier und Spiegel: Traditionen des Christusbildes und die Bildkonzepte der Renaissance*. Munich, 2002.

Many other photos, helpful references, materials, maps, addresses, and multilingual links to the Holy Face of Manoppello are found at the following address on the worldwide web: www.holyfaceofmanoppello.blogspot.com.

SOURCES FOR ILLUSTRATIONS

Page 6: Stephanus Plannck (attributed to), Mirabilia Urbis Romae, ca. 1486, Vatican City, Biblioteca Apostolica Vaticana, Inc. VI; pages 12, 32, 42, 56, 70, 78, 84, 118, 158, 170, 194, 204, 226, 256, 270, 300, and 312, photos: Paul Badde; page 98: with the kind permission of the chapter of Saint Peter's, Vatican City; page 106: with the kind permission of the Archdiocese of Turin; page 118: photo by Stefan Meier, Rome; page 218: photo by Georg Gerster, Zürich, 1968; page 238: illustration from *El Santo Sudario de Oviedo* (Ediciones Madù, Grande [Asturias]); page 290: illustration from: *Biblia, Das ist: Die gantze Heilige Schrift, Alten und Neuen Testaments*, Nach der Teutschen Übersetzung D. Martin Luthers (Erfurt, 1735); page 321: the first sketch of the *Volto Santo* of Manoppello by Sister Blandina Paschalis Schlömer, O.C.S.O., from 1985; page 322: photo by Raphaela Pallin, Vienna.

Colored Picture Section
Pages 1 and 2: Paul Badde; page 3: Stefan Meier, Rome; page 4: Dorothea Link, Enkirch; page 5: Paul Badde; page 6: with the kind permission of the Sacristy of the Sistine Chapel; page 7: Paul Badde (Church of Saint Bartholomew in Genoa); page 8: Paul Badde (Church of Saint Cecilia in Rome, Städel Museum in Frankfurt-am-Main); page 9: Paul Badde (Louvre, Paris, and Alte Pinakothek, Munich); pages 10, 11, 12, and 13: Paul Badde;

page 14: (above) Paul Badde, (below) AP; page 15: (above) Paul Badde, (below) *Osservatore Romano*; page 16: Paul Badde.

ACKNOWLEDGMENTS

I am most grateful to Fr. Carmine Cucinelli, O.F.M. Cap., Fr. Germano Franco di Pietro, O.F.M.Cap., Fr. Emilio Cucchinella, O.F.M.Cap., Fr. Lino Pupatti, O.F.M. Cap., Sr. Blandina Paschalis Schlömer, O.C.S.O., together with her sisters, Fr. Heinrich Pfeiffer, S.J., Fr. Herbert Douteil, C.S.Sp., Don Antonio Tedesco, Karlheinz Dietz, Chiara Vigo, Antonio Bini, Raymond Frost, Dorothea Link, Josefine Schiffer, Raphaela Pallin, Stefan Meier, Cornelia Schrader, Gerald Goesche, Gerhard Gnauck, Bernhard and Martin Müller, Hans D. Baumann, Andreas Löhr, my brother Hans-Peter, and many others, upon whose shoulders I had to climb again and again in writing this book over a period when my time was already overloaded—with a request for them to forgive me for the burdens I must sometimes have laid upon them this way. Quite particularly, I would like to thank at this time my wife Ellen, companion and joy of my old eyes, who has become the great source of happiness in my life— thank God.

Rome, February 12, 2006

APPENDIX

Pilgrimage to the shrine of the Holy Face
In Manoppello, Italy

Address of His Holiness Benedict XVI
Friday, 1 September 2006

Before entering the Shrine of Manoppello, the Holy Father greeted the faithful gathered outside it:

Dear Brothers and Sisters,

Thank you for this most cordial welcome. I see that the Church is a large family. Wherever the Pope goes the family meets with great joy.

For me this is a sign of lively faith, of communion and of the peace that faith creates, and I am deeply grateful to you for this welcome. Thus, I see on your faces the full beauty of this Region of Italy here.

A special greeting to the sick: we know that the Lord is especially close to you, helps you and accompanies you in your sufferings. You are in our prayers, and pray for us, too!

I offer a special greeting to the young people and children making their First Communion. Thank you for your enthusiasm and for your faith.

As the Psalms say, we are all "seeking the Face of the Lord". And this is also the meaning of my Visit. Let us seek together to know the Face of the Lord ever better, and in the Face of the Lord let us find this impetus of love and peace which also reveals to us the path of our life.

Thank you, and my best wishes to you all!

* * *

Venerable Brother in the Episcopate,

Dear Brothers and Sisters,

First of all, I must once again say a heartfelt "thank you" for this welcome, for your words, Your Excellency, so profound, so friendly, for the expression of your friendship and for the deeply meaningful gifts: the Face of Christ venerated here, for me, for my house, and then the gifts of your land that express the beauty and generosity of the earth, of the people who live and work here, and the goodness of the Creator himself. I simply want to thank the Lord for today's simple, family meeting in a place where we can meditate on the mystery of divine love, contemplating the image of the Holy Face.

I extend my most heartfelt gratitude to all of you present here for your cordial welcome and for the dedication and discretion with which you have supported my private pilgrimage, which nevertheless, as an ecclesial pilgrimage, cannot be entirely private.

I greet and thank in particular, I repeat, your Archbishop, a longstanding friend. We worked together in the Theological Commission. And in many conversations I always learned from his wisdom, and also from his books.

Thank you for your gifts which I very much appreciate as "signs", as Archbishop Forte has called them. Indeed, they are signs of the affective and effective communion which binds the people of this beloved Abruzzi Region to the Successor of Peter.

I address a special greeting to you, priests, men and women religious and seminarians gathered here. I am particularly glad to see a large number of seminarians: the future of the Church in our midst. Since it is impossible to meet the entire diocesan Community—perhaps that will be for another time—I am glad that you are representing it, people already dedicated to the priestly ministry and the consecrated life or who are on the way to the priesthood.

You are people whom I like to think of as in love with Christ, attracted by him and determined to make your own life a continuous quest for his Holy Face.

Lastly, I address a grateful thought to the community of the Capuchin Fathers who are offering us hospitality and who for centuries have cared for this Shrine, the goal of so many pilgrims.

During my pause for prayer just now, I was thinking of the first two Apostles who, urged by John the Baptist, followed Jesus to the banks of the Jordan River, as we read at the beginning of John's Gospel (cf. 1: 35–37).

The Evangelist recounts that Jesus turned around and asked them: "'What do you seek?'. And they answered him, 'Rabbi ... where are you staying?'. And he said to them, 'Come and see'" (cf. Jn 1: 38–39).

That very same day, the two who were following him had an unforgettable experience which prompted them to say: "We have found the Messiah" (Jn 1: 41).

The One whom a few hours earlier they had thought of as a simple "rabbi" had acquired a very precise identity: the identity of Christ who had been awaited for centuries.

But, in fact, what a long journey still lay ahead of those disciples!

They could not even imagine how profound the mystery of Jesus of Nazareth could be or how unfathomable, inscrutable, his "Face" would prove, so that even after living with Jesus for three years, Philip, who was one of them, was to hear him say at the Last Supper: "Have I been with you so long, and yet you do not know me, Philip?". And then the words that sum up the novelty of Jesus' revelation: "He who has seen me has seen the Father" (Jn 14: 9).

Only after his Passion when they encountered him Risen, when the Spirit enlightened their minds and their hearts, would the Apostles understand the significance of the words Jesus had spoken and recognize him as the Son of God, the Messiah promised for the world's redemption. They were then to become his unflagging messengers, courageous witnesses even to martyrdom.

"He who has seen me has seen the Father". Yes, dear brothers and sisters, to "see God" it is necessary to know Christ and to let oneself be moulded by his Spirit who guides believers "into all the truth" (cf. Jn 16: 13). Those who meet Jesus, who let themselves be attracted by him and are prepared to follow him even to the point of sacrificing their lives, personally experience, as he did on the Cross, that only the "grain of wheat" that falls into the earth and dies, bears "much fruit" (Jn 12: 24).

This is the path of Christ, the way of total love that overcomes death: he who takes it and "hates his life in this world will keep it for eternal life" (Jn 12: 25). In other words, he lives in God already on this earth, attracted and transformed by the dazzling brightness of his Face.

This is the experience of God's true friends, the saints who, in the brethren, especially the poorest and neediest, recognized and loved the Face of that God, lovingly contemplated for hours in prayer. For us they are encouraging examples to imitate; they assure us that if we follow this path, the way of love, with fidelity, we too, as the Psalmist sings, will be satisfied with God's presence (cf. Ps 17[16]: 15).

"*Jesu . . . quam bonus te quaerentibus!*—How kind you are, Jesus, to those who seek you!". This is what we have just sung in the ancient hymn "*Jesu, dulcis memoria*" [Jesus, the very thought of you], which some people attribute to St Bernard.

It is a hymn that acquires rare eloquence in the Shrine dedicated to the Holy Face, which calls to mind Psalm 24[23]: "Such is the generation of those who seek him, who seek the face of the God of Jacob" (v. 6).

But which is "the generation" of those who seek the Face of God, which generation deserves to "ascend the hill of the Lord" and "stand in his holy place"?

The Psalmist explains: it consists of those who have "clean hands and a pure heart", who do not speak falsehoods, who do not "swear deceitfully" to their neighbour (cf. vv. 3–4). Therefore, in order to enter into communion with Christ and to contemplate his Face, to recognize the Lord's Face in the faces of the brethren and in daily events, we require "clean hands and a pure heart".

Clean hands, that is, a life illumined by the truth of love that overcomes indifference, doubt, falsehood and selfishness; and pure hearts are essential too, hearts enraptured by divine beauty, as the Little Teresa of Lisieux says in her prayer to the Holy Face, hearts stamped with the hallmark of the Face of Christ.

Dear priests, if the holiness of the Face of Christ remains impressed within you, pastors of Christ's flock, do not fear: the faithful entrusted to your care will also be infected with it and transformed.

And you, seminarians, who are training to be responsible guides of the Christian people, do not allow yourselves to be attracted by anything other than Jesus and the desire to serve his Church.

I would like to say as much to you, men and women religious, so that your activities may be a visible reflection of divine goodness and mercy.

"Your Face, O Lord, I seek": seeking the Face of Jesus must be the longing of all of us Christians; indeed, we are "the generation" which seeks his Face in our day, the Face of the "God of Jacob". If we persevere in our quest for the Face of the Lord, at the end of our earthly pilgrimage, he, Jesus, will be our eternal joy, our reward and glory for ever: "*Sis Jesu nostrum gaudium, qui es futurus praemium: sit nostra in te gloria, per cuncta semper saecula*".

This is the certainty that motivated the saints of your Region, among whom I would like to mention in particular Gabriel of Our Lady of Sorrows and Camillus de Lellis; our reverent remembrance and our prayer is addressed to them.

But let us now address a thought of special devotion to the "Queen of all the saints", the Virgin Mary, whom you venerate in the various shrines and chapels scattered across the valleys and mountains of the Abruzzi Region. May Our Lady, in whose face—more than in any other creature—we can recognize the features of the Incarnate

Word, watch over the families and parishes and over the cities and nations of the whole world.

May the Mother of the Creator also help us to respect nature, a great gift of God that we can admire here, looking at the marvellous mountains surrounding us. This gift, however, is exposed more and more to the serious risks of environmental deterioration and must therefore be defended and protected. This is urgently necessary, as Archbishop Forte noted and as is appropriately highlighted by the Day of Reflection and Prayer for the Safeguarding of Creation, which is being celebrated by the Church in Italy this very day.

Dear brothers and sisters, as I thank you once again for your presence and for your gifts, I invoke the Blessing of God upon you and upon all your loved ones with the ancient biblical formula: "May the Lord bless you and keep you: may the Lord make his face to shine upon you and be gracious to you: may the Lord lift up his countenance upon you and give you peace" (cf. Nm 6: 24–26). Amen!

INDEX

373